Central Europe

lonely planet

phrasebooks

Central Europe phrasebook
3rd edition – February 2007

Published by
Lonely Planet Publications Pty Ltd ABN 36 005 607 983
90 Maribyrnong St, Footscray, Victoria 3011, Australia

Lonely Planet Offices
Australia Locked Bag 1, Footscray, Victoria 3011
USA 150 Linden St, Oakland CA 94607
UK 72–82 Rosebery Ave, London, EC1R 4RW

Cover illustration
Europa by Yukiyoshi Kamimura

ISBN 978 1 74104 030 2

10 9 8 7 6 5 4 3 2

Printed by C&C Offset Printing Co Ltd, China

acknowledgments

This book is based on existing editions of Lonely Planet's phrasebooks as well as new content. It was developed with the help of the following people:

- Richard Nebeský for the Czech chapter
- Gunter Muehl for the German chapter
- Christina Mayer for the Hungarian chapter
- Piotr Czajkowski for the Polish chapter
- Katarina Nodrovicziova for the Slovak chapter
- Urška Pajer for the Slovene chapter

Editor Branislava Vladisavljevic would also like to thank Elmar Duenschede (German) and Hunor Csutoros (Hungarian) for additional language expertise.

Lonely Planet Language Products

Publishing Manager: Chris Rennie
Commissioning Editor: Karin Vidstrup Monk
Editor: Branislava Vladisavljevic
Assisting Editors: Vanessa Battersby & Francesca Coles
Managing Editor: Annelies Mertens
Project Manager: Adam McCrow

Layout Designers: Clara Monitto & David Kemp
Managing Layout Designer: Sally Darmody
Cartographer: Wayne Murphy
Series Designer & Illustrations: Yukiyoshi Kamimura
Production Manager: Jennifer Bilos

contents

Central Europe

Czech
German
Hungarian

Baltic Sea

Lithuania

Kaliningrad
(Russia)

Belarus

Gdańsk

POLAND

Poznań

⊛ *Warsaw*

Łódź

Wrocław

Ukraine

Kraków

Ostrava

REPUBLIC

Brno

SLOVAKIA

Prešov
Košice

Nitra

Miskolc

Vienna

⊛ *Bratislava*

Győr

Debrecen

Graz

⊛ *Budapest*

HUNGARY

Maribor

Szeged

Celje

Pécs

Croatia

Moldova

Romania

Serbia

Bosnia and
Hercegovina

Polish

Slovak

Slovene

Note: Language areas are approximate only.
For more details see the relevant introduction.

EUROPE

central europe – at a glance

One of the rewarding things about travelling through Central Europe is the rich variety of cuisine, customs, architecture and history. The flipside of course is that you'll encounter a number of very different languages. Most languages spoken in Central Europe belong to what's known as the Indo-European language family, believed to have originally developed from one language spoken thousands of years ago.

German belongs to the Germanic branch of the Indo European language family and is quite closely related to English. You should find that many basic words in German are similar to English words. The Slavic languages originated north of the Carpathians and are now divided into Eastern, Western and Southern subgroups. Czech, Slovak and Polish all belong to the Western subgroup of the Slavic language family, while Slovene belongs to the Southern subgroup. Fortunately, (for travellers at least), all these Central European Slavic languages are written in the Latin alphabet. Hungarian is something of a linguistic oddity within Europe. Though classified as a member of the Finno-Ugric language group, making it a distant relative of Finnish, it has no other significant similarities to any other language in Europe – or the world for that matter.

did you know?

- The European Union (EU) was established by the Maastricht Treaty in 1992. It developed from the European Economic Community, founded by the Treaty of Rome in 1957. Since the 2004 enlargement, it has 25 member states and 20 official languages.
- The EU flag is a circle of 12 gold stars on a blue background – the number 12 representing wholeness.
- The EU anthem is the 'Ode to Joy' from Beethoven's Ninth Symphony.
- Europe Day, 9 May, commemorates the 1950 declaration by French Foreign Minister Robert Schuman which marked the creation of the European Union.
- The euro has been in circulation since E-Day, 1 January 2002. The euro's symbol (€) was inspired by the Greek letter epsilon (ε) – Greece being the cradle of European civilisation and ε being the first letter of the word 'Europe'.
- The Eurovision Song Contest, held each May, has been running since 1956. For the larger part of the competition's history, the performers were only allowed to sing in their country's national language, but that's no longer the case.

Czech

czech alphabet

A a uh	*Á á* a	*B b* bair	*C c* tsair	*Č č* chair
D d dair	*Ď ď* dyair	*E e* e	*É é* dloh·hair air	*Ě ě* e s *hach*·kem
F f ef	*G g* gair	*H h* ha	*Ch ch* cha	*I i* ee
Í í dloh·hair ee	*J j* yair	*K k* ka	*L l* el	*M m* em
N n en	*Ň ň* en´	*O o* o	*P p* pair	*Q q* kair
R r er	*Ř ř* erzh	*S s* es	*Š š* esh	*T t* tair
Ť ť tyair	*U u* u	*Ú ú* dloh·hair u	*Ů ů* u s *krohzh*·kem	*V v* vair
W w dvo·yi·tair vair	*X x* iks	*Y y* ip·si·lon	*Ý ý* dloh·hee ip·si·lon	*Z z* zet
Ž ž zhet				

czech

introduction

Czech (*čeština* chesh·tyi·nuh), the language which gave us words such as *dollar*, *pistol* and *robot*, has a turbulent history. The Czech Republic may now be one of the most stable and well-off Eastern European countries, but over the centuries the land and the language have been regularly swallowed and regurgitated by their neighbours. In 1993 the Velvet Divorce ended the patched-together affair that was Czechoslovakia, and allowed Czech to go its own way after being tied to Slovak for over 70 years.

Both Czech and Slovak belong to the western branch of the Slavic language family, pushed westward with the Slavic people by the onslaught of the Huns, Avars, Bulgars and Magyars in the 5th and 6th centuries. Czech is also related to Polish, though not as closely as to Slovak – adults in Slovakia and the Czech Republic can generally understand one another, although younger people who have not been exposed to much of the other language may have more difficulty.

The earliest written literature dates from the 13th century upswing in Czech political power, which continued for several centuries. In the 17th century, however, the Thirty Years War nearly caused literature in Czech to become extinct. Fortunately, the national revival of the late 18th century brought it to the forefront again, at least until the 20th century, when first Nazi and then Communist rule pressed it into a subordinate position once more.

Many English speakers flinch when they see written Czech, especially words like *prst* prst (finger) and *krk* krk (neck) with no apparent vowels, and the seemingly unpronounceable clusters of consonants in phrases like *čtrnáct dní* chtr·natst dnyee (fortnight). Don't despair! With a little practice and the coloured pronunciation guides in this chapter you'll be enjoying the buttery mouthfeel of Czech words in no time. Czech also has one big advantage in the pronunciation stakes – each Czech letter is always pronounced exactly the same way, so once you've got the hang of the Czech alphabet you'll be able to read any word put before you with aplomb. Thank religious writer and martyr Jan Hus for this – he reformed the spelling system in the 15th and 16th centuries and introduced the *háček* ha·chek (ˇ) and the various other accents you'll see above Czech letters.

So, whether you're visiting the countryside or marvelling at Golden Prague, launch into this Czech chapter and your trip will be transformed into a truly memorable one.

pronunciation

vowel sounds

The Czech vowel system is relatively easy to master and most sounds have equivalents in English.

symbol	english equivalent	czech example	transliteration
a	father	*já*	ya
ai	aisle	*krajka*	*krai*·kuh
air	hair	*veliké*	ve·lee·*kair*
aw	law	*balcón*	*bal*·kawn
e	bet	*pes*	pes
ee	see	*prosím*	pro·*seem*
ey	hey	*dej*	dey
i	bit	*kolik*	*ko*·lik
o	pot	*noha*	*no*·huh
oh	oh	*koupit*	*koh*·pit
oo	zoo	*ústa*	*oo*·stuh
oy	toy	*výstroj*	*vee*·stroy
ow	how	*autobus*	*ow*·to·bus
u	put	*muž*	muzh
uh	run	*nad*	n d

word stress

Word stress in Czech is easy – it's always on the first syllable of the word. Stress is marked with italics in the pronunciation guides in this chapter as a reminder.

consonant sounds

The consonants in Czech are mostly the same as in English, with the exception of the kh sound, the r sound (which is rolled as it is in Spanish) and the rzh sound.

symbol	english equivalent	czech example	transliteration
b	**bed**	*bláto*	*bla*·to
ch	**cheat**	*odpočinek*	ot·po·**chi**·nek
d	**dog**	*nedávný*	ne·*dav*·nee
f	**fat**	*vyfotit*	vi·*fo*·tit
g	**go**	*vegetarián*	ve·ge·*tuh*·ri·an
h	**hat**	*zahrady*	zuh·*hruh*·di
k	**kit**	*navěky*	na·vye·**ki**
kh	**loch**	*kuchyně*	ku·**khi**·nye
l	**lot**	*loni*	*lo*·nyi
m	**man**	*menší*	*men*·shee
n	**not**	*nízký*	*nyeez*·kee
p	**pet**	*dopis*	*do*·pis
r	**run** (rolled)	*rok*	rok
rzh	**rolled r followed by zh**	*řeka*	*rzhe*·kuh
s	**sun**	*slovo*	*slo*·vo
sh	**shot**	*pošta*	*posh*·tuh
t	**top**	*fronta*	*fron*·tuh
ts	**hats**	*co*	tso
v	**very**	*otvor*	*ot*·vor
y	**yes**	*již*	yizh
z	**zero**	*zmiz*	zmiz
zh	**pleasure**	*už*	uzh
'	**a slight y sound**	*promiňte*	*pro*·min'·te

tools

language difficulties

Do you speak English?
  Mluvíte anglicky? — mlu·vee·te uhn·glits·ki

Do you understand?
  Rozumíte? — ro·zu·mee·te

I understand.
  Rozumím. — ro·zu·meem

I don't understand.
  Nerozumím. — ne·ro·zu·meem

What does (*knedlík*) mean?
  Co znamená (knedlík)? — tso znuh·me·na (kned·leek)

How do you ...? — *Jak se ...?* — yuhk se ...
  pronounce this — *toto vyslovuje* — toh·to vis·lo·vu·ye
  write (*krtek*) — *píše (krtek)* — pee·she (kr·tek)

Could you please ...? — *Prosím, můžete ...?* — pro·seem moo·zhe·te ...
  repeat that — *to opakovat* — to o·puh·ko·vuht
  speak more slowly — *mluvit pomaleji* — mlu·vit po·muh·le·yi
  write it down — *to napsat* — to nuhp·suht

numbers

0	*nula*	nu·luh	16	*šestnáct*	shest·natst	
1	*jeden* m	ye·den	17	*sedmnáct*	se·dm·natst	
	jedna f	yed·na	18	*osmnáct*	o·sm·natst	
	jedno n	yed·no	19	*devatenáct*	de·vuh·te·natst	
2	*dva/dvě* m/f&n	dvuh/dvye	20	*dvacet*	dvuh·tset	
3	*tři*	trzhi	21	*dvacet jedna*	dvuh·tset yed·nuh	
4	*čtyři*	chti·rzhi		*jednadvacet*	yed·nuh·dvuh·tset	
5	*pět*	pyet	22	*dvacet dva*	dvuh·tset dvuh	
6	*šest*	shest		*dvaadvacet*	dvuh·uh·dvuh·tset	
7	*sedm*	se·dm	30	*třicet*	trzhi·tset	
8	*osm*	o·sm	40	*čtyřicet*	chti·rzhi·tset	
9	*devět*	de·vyet	50	*padesát*	puh·de·sat	
10	*deset*	de·set	60	*šedesát*	she·de·sat	
11	*jedenáct*	ye·de·natst	70	*sedmdesát*	se·dm·de·sat	
12	*dvanáct*	dvuh·natst	80	*osmdesát*	o·sm·de·sat	
13	*třináct*	trzhi·natst	90	*devadesát*	de·vuh·de·sat	
14	*čtrnáct*	chtr·natst	100	*sto*	sto	
15	*patnáct*	puht·natst	1000	*tisíc*	tyi·seets	

time & dates

What time is it?	*Kolik je hodin?*	ko·lik ye ho·dyin
It's one o'clock.	*Je jedna hodina.*	ye yed·nuh ho·dyi·nuh
It's (10) o'clock.	*Je (deset) hodin.*	ye (de·set) ho·dyin
Quarter past (10).	*Čtvrt na (jedenáct).*	chtvrt nuh (ye·de·natst)
	(lit: quarter of eleven)	
Half past (10).	*Půl (jedenácté).*	pool (ye·de·nats·tair)
	(lit: half eleven)	
Quarter to (eleven).	*Třičtvrtě na (jedenáct).*	trzhi·chtvr·tye nuh (ye·de·natst)
At what time?	*V kolik hodin?*	f ko·lik ho·dyin
At ...	*V ...*	f ...
am (midnight–8am)	*ráno*	ra·no
am (8am–noon)	*dopoledne*	do·po·led·ne
pm (noon–7pm)	*odpoledne*	ot·po·led·ne
pm (7pm–midnight)	*večer*	ve·cher

Monday	pondělí	pon·dye·lee
Tuesday	úterý	oo·te·ree
Wednesday	středa	strzhe·duh
Thursday	čtvrtek	chtvr·tek
Friday	pátek	pa·tek
Saturday	sobota	so·bo·tuh
Sunday	neděle	ne·dye·le

January	leden	le·den
February	únor	oo·nor
March	březen	brzhe·zen
April	duben	du·ben
May	květen	kvye·ten
June	červen	cher·ven
July	červenec	cher·ve·nets
August	srpen	sr·pen
September	září	za·rzhee
October	říjen	rzhee·yen
November	listopad	li·sto·puht
December	prosinec	pro·si·nets

What date is it today?
Kolikátého je dnes?   ko·li·ka·tair·ho ye dnes

It's (18 October).
Je (osmnáctého října).   ye (o·sm·nats·tair·ho rzheey·nuh)

last night	včera v noci	fche·ruh v no·tsi
last week/month	minulý týden/měsíc	mi·nu·lee tee·den/mye·seets
last year	vloni	vlo·nyi

next ...	příští ...	przheesh·tyee ...
week	týden	tee·den
month	měsíc	mye·seets
year	rok	rok

tomorrow/yesterday ...	zítra/včera ...	zee·truh/fche·ruh ...
morning (early/late)	ráno/dopoledne	ra·no/do·po·led·ne
afternoon	odpoledne	ot·po·led·ne
evening	večer	ve·cher

16

weather

What's the weather like?	Jaké je počasí?	yuh·kair ye po·chuh·see
It's ...		
cloudy	Je zataženo.	ye zuh·tuh·zhe·no
cold	Je chladno.	ye khluhd·no
hot	Je horko.	ye hor·ko
raining	Prší.	pr·shee
snowing	Sněží.	snye·zhee
sunny	Je slunečno.	ye slu·nech·no
warm	Je teplo.	ye tep·lo
windy	Je větrno.	ye vye·tr·no
spring	jaro n	yuh·ro
summer	léto n	lair·to
autumn	podzim m	pod·zim
winter	zima f	zi·muh

border crossing

I'm here ...	Jsem zde ...	ysem zde ...
in transit	v tranzitu	f truhn·zi·tu
on business	na služební cestě	nuh slu·zheb·nyee tses·tye
on holiday	na dovolené	nuh do·vo·le·nair

I'm here for ...	Jsem zde na ...	ysem zde nuh ...
(10) days	(deset) dní	(de·set) dnyee
(three) weeks	(tři) týdny	(trzhi) teed·ni
(two) months	(dva) měsíce	(dvuh) mye·see·tse

I'm going to (Valtice).
Jedu do (Valtic).   ye·du do (vuhl·tyits)

I'm staying at the (Hotel Špalíček).
Jsem ubytovaný/á v   ysem u·bi·to·vuh·nee/a v
(Hotelu Špalíček). m/f   (ho·te·lu shpuh·lee·chek)

I have nothing to declare.
Nemám nic k proclení.   ne·mam nyits k prots·le·nyee

I have something to declare.
Mám něco k proclení.   mam nye·tso k prots·le·nyee

That's not mine.
To není moje.   to ne·nyee mo·ye

transport

tickets & luggage

Where can I buy a ticket?
Kde koupím jízdenku? gde *koh*·peem *yeez*·den·ku

Do I need to book a seat?
Potřebuji místenku? pot·rzhe·bu·yi *mees*·ten·ku

One ... ticket to (Telč), please.	... do (Telče), prosím.	... do (tel·che) pro·seem
one-way	Jednosměrnou jízdenku	yed·no·smyer·noh yeez·den·ku
return	Zpáteční jízdenku	zpa·tech·nyee yeez·den·ku

I'd like to ... my ticket, please.	Chtěl/Chtěla bych ... mojí jízdenku, prosím. m/f	khtyel/khtye·luh bikh ... mo·yee yeez·den·ku pro·seem
cancel	zrušit	zru·shit
change	změnit	zmye·nyit
collect	vyzvednout	vi·zved·noht
confirm	potvrdit	pot·vr·dyit

I'd like a ... seat, please.	Chtěl/Chtěla bych ... m/f	khtyel/khtye·luh bikh ...
nonsmoking	nekuřácké místo	ne·ku·rzhats·kair mees·to
smoking	kuřácké místo	ku·rzhats·kair mees·to

How much is it?
Kolik to stojí? ko·lik to sto·yee

Is there a toilet?
Je tam toaleta? ye tuhm to·uh·le·tuh

Is there air conditioning?
Je tam klimatizace? ye tuhm kli·muh·ti·zuh·tse

How long does the trip take?
Jak dlouho trvá cesta? yuhk dloh·ho tr·va tses·tuh

Is it a direct route?
Je to přímá cesta? ye to przhee·ma tses·tuh

Where can I find a luggage locker?
Kde mohu najít zavazadlová schránka? gde mo·hu nuh·yeet zuh·vuh·zuhd·lo·va skhran·kuh

My luggage	*Moje zavazadlo*	*mo*·ye zuh·vuh·zuhd·lo
has been ...	*bylo ...*	*bi*·lo ...
damaged	*poškozeno*	*posh*·ko·ze·no
lost	*ztraceno*	*ztruh*·tse·no
stolen	*ukradeno*	*u*·kruh·de·no

getting around

Where does flight (OK25) arrive?
Kam přiletí let (OK25)? kuhm *przhi*·le·tyee let (*aw*·ka *dvuh*·tset pyet)

Where does flight (OK25) depart?
Kde odlítá let (OK25)? gde *od*·lee·ta let (*aw*·ka *dvuh*·tset pyet)

Where's (the) ...?	*Kde je ...?*	gde ye ...
arrivals hall	*příletová hala*	*przhee*·le·to·va *huh*·luh
departures hall	*odletová hala*	*od*·le·to·va *huh*·luh
duty-free shop	*prodejna*	*pro*·dey·nuh
	bezcelního zboží	*bez*·tsel·nyee·ho *zbo*·zhee
gate (12)	*východ k letadlu*	*vee*·khod k *le*·tuhd·lu
	(dvanáct)	(*dvuh*·natst)

Is this the ...	*Jede tento/tato ...*	ye·de ten·to/*tuh*·to ...
to (Mělník)? m/f	*do (Mělníka)?* m/f	do (*myel*·nyee·kuh)
bus	*autobus* m	*ow*·to·bus
train	*vlak* m	vluhk
tram	*tramvaj* f	*truhm*·vai
trolleybus	*trolejbus* m	*tro*·ley·bus

When's the	*V kolik jede*	f *ko*·lik ye·de
... bus?	*... autobus?*	... *ow*·to·bus
first	*první*	*prv*·nyee
last	*poslední*	*po*·sled·nyee
next	*příští*	*przhee*·shtyee

At what time does the bus/train leave?
V kolik hodin odjíždí f *ko*·lik ho·dyin *od*·yeezh·dyee
autobus/vlak? *ow*·to·bus/vluhk

How long will it be delayed?
Jak dlouho bude mít zpoždění? yuhk *dloh*·ho *bu*·de meet *zpozh*·dye·nyee

What's the next station/stop?
Která je příští stanice/zastávka? *kte*·ra ye *przheesh*·tyee *stuh*·nyi·tse/*zuhs*·taf·kuh

Does it stop at (Cheb)?
   Zastaví to v (Chebu)?   zuhs·tuh·vee to f (khe·bu)

Please tell me when we get to (Přerov).
   Prosím vás řekněte mi   pro·seem vas rzhek·nye·te mi
   kdy budeme v (Přerově).   kdi bu·de·me f (przhe·ro·vye)

How long do we stop here?
   Jak dlouho zde budeme stát?   yuhk dloh·ho zde bu·de·me stat

Is this seat available?
   Je toto místo volné?   ye to·to mees·to vol·nair

That's my seat.
   To je mé místo.   to ye mair mees·to

I'd like a taxi ...	*Potřebuji taxíka ...*	po·trzhe·bu·yi tuhk·see·kuh ...
at (9am)	*v (devět hodin*	f (de·vyet ho·dyin
	dopoledne)	do·po·led·ne)
now	*teď*	teď
tomorrow	*zítra*	zee·truh

Is this taxi available?
   Je tento taxík volný?   ye ten·to tuhk·seek vol·nee

How much is it to ...?
   Kolik stojí jízdenka do ...?   ko·lik sto·yee yeez·den·kuh do ...

Please put the meter on.
   Prosím zapněte taxametr.   pro·seem zuhp·nye·te tuhk·suh·me·tr

Please take me to (this address).
   Prosím odvezte mě na (tuto adresu).   pro·seem od·ves·te mye na (tu·to uh·dre·su)

Please ...	*Prosím ...*	pro·seem ...
slow down	*zpomalte*	spo·muhl·te
stop here	*zastavte zde*	zuhs·tuhf·te zde
wait here	*počkejte zde*	poch·key·te zde

car, motorbike & bicycle hire

I'd like to hire	*Chtěl/Chtěla bych*	khtyel/khtye·luh bikh
a ...	*si půjčit ...* m/f	si pooy·chit ...
bicycle	*kolo*	ko·lo
car	*auto*	ow·to
motorbike	*motorku*	mo·tor·ku

with ...	s ...	s ...
a driver	řidičem	rzhi·dyi·chem
air conditioning	klimatizací	kli·muh·ti·zuh·tsee
antifreeze	nemrznoucí směsí	ne·mrz·noh·tsee smye·see
snow chains	sněhovými řetězy	snye·ho·vee·mi rzhe·tye·zi

How much for	Kolik stojí	ko·lik sto·yee
... hire?	půjčení na ...?	pooy·che·nyee nuh ...
hourly	hodinu	ho·dyi·nu
daily	den	den
weekly	týden	tee·den

air	vzduch m	vz·dukh
oil	olej m	o·ley
petrol	benzin m	ben·zin
tyre	pneumatika f	pne·u·muh·ti·kuh

I need a mechanic.	Potřebuji mechanika.	pot·rzhe·bu·yi me·khuh·ni·kuh
I've run out of petrol.	Došel mi benzin.	do·shel mi ben·zin
I have a flat tyre.	Mám defekt.	mam de·fekt

directions

Where's the ...?	Kde je ...?	gde ye ...
bank	banka	buhn·kuh
city centre	centrum	tsen·trum
hotel	hotel	ho·tel
market	trh	trh
police station	policejní stanice	po·li·tsey·nyee stuh·nyi·tse
post office	pošta	posh·tuh
public toilet	veřejný záchod	ve·rzhey·nee za·khod
tourist office	turistická informační kancelář	tu·ris·tits·ka in·for·muhch·nye kuhn·tse·larzh

Is this the road to (Cheb)?
Vede tato silnice do (Chebu)?   ve·de tuh·to sil·ni·tse do (khe·bu)

Can you show me (on the map)?
Můžete mi to ukázat (na mapě)?   moo·zhe·te mi to u·ka·zuht (nuh muh·pye)

What's the address?
Jaká je adresa? — yuh·ka ye uh·dre·suh

How far is it?
Jak je to daleko? — yuhk ye to duh·le·ko

How do I get there?
Jak se tam dostanu? — yuhk se tuhm dos·tuh·nu

Turn ...	Odbočte ...	od·boch·te ...
at the corner	za roh	zuh rawh
at the traffic lights	u semaforu	u se·muh·fo·ru
left/right	do leva/prava	do le·vuh/pruh·vuh

It's ...	Je to ...	ye to ...
behind ...	za ...	zuh ...
far away	daleko	duh·le·ko
here	zde	zde
in front of ...	před ...	przhed ...
left	na levo	nuh le·vo
near	blízko	bleez·ko
next to ...	vedle ...	ved·le ...
on the corner	na rohu	nuh ro·hu
opposite ...	naproti ...	nuh·pro·tyi ...
right	na pravo	nuh pruh·vo
straight ahead	přímo	przhee·mo
there	tam	tuhm

by bus	autobusem	ow·to·bu·sem
by taxi	taxikem	tuhk·si·kem
by train	vlakem	vluh·kem
on foot	pěšky	pyesh·ki

north	sever	se·ver
south	jih	yih
east	východ	vee·khod
west	západ	za·puhd

signs

Vchod/Východ	vkhod/*vee*-khod	**Entrance/Exit**
Otevřeno/Zavřeno	o-te-vrzhe-no/*zuh*-vrzhe-no	**Open/Closed**
Volné pokoje	*vol*-nair po-ko-ye	**Rooms Available**
Obsazeno	*op*-suh-ze-no	**No Vacancies**
Informace	*in*-for-muh-tse	**Information**
Policejní stanice	po-li-tsey-nyee *stuh*-nyi-tse	**Police Station**
Zakázáno	*zuh*-ka-za-no	**Prohibited**
Záchody	za-kho-di	**Toilets**
Páni	*pa*-nyi	**Men**
Ženy	zhe-ni	**Women**
Horké/Studené	hor-kair/*stu*-de-nair	**Hot/Cold**

accommodation

finding accommodation

Where's a ...?	*Kde je ...?*	gde ye ...
camping ground	*tábořiště*	*ta*-bo-rzhish-tye
guesthouse	*penzion*	*pen*-zi-on
hotel	*hotel*	*ho*-tel
youth hostel	*mládežnická*	*mla*-dezh-nyits-ka
	ubytovna	*u*-bi-tov-nuh

Can you recommend	*Můžete mi doporučit*	moo-zhe-te mi *do*-po-ru-chit
somewhere ...?	*něco ...?*	*nye*-tso ...
cheap	*levného*	*lev*-nair-ho
good	*dobrého*	*dob*-rair-ho
nearby	*nejbližšího*	*ney*-blizh-shee-ho

I'd like to book a room, please.
Chtěl/Chtěla bych   khtyel/*khtye*-luh bikh
rezervovat pokoj, prosím. m/f   re-zer-vo-vuht *po*-koy pro-seem

I have a reservation.
Mám rezervaci.   mam re-zer-vuh-tsi

My name is ...
Mé jméno je ...   mair *ymair*-no ye ...

Do you have a double room?
Máte pokoj s manželskou postelí?   ma-te *po*-koy s *muhn*-zhels-koh *pos*-te-lee

Do you have a ... room?	*Máte ... pokoj?*	ma·te ... po·koy
single	*jednolůžkový*	yed·no·loozh·ko·vee
twin	*dvoulůžkový*	dvoh·loozh·ko·vee

How much is it per ...?	*Kolik to stojí ...?*	ko·lik to sto·yee ...
night	*na noc*	nuh nots
person	*za osobu*	zuh o·so·bu

Can I pay ...?	*Mohu zaplatit ...?*	mo·hu zuh·pluh·tyit ...
by credit card	*kreditní kartou*	kre·dit·nyee kuhr·toh
with a travellers cheque	*cestovním šekem*	tses·tov·nyeem she·kem

For (three) nights/weeks.
Na (tři) noci/týdny.   nuh (trzhi) no·tsi/teed·ni

From (2 July) to (6 July).
Od (druhého července)   od (dru·hair·ho cher·ven·tse)
do (šestého července).   do (shes·tair·ho cher·ven·tse)

Can I see it?
Mohu se na něj podívat?   mo·hu se na nyey po·dyee·vuht

Am I allowed to camp here?
Mohu zde stanovat?   mo·hu zde stuh·no·vuht

Where can I find a camping ground?
Kde mohu najít stanový tábor?   gde mo·hu nuh·yeet stuh·no·vee ta·bor

requests & queries

When's breakfast served?
V kolik se podává snídaně?   f ko·lik se po·da·va snyee·duh·nye

Where's breakfast served?
Kde se podává snídaně?   gde se po·da·va snyee·duh·nye

Please wake me at (seven).
Prosím probuďte mě v (sedm).   pro·seem pro·bud'·te mye f (se·dm)

Could I have my key, please?
Můžete mi dát můj klíč, prosím?   moo·zhe·te mi dat mooy kleech pro·seem

Can I get another (blanket)?
Mohu dostat další (deku)?   mo·hu dos·tuht duhl·shee (de·ku)

Do you have a/an ...?	Máte ...?	ma·te ...
elevator	výtah	vee·tah
safe	trezor	tre·zor

The room is too ...	Je moc ...	ye mots ...
expensive	drahý	druh·hee
noisy	hlučný	hluch·nee
small	malý	muh·lee

The ... doesn't work.	... nefunguje.	... ne·fun·gu·ye
air conditioning	Klimatizace	kli·muh·ti·zuh·tse
fan	Větrák	vye·trak
toilet	Toaleta	to·uh·le·tuh

This ... isn't clean.	Tento ... neni čistý.	ten·to ... ne·nyi chis·tee
pillow	polštář	pol·shtarzh
towel	ručník	ruch·nyeek

checking out

What time is checkout?
V kolik hodin máme vyklidit pokoj?   f ko·lik ho·dyin ma·me vi·kli·dyit po·koy

Can I leave my luggage here?
Mohu si zde nechat zavazadla?   mo·hu si zde ne·khuht zuh·vuh·zuhd·luh

Could I have	Můžete mi vratit	moo·zhe·te mi vra·tyit
my ..., please?	..., prosím?	... pro·seem
deposit	zálohu	za·lo·hu
passport	pas	puhs
valuables	cennosti	tse·nos·tyi

communications & banking

the internet

Where's the local Internet café?
Kde je místní internetová kavárna?   gde ye meest·nyee in·ter·ne·to·va kuh·var·nuh

How much is it per hour?
Kolik to stojí na hodinu?   ko·lik to sto·yee nuh ho·dyi·nu

I'd like to ...	Chtěl/Chtěla bych ... m/f	khtyel/khtye·luh bikh ...
check my email	zkontrolovat	skon·tro·lo·vuht
	můj email	mooy ee·meyl
get Internet	přístup na	przhees·tup nuh
access	internet	in·ter·net
use a printer	použít tiskárnu	po·u·zheet tyis·kar·nu
use a scanner	použít skener	po·u·zheet ske·ner

mobile/cell phone

I'd like a ...	Chtěl/Chtěla bych ... m/f	ktyel/khtye·luh bikh ...
mobile/cell phone for hire	si půjčit mobil	si pooy·chit mo·bil
SIM card for your network	SIM kartu pro vaší síť	sim kuhr·tu pro vuh·shee seet'

| What are the rates? | Jaké jsou tarify? | yuh·kair ysoh tuh·ri·fi |

telephone

What's your phone number?
Jaké je vaše telefonní číslo?   yuh·kair ye vuh·she te·le·fo·nyee chees·lo

The number is ...
Číslo je ...   chees·lo ye ...

Where's the nearest public phone?
Kde je nejbližší veřejný telefon?   gde ye ney·blizh·shee ve·rzhey·nee te·le·fon

I'd like to buy a phonecard.
Chtěl/Chtěla bych koupit   ktyel/khtye·luh bikh koh·pit
telefonní kartu. m/f   te·le·fo·nyee kuhr·tu

I want to ...	Chtěl/Chtěla bych ... m/f	ktyel/khtye·luh bikh ...
call (Singapore)	telefonovat do (Singapůru)	te·le·fo·no·vuht do sin·guh·poo·ru
make a local call	si zavolat místně	si zuh·vo·luht meest·nye
reverse the charges	telefonovat na účet volaného	te·le·fo·no·vuht na oo·chet vo·luh·nair·ho

How much does ... cost?	Kolik stojí ...?	ko·lik sto·yee ...
a (three)-minute	(tří) minutový	(trzhe) mi·nu·to·vee
call	hovor	ho·vor
each extra minute	každá další	kuzh·da duhl·shee
	minuta	mi·nu·tuh

(Seven crowns) per minute.
(Sedm korun) za jednu minutu.   (se·dm ko·run) zuh yed·nu mi·nu·tu

post office

I want to send a ...	Chci poslat ...	khtsi po·sluht ...
fax	fax	fuhks
letter	dopis	do·pis
parcel	balík	buh·leek
postcard	pohled	po·hled

I want to buy a/an ...	Chci koupit ...	khtsi koh·pit ...
envelope	obálku	o·bal·ku
stamp	známku	znam·ku

Please send it by	Prosím vás pošlete	pro·seem vas po·shle·te
... to (Australia).	to ... do (Austrálie).	to ... do (ow·stra·li·ye)
airmail	letecky poštou	le·tets·ki posh·toh
express mail	expresní poštou	eks·pres·nyee posh·toh
registered mail	doporučenou poštou	do·po·ru·che·noh posh·toh
surface mail	obyčejnou poštou	o·bi·chey·noh posh·toh

Is there any mail for me?
Mám zde nějakou poštu?   mam zde nye·yuh·koh posh·tu

bank

I'd like to ...	Chtěl/Chtěla bych ... m/f	kthyel/khtye·luh bikh ...
Where can I ...?	Kde mohu ...?	gde mo·hu ...
arrange a transfer	převést peníze	przhe·vairst pe·nyee·ze
cash a cheque	proměnit šek	pro·mye·nyit shek
change a travellers	proměnit	pro·mye·nyit
cheque	cestovní šek	tses·tov·nyee shek
change money	vyměnit peníze	vi·mye·nyit pe·nyee·ze
get a cash advance	zálohu v hotovosti	za·lo·hu v ho·to·vos·tyi
withdraw money	vybrat peníze	vi·bruht pe·nyee·ze

Where's a/an ...? *Kde je ...?* gde ye ...
   ATM *bankomat* buhn-ko-muht
   foreign exchange *směnárna* smye-nar-nuh
   office

What's the ...? *Jaký je ...?* yuh-kee ye ...
   charge for that *poplatek za to* po-pluh-tek zuh to
   exchange rate *devizový kurz* de-vi-zo-vee kurz

It's ... *Je to ...* ye to ...
   (12) crowns *(dvanáct) korun* (dvuh-natst) ko-run
   (five) euros *(pět) eur* (pyet) e-ur
   free *bez poplatku* bez po-pluht-ku

What time does the bank open?
Jaké jsou úřední hodiny? yuh-kair ysoh oo-rzhed-nyee ho-dyi-ni

Has my money arrived yet?
Přišly už moje peníze? przhi-shli uzh mo-ye pe-nyee-ze

sightseeing

getting in

What time does it open/close?
V kolik hodin otevírají/ f ko-lik ho-dyin o-te-vee-ruh-yee/
zavírají? zuh-vee-ruh-yee

What's the admission charge?
Kolik stojí vstupné? ko-lik sto-yee vstup-nair

Is there a discount for students/children?
Máte slevu pro studenty/děti? ma-te sle-vu pro stu-den-ti/dye-tyi

I'd like a ... *Chtěl/Chtěla bych ...* m/f khtyel/khtye-luh bikh ...
   catalogue *katalog* kuh-tuh-log
   guide *průvodce* proo-vod-tse
   local map *mapu okolí* ma-pu o-ko-lee

I'd like to see ...
Chtěl/Chtěla bych vidět ... m/f   khtyel/khtye·luh bikh *vi*·dyet ...

What's that?
Co je to?   tso ye to

Can I take a photo of this?
Mohu toto fotografovat?   mo·hu *to*·to *fo*·to·gruh·fo·vuht

Can I take a photo of you?
Mohu si vás vyfotit?   mo·hu si vas *vi*·fo·tyit

tours

When's the next ...?	*Kdy je příští ...?*	gdi ye przheesh·tyee ...
day trip	*celodenní výlet*	tse·lo·de·nyee vee·let
tour	*okružní jízda*	o·kruzh·nyee yeez·duh

Is ... included?	*Je zahrnuto/a ...?* n/f	ye zuh·hr·nu·to/a ...
accommodation	*ubytování* n	u·bi·to·va·nyee
the admission charge	*vstupné* n	fstup·nair
food	*strava* f	struh·vuh
transport	*doprava* f	do·pruh·vuh

How long is the tour?
Jak dlouho bude trvat   yuhk *dloh*·ho *bu*·de *tr*·vuht
tento zájezd?   ten·to *za*·yezd

What time should we be back?
V kolik hodin se máme vrátit?   f *ko*·lik *ho*·dyin se *ma*·me *vra*·tyit

sightseeing		
castle	*hrad* m	hruhd
cathedral	*katedrála* f	kuh·te·dra·luh
church	*kostel* m	kos·tel
main square	*hlavní náměstí* n	hluhv·nyee na·myes·tyee
monastery	*klášter* m	klash·ter
monument	*památník* m	puh·mat·nyeek
museum	*muzeum* f	mu·ze·um
old city	*staré město* n	stuh·rair myes·to
palace	*palác* m	puh·lats
ruins	*zříceniny* f pl	zrzhee·tse·nyi·ni
stadium	*stadion* m	stuh·di·yon
statue	*socha* f	so·khuh

shopping

enquiries

Where's a ...?	Kde je ...?	gde ye ...
bank	banka	buhn·kuh
bookshop	knihkupectví	knyikh·ku·pets·tvee
camera shop	foto potřeby	fo·to pot·rzhe·bi
department store	obchodní dům	op·khod·nyee doom
grocery store	smíšené zboží	smee·she·nair zbo·zhee
market	tržnice	tr·zhnyi·tse
newsagency	tabák	tuh·bak
supermarket	samoobsluha	suh·mo·op·slu·huh

Where can I buy (a padlock)?
Kde si mohu koupit (zámek)? gde si mo·hu koh·pit (za·mek)

I'm looking for ....
Hledám ... hle·dam ...

Can I look at it?
Mohu se na to podívat? mo·hu se nuh to po·dyee·vuht

Do you have any others?
Máte ještě jiné? ma·te yesh·tye yi·nair

Does it have a guarantee?
Je na to záruka? ye nuh to za·ru·kuh

Can I have it sent abroad?
Můžete mi to poslat moo·zhe·te mi to pos·luht
do zahraničí? do zuh·hruh·nyi·chee

Can I have my ... repaired?
Můžete zde opravit ...? moo·zhe·te zde o·pruh·vit ...

It's faulty.
Je to vadné. ye to vuhd·nair

I'd like ...,	*Chtěl/Chtěla bych*	khtyel/khtye·la bikh
please.	*..., prosím.* m/f	... pro·seem
a bag	*tašku*	tuhsh·ku
a refund	*vrátit peníze*	vra·tyit pe·nyee·ze
to return this	*toto vrátit*	to·to vra·tyit

paying

How much is it?
Kolik to stojí? — ko·lik to sto·yee

Can you write down the price?
Můžete mi napsat cenu? — moo·zhe·te mi nuhp·suht tse·nu

That's too expensive.
To je moc drahé. — to ye mots druh·hair

What's your lowest price?
Jaká je vaše konečná cena? — yuh·ka ye vuh·she ko·nech·na tse·nuh

I'll give you (200 crowns).
Dám vám (dvěstě korun). — dam vam (dvye·stye ko·run)

There's a mistake in the bill.
Na účtu je chyba. — nuh ooch·tu ye khi·buh

Do you accept ...?	*Mohu platit ...?*	mo·hu pluh·tyit ...
credit cards	*kreditními kartami*	kre·dit·nyee·mi kuhr·tuh·mi
debit cards	*platebními*	pluh·teb·nyee·mi
	kartami	kuhr·tuh·mi
travellers cheques	*cestovními šeky*	tses·tov·nyee·mi she·ki
I'd like ..., please.	*Můžete mi dát*	moo·zhe·te mi dat
	..., prosím?	... pro·seem
a receipt	*účet*	oo·chet
my change	*mé drobné*	mair drob·nair

clothes & shoes

Can I try it on?	*Mohu si to zkusit?*	mo·hu si to sku·sit
My size is (40).	*Mám číslo (čtyřicet).*	mam chee·slo (chti·rzhi·tset)
It doesn't fit.	*Nepadne mi to.*	ne·puhd·ne mi to
small	*malý*	muh·le
medium	*střední*	strzhed·nyee
large	*velký*	vel·keeh

books & music

I'd like a ...	Chtěl/Chtěla bych ... m/f	khtyel/khtye·luh bikh ...
newspaper	noviny	no·vi·ni
(in English)	(v angličtině)	(f uhn·glich·tyi·nye)
pen	propisovací pero	pro·pi·so·vuh·tsee pe·ro

Is there an English-language bookshop?

Je tam knihkupectví	ye tuhm knyih·ku·pets·tvee
s anglickýma knihama?	s uhn·glits·kee·muh knyi·huh·muh

I'm looking for something by (Kabát).

Hledám něco od (Kabátu).	hle·dam nye·tso od (kuh·ba·tu)

Can I listen to this?

Mohu si to poslechnout?	mo·hu si to po·slekh·noht

photography

Can you ...?	Můžete ...?	moo·zhe·te ...
develop this film	vyvolat tento film	vi·vo·luht ten·to film
load my film	vložit můj film	vlo·zhit mooy film
transfer photos	uložit fotografie	u·lo·zhit fo·to·gruh·fi·ye
from my camera	z mého	z mair·ho
to CD	fotoaparátu	fo·to·uh·puh·ra·tu
	na CD	nuh tsair·dairch·ko

I need a/an ... film	Potřebuji ... film	pot·rzhe·bu·yi ... film
for this camera.	pro tento fotoaparát.	pro ten·to fo·to·uh·puh·rat
APS	APS	a·pair·es
B&W	černobílý	cher·no·bee·lee
colour	barevný	buh·rev·nee
slide	diapozitivní	di·uh·po·zi·tiv·nyee
(200) speed	film s citlivostí	film s tsit·li·vos·tyee
	(dvěstě)	(dvye·stye)

When will it be ready?	Kdy to bude hotové?	gdi to bu·de ho·to·vair

meeting people

greetings, goodbyes & introductions

Hello/Hi.	*Ahoj/Čau.*	*uh·hoy/chow*
Good night.	*Dobrou noc.*	*do·broh nots*
Goodbye.	*Na shledanou.*	*nuh·skhle·duh·noh*
Bye.	*Ahoj/Čau.*	*uh·hoy/chow*
See you later.	*Na viděnou.*	*nuh vi·dye·noh*

Mr/Mrs	*pan/paní*	*puhn/puh·nyee*
Miss	*slečna*	*slech·nuh*

How are you?	*Jak se máte/máš?* pol/inf	*yuhk se ma·te/mash*
Fine. And you?	*Dobře. A vy/ty?* pol/inf	*dob·rzhe a vi/ti*
What's your name?	*Jak se jmenujete/* *jmenuješ?* pol/inf	*yuhk se yme·nu·ye·te/* *yme·nu·yesh*
My name is …	*Jmenuji se …*	*yme·nu·yi se …*
I'm pleased to meet you.	*Těší mě.*	*tye·shee mye*

This is my …	*To je můj/moje …* m/f	*to ye mooy/mo·ye …*
boyfriend	*přítel*	*przhee·tel*
brother	*bratr*	*bruh·tr*
daughter	*dcera*	*dtse·ruh*
father	*otec*	*o·tets*
friend	*přítel* m	*przhee·tel*
	přítelkyně f	*przhee·tel·ki·nye*
girlfriend	*přítelkyně*	*przhee·tel·ki·nye*
husband	*manžel*	*muhn·zhel*
mother	*matka*	*muht·kuh*
partner (intimate)	*partner/partnerka* m/f	*puhrt·ner/puhrt·ner·kuh*
sister	*sestra*	*ses·truh*
son	*syn*	*sin*
wife	*manželka*	*muhn·zhel·kuh*

Here's my …	*Zde je moje …*	*zde ye mo·ye …*
What's your …?	*Jaké/Jaká je* *vaše …?* n/f	*yuh·kair/yuh·ka ye* *vuh·she …*
(email) address	*(email) adresa* f	*(ee·meyl) uh·dre·suh*
fax number	*faxové číslo* n	*fuhk·so·vair chees·lo*
phone number	*telefonní číslo* n	*te·le·fo·nyee chees·lo*

occupations

What's your occupation?
Jaké je vaše povolání? — yuh·kair ye vuh·she po·vo·la·nyee

I'm a/an ...	Jsem ...	ysem ...
artist	*umělec/umělkyně* m/f	*u*·mye·lets/*u*·myel·ki·nye
businessperson	*obchodník* m&f	*ob*·khod·nyeek
farmer	*zemědělec* m	*ze*·mye·dye·lets
	zemědělkyně f	*ze*·mye·dyel·ki·nye
manual worker	*dělník* m&f	*dyel*·nyeek
office worker	*úředník* m	*oo*·rzhed·nyeek
	úřednice f	*oo*·rzhed·nyi·tse
scientist	*vědec/vědkyně* m/f	*vye*·dets/*vyeď*·ki·nye

background

Where are you from?	Odkud jste?	ot·kud yste
I'm from ...	Jsem z ...	ysem s ...
Australia	*Austrálie*	ow·stra·li·ye
Canada	*Kanady*	*kuh*·nuh·di
England	*Anglie*	*uhn*·gli·ye
New Zealand	*Nového Zélandu*	no·vair·ho zair·luhn·du
the USA	*Ameriky*	*uh*·meh·ri·ki

Are you married?	Jste ženatý/vdaná? m/f	yste zhe·nuh·tee/fduh·na
I'm married.	Jsem ženatý/vdaná. m/f	ysem zhe·nuh·tee/fduh·na
I'm single.	Jsem svobodný/á. m/f	ysem svo·bod·nee/a

age

How old ...?	Kolik ...?	ko·lik ...
are you	*je vám let* pol	ye vam let
	ti je let inf	ti ye let
is your daughter	*let je vaší dceři*	let ye vuh·shee dtse·rzhi
is your son	*let je vašemu synovi*	let ye vuh·she·mu si·no·vi

I'm ... years old.	Je mi ... let.	ye mi ... let
He's ... years old.	Je mu ... let.	ye mu ... let
She's ... years old.	Jí je ... let.	yee ye ... let

PEGASUS FINE BOOKS & CDS
1855 SOLANO AVE

BERKELEY, CA 94707
(510) 525-6888

B   01738 11/04/2007 07:53 PM

00001   1 Used Book   6.00   6.00

       1   Subtotal: 6.00
                   Tax: 0.53
CLERK   Total Due: 6.53
                   Bank Card   6.53

            Thank You!
Merchandise may be exchanged with
receipt for store credit only
within 7 days.

feelings

Are you ...?	Jste ...?	yste ...
I'm/I'm not ...	Jsem/Nejsem ...	ysem/ney·sem ...
happy	šťastný/šťastná m/f	shtyuhst·nee/shtyuhst·na
hungry	hladový/hladová m/f	hluh·do·vee/hluh·do·va
sad	smutný/smutná m/f	smut·nee/smut·na
thirsty	žíznivý/žíznivá m/f	zheez·nyi·vee/zheez·nyi·va
Are you ...?	Je vám ...?	ye vam ...
I'm/I'm not ...	Je/Neni mi ...	ye/ne·nyi mi ...
cold	zima	zi·muh
hot	horko	hor·ko

entertainment

going out

Where can I find ...?	Kde mohu najít ...?	gde mo·hu nuh·yeet ...
clubs	kluby	klu·bi
gay venues	homosexuální	ho·mo·sek·su·al·nyee
	zábavné podniky	za·buhv·nair pod·ni·ki
pubs	hospody	hos·po·di
I feel like going	Rád bych šel ... m	rad bikh shel ...
to a/the ...	Ráda bych šla ... f	ra·duh bikh shluh ...
concert	na koncert	nuh kon·tsert
movies	do kina	do ki·nuh
party	na mejdan/	nuh mey·duhn/
	večírek	ve·chee·rek
theatre	na hru	nuh hru
restaurant	do restaurace	do res·tow·ruh·tse

interests

Do you like to ...?		
go to concerts	Chodíte na koncerty?	kho·dyee·te nuh kon·tser·ti
dance	Tancujete?	tuhn·tsu·ye·te
listen to music	Posloucháte hudbu?	po·sloh·kha·te hud·bu

Do you like ...?	Máte rád/ráda ...? m/f	ma·te rad/ra·duh ...
I like ...	Mám rád/ráda ... m/f	mam rad/ra·duh ...
I don't like ...	Nemám rád/ráda ... m/f	ne·mam rad/ra·duh ...
art	umění	u·mye·nyee
cooking	vaření	vuh·rzhe·nyee
movies	filmy	fil·mi
reading	čtení	chte·nyee
sport	sport	sport
travelling	cestování	tses·to·va·nyee

food & drink

finding a place to eat

Can you	Můžete	moo·zhe·te
recommend a ...?	doporučit ...?	do·po·ru·chit ...
café	kavárnu	kuh·var·nu
pub	hospodu	hos·po·du
restaurant	restauraci	res·tow·ruh·tsi
I'd like ..., please.	Chtěl/Chtěla bych	khtyel/khtye·luh bikh
	..., prosím. m/f	... pro·seem
a table for (five)	stůl pro (pět)	stool pro (pyet)
the nonsmoking	nekuřáckou	ne·ku·rzhats·koh
section	místnost	meest·nost
the smoking section	kuřáckou místnost	ku·rzhats·koh meest·nost

ordering food

breakfast	snídaně f	snee·duh·nye
lunch	oběd m	o·byed
dinner	večeře f	ve·che·rzhe
snack	občerstvení n	ob·cherst·ve·nyee
What would you	Co byste doporučil/	tso bis·te do·po·ru·chil/
recommend?	doporučila? m/f	do·po·ru·chi·luh

I'd like (the) ...,	Chtěl/Chtěla bych	khtyel/khtye·luh bikh
please.	..., prosím. m/f	... pro·seem
bill	účet	oo·chet
drink list	nápojový lístek	na·po·yo·vee lees·tek
menu	jídelníček	yee·del·nyee·chek
that dish	ten pokrm	ten po·krm

drinks

(cup of) coffee ...	(šálek) kávy ...	(sha·lek) ka·vi ...
(cup of) tea ...	(šálek) čaje ...	(sha·lek) chuh·ye ...
with milk	s mlékem	s mlair·kem
without sugar	bez cukru	bez tsu·kru
(orange) juice	(pomerančový) džus m	(po·me·ruhn·cho·vee) dzhus
soft drink	nealkoholický nápoj m	ne·uhl·ko·ho·lits·kee na·poy
(hot) water	(horká) voda f	(hor·ka) vo·duh
... mineral water	... minerální voda	... mi·ne·ral·nyee vo·duh
sparkling	perlivá	per·li·va
still	neperlivá	ne·per·li·va

in the bar

I'll have a ...	Dám si ...	dam si ...
I'll buy you a drink.	Zvu vás/tě na	zvu vas/tye nuh
	sklenku. pol/inf	sklen·ku
What would you like?	Co byste si přál/	tso bis·te si przhal/
	přála? m/f	przha·la
Cheers!	Na zdraví!	nuh zdruh·vee
brandy	brandy f	bruhn·di
champagne	šampaňské n	shuhm·puhn'·skair
cocktail	koktejl m	kok·teyl
a shot of (whisky)	panák (whisky)	puh·nak (vis·ki)
a bottle/jug of beer	láhev/džbán piva	la·hef/dzhban pi·vuh
a bottle/glass	láhev/skleničku	la·hef/skle·nyich·ku
of ... wine	... vína	... vee·nuh
red	červeného	cher·ve·nair·ho
sparkling	šumivého	shu·mi·vair·ho
white	bílého	bee·lair·ho

self-catering

What's the local speciality?
Co je místní specialita?   tso ye *meest*·nyee spe·tsi·uh·li·tuh

What's that?
Co to je?   tso to ye

How much is (500 grams of cheese)?
Kolik stojí (padesát   *ko*·lik *sto*·yee (puh·de·sat
deka sýra)?   de·kuh see·ruh)

I'd like ...	*Chtěl/Chtěla bych ...* m/f	khtyel/*khtye*·luh bikh ...
200 grams	*dvacet deka*	*dvuh*·tset de·kuh
(two) kilos	*(dvě) kila*	(dvye) *ki*·luh
(three) pieces	*(tři) kusy*	(trzhi) *ku*·si
(six) slices	*(šest) krajíců*	(shest) *kruh*·yee·tsoo

Less.	*Méně.*	*mair*·nye
Enough.	*Stačí.*	*stuh*·chee
More.	*Trochu více.*	*tro*·khu *vee*·tse

special diets & allergies

Is there a vegetarian restaurant near here?
Je zde blízko vegetariánská   ye zde *blees*·ko ve·ge·tuh·ri·ans·ka
restaurace?   res·tow·ruh·tse

Do you have vegetarian food?
Máte vegetariánská jídla?   ma·te ve·ge·tuh·ri·ans·ka *yeed*·luh

Could you prepare a meal without ...?
Mohl/Mohla by jste   *mo*·hl/*mo*·hluh bi yste
připravit jídlo bez ...? m/f   *przhi*·pruh·vit *yeed*·lo bez ...

butter	*máslo* n	*mas*·lo
eggs	*vejce* n pl	*vey*·tse
meat stock	*bujón* m	*bu*·yawn

I'm allergic to ...	*Mám alergii na ...*	mam uh·*ler*·gi·yi nuh ...
dairy produce	*mléčné výrobky*	*mlair*·chnair *vee*·rob·ki
gluten	*lepek*	*le*·pek
MSG	*glutaman sodný*	*glu*·tuh·muhn *sod*·nee
nuts	*ořechy*	*o*·rzhe·khi
seafood	*plody moře*	*plo*·di *mo*·rzhe

menu reader

boršč m	*borshch*	*beetroot soup*
bramboračka f	*bruhm-bo-ruhch-kuh*	*thick soup of potatoes & mushrooms*
bramborák m	*bruhm-bo-rak*	*potato cake*
čevapčiči n pl	*che-vuhp-chi-chi*	*fried or grilled minced veal, pork & mutton made into cone-like shapes*
dršťky f pl	*drsht-ki*	*sliced tripe*
dušená roštěnka f	*du-she-na rosh-tyen-kuh*	*braised beef slices in sauce*
fazolová polévka f	*fuh-zo-lo-va po-lairf-kuh*	*bean soup*
guláš m	*gu-lash*	*thick, spicy stew, usually made with beef & potatoes*
gulášová polévka f	*gu-la-sho-va po-lairf-kuh*	*beef goulash soup*
houskové knedlíky m pl	*hohs-ko-vair kned-lee-ki*	*bread dumplings*
hovězí guláš n	*ho-vye-zee gu-lash*	*beef stew, sometimes served with dumplings*
hrachová polévka f	*hra-kho-va po-lairf-kuh*	*thick pea soup with bacon*
hranolky f pl	*hruh-nol-ki*	*French fries*
jablečný závin m	*yuh-blech-nee za-vin*	*apple strudel*
jelito n	*ye-li-to*	*black pudding*
karbanátek m	*kuhr-buh-na-tek*	*hamburger with breadcrumbs, egg, diced bread roll & onions*
klobása f	*klo-ba-suh*	*thick sausage*
koprová polévka f	*kop-ro-va po-lairf-kuh*	*dill & sour cream soup*

menu reader – CZECH

krokety f pl	*kro-ke-ti*	deep-fried mashed potato balls
kuřecí polévka s nudlemi f	*ku-rzhe-tsee po-lairf-kuh s nud-le-mi*	chicken noodle soup
kuře na paprice n	*ku-rzhe nuh puh-pri-tse*	chicken boiled in spicy paprika cream sauce
lečo n	*le-cho*	stewed onions, capsicums, tomatoes, eggs & sausage
míchaná vejce f pl	*mee-khuh-na vey-tse*	scrambled eggs
nudlová polévka f	*nud-lo-va po-lairf-kuh*	noodle soup made from chicken broth with vegetables
oplatka f	*o-pluht-kuh*	large paper-thin waffle
ovocné knedlíky m pl	*o-vots-nair kned-lee-ki*	fruit dumplings
palačinka f	*puh-luh-chin-kuh*	crepe • pancake
plněná paprika f	*pl-nye-na puh-pri-kuh*	capsicum stuffed with minced meat & rice, in tomato sauce
Pražská šunka f	*pruhzh-ska shun-kuh*	Prague ham – ham pickled in brine & spices & smoked over a fire
přírodní řízek m	*przhee-rod-nyee rzhee-zek*	pork or veal schnitzel without breadcrumbs
rizoto n	*ri-zo-to*	a mixture of pork, onions, peas & rice
ruské vejce n pl	*rus-kair vey-tse*	hard-boiled eggs & ham, topped with mayonnaise & caviar
rybí polévka f	*ri-bee po-lairf-kuh*	fish soup usually made with carp & some carrots, potatoes & peas
smažený květák s bramborem m	*smuh-zhe-nee kvye-tak s bruhm-bo-rem*	cauliflower florets fried in breadcrumbs & served with boiled potatoes & tartar sauce
svíčková na smetaně f	*sveech-ko-va nuh sme-ta-nye*	roast beef & dumplings in carrot cream sauce, topped with lemon, cranberries & whipped cream
tvarohový koláč m	*tvuh-ro-ho-vee ko-lach*	pastry with cottage cheese & raisins

emergencies

basics

Help!	*Pomoc!*	po·mots
Stop!	*Zastav!*	zuhs·tuhf
Go away!	*Běžte pryč!*	byezh·te prich
Thief!	*Zloděj!*	zlo·dyey
Fire!	*Hoří!*	ho·rzhee
Watch out!	*Pozor!*	po·zor
Call …!	*Zavolejte …!*	zuh·vo·ley·te …
a doctor	*lékaře*	lair·kuh·rzhe
an ambulance	*sanitku*	suh·nit·ku
the police	*policii*	po·li·tsi·yi

It's an emergency.
To je naléhavý případ. to ye nuh·lair·huh·vee przhee·puhd

Could you help me, please?
Můžete prosím pomoci? moo·zhe·te pro·seem po·mo·tsi

Can I use the phone?
Mohu si zatelefonovat? mo·hu si zuh·te·le·fo·no·vuht

I'm lost.
Zabloudil/Zabloudila jsem. m/f zuh·bloh·dyil/zuh·bloh·dyi·luh ysem

Where are the toilets?
Kde jsou toalety? gde ysoh to·uh·le·ti

police

Where's the police station?
Kde je policejní stanice? gde ye po·li·tsey·nyee stuh·nyi·tse

I want to report an offence.
Chci nahlásit trestný čin. khtsi nuh·hla·sit trest·nee chin

I have insurance.
Jsem pojištěný/pojištěná. m/f ysem po·yish·tye·nee/po·yish·tye·na

I've been …	… *mě.*	… mye
assaulted	*Přepadli*	przhe·puhd·li
raped	*Znásilnili*	zna·sil·nyi·li
robbed	*Okradli*	o·kruhd·li

I've lost my ...	Ztratil/Ztratila jsem ... m/f	ztruh·tyil/ztruh·tyi·luh ysem ...
My ... was/were stolen.	Ukradli mě ...	u·kruhd·li mye ...
backpack	batoh	buh·tawh
credit card	kreditní kartu	kre·dit·nyee kuhr·tu
bag	zavazadlo	zuh·vuh·zuhd·lo
handbag	kabelku	kuh·bel·ku
jewellery	šperky	shper·ki
money	peníze	pe·nyee·ze
passport	pas	puhs
travellers cheques	cestovní šeky	tses·tov·nyee she·ki
wallet	peněženku	pe·nye·zhen·ku
I want to contact my ...	Potřebuji se obrátit na ...	pot·rzhe·bu·yi se o·bra·tyit nuh ...
consulate	můj konzulát	mooy kon·zu·lat
embassy	mé velvyslanectví	mair vel·vi·sluh·nets·tvee

health

medical needs

Where's the nearest ...?	Kde je nejbližší ...?	gde ye ney·blizh·shee ...
dentist	zubař	zu·buhrzh
doctor	lékař	lair·kuhrzh
hospital	nemocnice	ne·mots·nyi·tse
(night) pharmacist	(non-stop) lékárník	(non·stop) lair·kar·nyeek

I need a doctor (who speaks English).

Potřebuji (anglickomluvícího) doktora.　　pot·rzhe·bu·yi (uhn·glits·kom·lu·vee·tsee·ho) dok·to·ruh

Could I see a female doctor?

Mohla bych být vyšetřená lékařkou?　　mo·hluh bikh beet vi·shet·rzhe·na lair·kuhrzh·koh

I've run out of my medication.

Došli mi léky.　　dosh·li mi lair·ki

symptoms, conditions & allergies

I'm sick.	Jsem nemocný/ nemocná. m/f	ysem ne·mots·nee/ ne·mots·na
It hurts here.	Tady to bolí.	tuh·di to bo·lee
I have (a) ...	Mám ...	mam ...

asthma	astma n	uhst·muh
bronchitis	zánět průdušek m	za·nyet proo·du·shek
constipation	zácpa f	zats·puh
cough n	kašel m	kuh·shel
diarrhoea	průjem m	proo·yem
fever	horečka f	ho·rech·kuh
headache	bolesti hlavy f	bo·les·tyi hluh·vi
heart condition	srdeční porucha f	sr·dech·nyee po·ru·khuh
nausea	nevolnost f	ne·vol·nost
pain n	bolest f	bo·lest
sore throat	bolest v krku f	bo·lest f kr·ku
toothache	bolení zubu n	bo·le·nyee zu·bu

I'm allergic to ...	Jsem alergický/ alergická na ... m/f	ysem uh·ler·gits·kee/ uh·ler·gits·ka nuh ...
antibiotics	antibiotika	uhn·ti·bi·o·ti·kuh
anti-inflammatories	protizánětlivé léky	pro·tyi·za·nyet·li·vair lair·ki
aspirin	aspirin	uhs·pi·rin
bees	včely	fche·li
codeine	kodein	ko·deyn
penicillin	penicilin	pe·ni·tsi·lin

antiseptic	antiseptický prostředek m	uhn·ti·sep·tits·kee prost·rzhe·dek
bandage	obvaz m	ob·vuhz
condoms	prezervativy m pl	pre·zer·vuh·ti·vi
contraceptives	antikoncepce f	uhn·ti·kon·tsep·tse
diarrhoea medicine	lék na průjem m	lairk nuh proo·yem
insect repellent	prostředek na hubení hmyzu m	pros·trzhe·dek nuh hu·be·nyee hmi·zu
laxatives	projímadla m pl	pro·yee·muhd·la
painkillers	prášky proti bolesti m pl	prash·ki pro·tyi bo·les·tyi
rehydration salts	iontový nápoj m	yon·to·vee na·poy
sleeping tablets	prášky na spaní m pl	prash·ki nuh spuh·nyee

english–czech dictionary

Czech nouns in this dictionary have their gender indicated by ⓜ (masculine), ⓕ (feminine) or ⓝ (neuter). If it's a plural noun, you'll also see pl. Adjectives are given in the masculine form only. Words are also marked as a (adjective), v (verb), sg (singular), pl (plural), inf (informal) or pol (polite) where necessary.

A

accident *nehoda* ⓕ ne-ho-duh
accommodation *ubytování* ⓝ
   u-bi-to-va-nyee
adaptor *adaptor* ⓜ uh-duhp-tor
address *adresa* ⓕ uh-dre-suh
after *po* po
air-conditioned *klimatizovaný* klí-muh-ti-zo-vuh-nee
airplane *letadlo* ⓝ le-tuhd-lo
airport *letiště* ⓝ le-tyish-tye
alcohol *alkohol* ⓜ uhl-ko-hol
all a *všichni* vshikh-nyi
allergy *alergie* ⓕ uh-ler-gi-ye
ambulance *ambulance* ⓕ uhm-bu-luhn-tse
and a uh
ankle *kotník* ⓜ kot-nyeek
arm *paže* ⓕ puh-zhe
ashtray *popelník* ⓜ po-pel-nyeek
ATM *bankomat* ⓜ buhn-ko-muht

B

baby *nemluvně* ⓝ nem-luv-nye
back (body) *záda* za-duh
backpack *batoh* ⓜ buh-tawh
bad *špatný* shpuht-nee
bag *taška* ⓕ tuhsh-kuh
baggage claim *výdej zavazadel* ⓜ
   vee-dey zuh-vuh-zuh-del
bank *banka* ⓕ buhn-kuh
bar *bar* ⓜ buhr
bathroom *koupelna* ⓕ koh-pel-nuh
battery *baterie* ⓕ buh-te-ri-ye
beautiful *krásný* kras-nee
bed *postel* ⓕ pos-tel
beer *pivo* ⓝ pi-vo
before *před* przhed
behind *za* zuh
bicycle *kolo* ⓝ ko-lo
big *velký* vel-kee
bill *účet* ⓜ oo-chet
black *černý* cher-nee

blanket *deka* ⓕ de-kuh
blood group *krevní skupina* ⓕ
   krev-nyee sku-pi-nuh
blue *modrý* mod-ree
book (make a reservation) v *objednat* ob-yed-nuht
bottle *láhev* ⓕ la-hef
bottle opener *otvírák na láhve* ⓜ
   ot-vee-rak nuh lah-ve
boy *chlapec* ⓜ khluh-pets
brakes (car) *brzdy* ⓕ pl brz-di
breakfast *snídaně* ⓕ snee-duh-nye
broken (faulty) *zlomený* zlo-me-nee
bus *autobus* ⓜ ow-to-bus
business *obchod* ⓜ op-khod
buy *koupit* koh-pit

C

café *kavárna* ⓕ kuh-var-nuh
camera *fotoaparát* ⓜ fo-to-uh-puh-rat
camp site *autokempink* ⓜ ow-to-kem-pink
cancel *zrušit* zru-shit
can opener *otvírák na konzervy* ⓜ
   ot-vee-rak nuh kon-zer-vi
car *auto* ⓝ ow-to
cash *hotovost* ⓕ ho-to-vost
cash (a cheque) v *inkasovat šek* in-kuh-so-vuht shek
cell phone *mobil* ⓜ mo-bil
centre *střed* ⓜ strzhed
change (money) v *vyměnit* vi-mye-nyit
cheap *levný* lev-nee
check (bill) *účet* ⓜ oo-chet
check-in *recepce* ⓕ re-tsep-tse
chest *hruď* ⓕ hrud'
child *dítě* ⓝ dyee-tye
cigarette *cigareta* ⓕ tsi-guh-re-tuh
city *město* ⓝ myes-to
clean a *čistý* chis-tee
closed *zavřený* zuh-vrzhe-nee
coffee *káva* ⓕ ka-vuh
coins *mince* ⓕ min-tse
cold a *chladný* khluhd-nee
collect call *hovor na účet volaného* ⓜ
   ho-vor nuh oo-chet vo-luh-nair-ho

come *přijít* przhi-yeet
computer *počítač* ⓜ po-chee-tuhch
condom *prezervativ* ⓜ pre-zer-vuh-tif
contact lenses *kontaktní čočky* ① pl
kon-tuhkt-nyee choch-ki
cook v *vařit* vuh-rzhit
cost *cena* ① tse-nuh
credit card *kreditní karta* ①
kre-dit-nyee kuhr-tuh
cup *šálek* ⓜ sha-lek
currency exchange *směnárna* ① smye-nar-nuh
customs (immigration) *celnice* ① tsel-ni-tse
Czech a *český* ches-kee
Czech (language) *čeština* ① chesh-tyi-nuh
Czech Republic *Česká republika* ①
ches-ka re-pu-bli-kuh

D

dangerous *nebezpečný* ne-bez-pech-nee
date (time) *schůzka* ① skhooz-kuh
day *den* ⓜ den
delay *zpoždění* ⓝ zpozh-dye-nyee
dentist *zubař/zubařka* ⓜ/① zu-buhrzh/zu-buhrzh-kuh
depart *odjet* od-yet
diaper *plénka* ① plairn-kuh
dictionary *slovník* ⓜ slov-nyeek
dinner *večeře* ⓝ ve-che-rzhe
direct *přímý* przhee-mee
dirty *špinavý* shpi-nuh-vee
disabled *invalidní* in-vuh-lid-nyee
discount *sleva* ① sle-vuh
doctor *doktor/doktorka* ⓜ/① dok-tor/dok-tor-kuh
double bed *manželská postel* ① muhn-zhels-ka pos-tel
double room *dvoulůžkový pokoj* ⓜ
dvoh-loozh-ko-vee po-koy
drink *nápoj* ⓜ na-poy
drive v *řídit* rzhee-dyit
drivers licence *řidičský průkaz* ⓜ
rzhi-dyich-skee proo-kuhz
drugs (illicit) *drogy* ① pl dro-gi
dummy (pacifier) *dudlík* ⓝ dud-leek

E

ear *ucho* ⓝ u-kho
east *východ* ⓜ vee-khod
eat *jíst* yeest
economy class *turistická třída* ① tu-ris-tits-ka trzhee-duh
electricity *elektřina* ① e-lek-trzhi-nuh
elevator *výtah* ⓜ vee-tuh
email *email* ⓜ ee-meyl

embassy *velvyslanectví* ⓝ vel-vi-sluh-nets-tvee
emergency *pohotovost* ① po-ho-to-vost
English (language) *angličtina* ① uhn-glich-tyi-nuh
entrance *vstup* ⓜ vstup
evening *večer* ⓜ ve-cher
exchange rate *směnný kurs* ⓜ smye-nee kurz
exit *východ* ⓜ vee-khod
expensive *drahý* druh-hee
express mail *expresní zásilka* ① eks-pres-nyee za-sil-kuh
eye *oko* ⓝ o-ko

F

far *daleko* duh-le-ko
fast *rychlý* rikh-lee
father *otec* ⓜ o-tets
film (camera) *film* ⓜ film
finger *prst* ⓜ prst
first-aid kit *lékárnička* ① lair-kar-nyich-kuh
first class *první třída* ① prv-nyee trzhee-duh
fish *ryba* ① ri-buh
food *jídlo* ⓝ yeed-lo
foot *chodidlo* ⓝ kho-dyid-lo
fork *vidlička* ① vid-lich-kuh
free (of charge) *bezplatný* bez-pluht-nee
friend *přítel/přítelkyně* ⓜ/①
przhee-tel/przhee-tel-ki-nye
fruit *ovoce* ⓝ o-vo-tse
full *plný* pl-nee
funny *legrační* le-gruhch-nyee

G

gift *dar* ⓜ duhr
girl *dívka* ① dyeef-kuh
glass (drinking) *sklenička* ① skle-nyich-kuh
glasses *brýle* ① pl bree-le
go *jít* yeet
good *dobrý* do-bree
green *zelený* ze-le-nee
guide *průvodce* ⓜ proo-vod-tse

H

half *polovina* ① po-lo-vi-nuh
hand *ruka* ① ru-kuh
handbag *kabelka* ① kuh-bel-kuh
happy *šťastný* shtyast-nee
have *mít* meet
he *on* on
head *hlava* ① hluh-vuh
heart *srdce* ⓝ srd-tse

heat *horko* ⓝ hor-ko
heavy *těžký* tyezh-kee
help v *pomoci* po-mo-tsi
here *tady* tuh-di
high *vysoký* vi-so-kee
highway *dálnice* ① dal-nyi-tse
hike v *trampovat* truhm-po-vuht
holiday *svátek* ⓜ sva-tek
homosexual *homosexuál* ⓜ ho-mo-sek-su-al
hospital *nemocnice* ① ne-mots-nyi-tse
hot *horký* hor-kee
hotel *hotel* ⓜ ho-tel
hungry *hladový* hluh-do-vee
husband *manžel* ⓜ muhn-zhel

I

I *já* ya
identification (card) *osobní doklad* ①
  o-sob-nyee dok-luhd
ill *nemocný* ne-mots-nee
important *důležitý* doo-le-zhi-tee
included *včetně* fchet-nye
injury *zranění* ⓝ zruh-nye-nyee
insurance *pojištění* ⓝ po-yish-tye-nyee
Internet *internet* ⓜ in-ter-net
interpreter *tlumočník/tlumočnice* ⓜ/①
  tlu-moch-nyeek/tlu-moch-nyi-tse

J

jewellery *šperky* ⓜ pl shper-ki
job *zaměstnání* ⓝ zuh-myest-na-nyee

K

key *klíč* ⓜ kleech
kilogram *kilogram* ⓜ ki-lo-gruhm
kitchen *kuchyň* ① ku-khin'
knife *nůž* ⓜ noozh

L

laundry (place) *prádelna* ① pra-del-nuh
lawyer *advokát/advokátka* ⓜ/①
  uhd-vo-kat/uhd-vo-kat-kuh
left (direction) *levý* le-vee
left-luggage office *úschovna zavazadel* ①
  oos-khov-nuh zuh-vuh-zuh-del
leg *noha* ① no-huh

lesbian *lesbička* ① les-bich-kuh
less *menší* men-shee
letter (mail) *dopis* ⓜ do-pis
lift (elevator) *výtah* ⓜ vee-tah
light *světlo* ⓝ svyet-lo
like v *mít rád* meet rad
lock *zámek* ⓜ za-mek
long *dlouhý* dloh-hee
lost *ztracený* ztruh-tse-nee
lost-property office *ztráty a nálezy* ①
  ztra-ti uh na-le-zi
love v *milovat* mi-lo-vuht
luggage *zavazadlo* ⓝ zuh-vuh-zuhd-lo
lunch *oběd* o-byed

M

mail *pošta* ① posh-tuh
man *muž* ⓜ muzh
map (of country) *mapa* ① muh-puh
map (of town) *plán* ⓜ plan
market *trh* ⓜ trh
matches *zápalky* ① pl za-puhl-ki
meat *maso* ⓝ muh-so
medicine *lék* ⓜ laik
menu *jídelní lístek* ⓜ yee-del-nyee lees-tek
message *zpráva* ① zpra-vuh
milk *mléko* ⓝ mlair-ko
minute *minuta* ① mi-nu-tuh
mobile phone *mobil* ⓜ mo-bil
money *peníze* ⓜ pl pe-nyee-ze
month *měsíc* ⓜ mye-seets
morning *ráno* ⓝ ra-no
mother *matka* ① muht-kuh
motorcycle *motorka* ① mo-tor-kuh
motorway *dálnice* ① dal-nyi-tse
mouth *ústa* ① oos-tuh
music *hudba* ① hud-buh

N

name *jméno* ⓝ ymair-no
napkin *ubrousek* ⓜ u-broh-sek
nappy *plenka* ① plen-kuh
near *blízko* bleez-ko
neck *krk* ⓜ krk
new *nový* no-vee
news *zprávy* ① pl zpra-vi
newspaper *noviny* ① pl no-vi-ni
night *noc* ① nots
no *ne* ne

noisy *hlučný hluch*-nee
nonsmoking *nekuřácký ne*-ku-rzhats-kee
north *sever* m *se*-ver
nose *nos* m nos
now *teď teď*
number *číslo* n chees-lo

O

oil (engine) *olej* m *o*-ley
old *starý stuh*-ree
one-way ticket *jednoduchá jízdenka* f
   yed-no-du-kha yeez-den-kuh
open a *otevřený o-tev*-rzhe-nee
outside *venku ven*-ku

P

package *balík* m *buh*-leek
paper *papír* m *puh*-peer
park (car) v *parkovat puhr*-ko-vuht
passport *pas* m puhs
pay *platit pluh*-tyit
pen *propiska* f *pro*-pis-kuh
petrol *benzín* m *ben*-zeen
pharmacy *lékárna* f *lair*-kar-nuh
phonecard *telefonní karta* f
   te-le-fo-nyee *kuhr*-tuh
photo *fotka* f *fot*-kuh
plate *talíř* m *tuh*-leerzh
police *policie* f po-li-tsi-ye
postcard *pohled* m *po*-hled
post office *pošta* f *posh*-tuh
pregnant *těhotná tye*-hot-na
price *cena* f *tse*-nuh

Q

quiet *tichý tyi*-khee

R

rain *déšť* m dairsht'
razor *břitva* f *brzhit*-vuh
receipt *stvrzenka* f *stvr*-zen-kuh
red *červený cher*-ve-nee
refund *vrácení peněz* n *vruh*-tse-nyee pe-nyez
registered mail *doporučená zásilka* f
   do-po-ru-che-na za-sil-kuh
rent v *pronajmout pro*-nai-moht

repair v *opravit o*-pruh-vit
reservation *rezervace* f *re*-zer-vuh-tse
restaurant *restaurace* f *res*-tow-ruh-tse
return v *vrátit se vra*-tyit se
return ticket *zpáteční jízdenka* f
   zpa-tech-nyee yeez-den-kuh
right (direction) *pravý pruh*-vee
road *silnice* f *sil*-nyi-tse
room *pokoj* m *po*-koy

S

safe a *bezpečný bez*-pech-nee
sanitary napkins *dámské vložky* f pl
   dams-kair vlozh-ki
seat *místo* n *mees*-to
send *poslat pos*-luht
service station *benzínová pumpa* f
   ben-zee-no-va pum-puh
sex *pohlaví* n *po*-hluh-vee
shampoo *šampon* m *shuhm*-pon
share (a dorm) *spoluobývat spo*-lu-o-bee-vuht
shaving cream *pěna na holení* f
   pye-nuh nuh ho-le-nyee
she *ona o*-nuh
sheet (bed) *prostěradlo* n *pros*-tye-ruhd-lo
shirt *košile* f *ko*-shi-le
shoes *boty* f pl *bo*-ti
shop *obchod* m *op*-khod
short *krátký krat*-kee
shower *sprcha* f *spr*-khuh
single room *jednolůžkový pokoj* m
   yed-no-loozh-ko-vee *po*-koy
skin *kůže* f *koo*-zhe
skirt *sukně* f *suk*-nye
sleep v *spát* spat
slowly *pomalu po*-muh-lu
small *malý muh*-lee
smoke (cigarettes) v *kouřit koh*-rzhit
soap *mýdlo* n *meed*-lo
some *několik nye*-ko-lik
soon *brzy br*-zi
south *jih* m yih
souvenir shop *obchod se suvenýry* m
   op-khod se su-ve-nee-ri
speak *říci rzhee*-tsi
spoon *lžíce* f *lzhee*-tse
stamp *známka* f *znam*-kuh
station (train) *nádraží* n *na*-druh-zhee
stomach *žaludek* m *zhuh*-lu-dek

stop v *zastavit* zuhs-tuh-vit

stop (bus) *zastávka* ① zuhs-taf-kuh

street *ulice* ① u-li-tse

student *student/studentka* ⓜ/①
stu-dent/stu-dent-kuh

sun *slunce* ⓝ slun-tse

sunscreen *opalovací krém* ⓝ o-puh-lo-vuh-tsee krairm

swim v *plavat* pluh-vuht

T

tampons *tampon* ⓜ tuhm-pon

taxi *taxík* ⓜ tuhk-seek

teaspoon *lžička* ① lzhich-kuh

teeth *zuby* ⓜ pl zu-bi

telephone *telefon* ⓜ te-le-fon

television *televize* ① te-le-vi-ze

temperature (weather) *teplota* ① te-plo-tuh

tent *stan* ⓜ stuhn

that (one) *tamten* tuhm-ten

they *oni* o-nyi

thirsty *žíznivý* zheez-nyi-vee

this (one) *tenhle* ten-hle

throat *hrdlo* ⓝ hrd-lo

ticket *vstupenka* ① fstu-pen-kuh

time *čas* ⓜ chuhs

tired *unavený* u-nuh-ve-nee

tissues *kosmetické kapesníčky* ⓜ pl
kos-me-tits-kair kuh-pes-neech-ki

today *dnes* dnes

toilet *toaleta* ① to-uh-le-tuh

tomorrow *zítra* zeet-ruh

tonight *dnes večer* dnes ve-cher

toothbrush *zubní kartáček* ⓜ zub-nyee kuhr-ta-chek

toothpaste *zubní pasta* ① zub-nyee puhs-tuh

torch (flashlight) *baterka* ① buh-ter-kuh

tour *okružní jízda* ① o-kruzh-nyee yeez-duh

tourist office *turistická informační kancelář* ①
tu-ris-tits-ka in-for-muhch-nyee kuhn-tse-larzh

towel *ručník* ⓜ ruch-nyeek

train *vlak* ⓜ vluhk

translate *přeložit* przhe-lo-zhit

travel agency *cestovní kancelář* ①
tses-tov-nyee kuhn-tse-larzh

travellers cheque *cestovní šek* ① tses-tov-nyee shek

trousers *kalhoty* ① pl kuhl-ho-ti

twin beds *dvoupostel* ① dvoh-pos-tel

tyre *pneumatika* ① pne-u-muh-ti-kuh

U

underwear *spodní prádlo* ⓝ spod-nyee prad-lo

urgent *naléhavý* nuh-lair-huh-vee

V

vacant *volný* vol-nee

vacation (from school) *prázdniny* ① prazd-nyi-ni

vacation (from work) *dovolená* ① do-vo-le-na

vegetable *zelenina* ① ze-le-nyi-nuh

vegetarian a *vegetariánský* ve-ge-tuh-ri-yans-kee

W

waiter/waitress *číšník/číšnice* ⓜ/①
cheesh-nyeek/cheesh-nyi-tse

wallet *peněženka* ① pe-nye-zhen-ka

walk v *jít* yeet

warm a *teplý* tep-lee

wash (something) *umýt* u-meet

watch *hodinky* ① pl ho-dyin-ki

water *voda* ① vo-duh

we *my* mi

weekend *víkend* ⓜ vee-kend

west *západ* ⓜ za-puhd

wheelchair *invalidní vozík* ⓜ in-vuh-lid-nyee vo-zeek

when *kdy* gdi

where *kde* gde

white *bílý* bee-lee

who *kdo* gdo

why *proč* proch

wife *manželka* ① muhn-zhel-kuh

window *okno* ⓝ ok-no

wine *víno* ⓝ vee-no

with s s

without *bez* bez

woman *žena* ① zhe-nuh

write *psát* p-sat

Y

yellow *žlutý* zhlu-tee

yes *ano* uh-no

yesterday *včera* fche-ruh

you sg inf *ty* ti

you sg pol&pl *vy* vi

German

german alphabet

A a a	*B b* be	*C c* tse	*D d* de	*E e* e
F f ef	*G g* ge	*H h* ha	*I i* i	*J j* yot
K k ka	*L l* el	*M m* em	*N n* en	*O o* o
P p pe	*Q q* ku	*R r* er	*S s* es	*T t* te
U u u	*V v* fau	*W w* ve	*X x* iks	*Y y* ewp·si·lon
Z z tset				

■ **german**

DEUTSCH

introduction

Romantic, flowing, literary . . . not usually how German (*Deutsch* doytsh) is described, but maybe it's time to reconsider. After all, this is the language that's played a major role in the history of Europe and remains one of the most widely spoken languages on the continent. It's taught throughout the world and chances are you're already familiar with a number of German words that have entered English – *kindergarten*, *kitsch* and *hamburger*, for example, are all of German origin.

German is spoken by around 100 million people, and is the official language of Germany, Austria and Liechtenstein, as well as one of the official languages of Belgium, Switzerland and Luxembourg. German didn't spread across the rest of the world with the same force as English, Spanish or French. Germany only became a unified nation in 1871 and never established itself as a colonial power. After the reunification of East and West Germany, however, German has become more important in global politics and economics. Its role in science has long been recognised and German literature lays claim to some of the most famous written works ever printed. Just think of the enormous influence of Goethe, Nietzsche, Freud and Einstein.

German is usually divided into two forms – Low German (*Plattdeutsch* plat-doytsh) and High German (*Hochdeutsch* hokh-doytsh). Low German is an umbrella term used for the dialects spoken in Northern Germany. High German is considered the standard form and is understood throughout German-speaking communities, from the Swiss Alps to the cosy cafés of Vienna; it's also the form used in this phrasebook.

Both German and English belong to the West Germanic language family, along with a number of other languages including Dutch and Yiddish. The primary reason why German and English have grown apart is that the Normans, on invading England in 1066, brought with them a large number of non-Germanic words. As well as the recognisable words, the grammar of German will also make sense to an English speaker. Even with a slight grasp of German grammar, you'll still manage to get your point across. On the other hand, German tends to join words together (while English uses a number of separate words) to express a single notion. You shouldn't be intimidated by this though – after a while you'll be able to tell parts of words and recognising 'the Football World Cup qualifying match' hidden within *Fussballweltmeisterschaftsqualifikationsspiel* won't be a problem at all!

pronunciation

vowel sounds

German vowels can be short or long, which influences the meaning of words. They're pronounced crisply and distinctly, so *Tee* (tea) is tey, not *tey*·ee.

symbol	english equivalent	german example	transliteration
a	**run**	*hat*	hat
aa	**father**	*habe*	*haa*·be
ai	**aisle**	*mein*	main
air	**fair**	*Bär*	bair
aw	**saw**	*Boot*	bawt
e	**bet**	*Männer*	*me*·ner
ee	**see**	*fliegen*	*flee*·gen
eu	**nurse**	*schön*	sheun
ew	**ee** pronounced with rounded lips	*zurück*	tsu·*rewk*
ey	as in 'bet', but longer	*leben*	*ley*·ben
i	**hit**	*mit*	mit
o	**pot**	*Koffer*	*ko*·fer
oo	**zoo**	*Schuhe*	*shoo*·e
ow	**now**	*Haus*	hows
oy	**toy**	*Leute, Häuser*	*loy*·te, *hoy*·zer
u	**put**	*unter*	*un*·ter

word stress

Almost all German words are pronounced with stress on the first syllable. While this is a handy rule of thumb, you can always rely on the coloured pronunciation guides, which show the stressed syllables in italics.

consonant sounds

All German consonant sounds exist in English except for the kh and r sounds. The kh sound is generally pronounced at the back of the throat, like the 'ch' in 'Bach' or the Scottish 'loch'. The r sound is pronounced at the back of the throat, almost like saying g, but with some friction, a bit like gargling.

symbol	english equivalent	german example	transliteration
b	bed	*Bett*	bet
ch	cheat	*Tschüss*	chews
d	dog	*dein*	dain
f	fat	*vier*	feer
g	go	*gehen*	*gey*·en
h	hat	*helfen*	*hel*·fen
k	kit	*kein*	kain
kh	loch	*ich*	ikh
l	lot	*laut*	lowt
m	man	*Mann*	man
n	not	*nein*	nain
ng	ring	*singen*	*zing*·en
p	pet	*Preis*	prais
r	run (throaty)	*Reise*	*rai*·ze
s	sun	*heiß*	hais
sh	shot	*schön*	sheun
t	top	*Tag*	taak
ts	hits	*Zeit*	tsait
v	very	*wohnen*	*vaw*·nen
y	yes	*ja*	yaa
z	zero	*sitzen*	*zi*·tsen
zh	pleasure	*Garage*	ga·*raa*·zhe

tools

language difficulties

Do you speak English?
Sprechen Sie Englisch?   shpre·khen zee eng·lish

Do you understand?
Verstehen Sie?   fer·shtey·en zee

I (don't) understand.
Ich verstehe (nicht).   ikh fer·shtey·e (nikht)

What does (Kugel) mean?
Was bedeutet (Kugel)?   vas be·doy·tet (koo·gel)

How do you ...?	*Wie ...?*	vee ...
pronounce this	*spricht man dieses Wort aus*	shprikht man dee·zes vort ows
write (Schweiz)	*schreibt man (Schweiz)*	shraipt man (shvaits)

Could you please ...?	*Könnten Sie ...?*	keun·ten zee ...
repeat that	*das bitte wiederholen*	das bi·te vee·der·haw·len
speak more slowly	*bitte langsamer sprechen*	bi·te lang·za·mer shpre·khen
write it down	*das bitte aufschreiben*	das bi·te owf·shrai·ben

essentials

Yes.	*Ja.*	yaa
No.	*Nein.*	nain
Please.	*Bitte.*	bi·te
Thank you.	*Danke.*	dang·ke
Thank you very much.	*Vielen Dank.*	fee·len dangk
You're welcome.	*Bitte.*	bi·te
Excuse me.	*Entschuldigung.*	ent·shul·di·gung
Sorry.	*Entschuldigung.*	ent·shul·di·gung

numbers

0	*null*	nul	16	*sechzehn*	zeks·tseyn	
1	*eins*	ains	17	*siebzehn*	zeep·tseyn	
2	*zwei*	tsvai	18	*achtzehn*	akht·tseyn	
3	*drei*	drai	19	*neunzehn*	noyn·tseyn	
4	*vier*	feer	20	*zwanzig*	tsvan·tsikh	
5	*fünf*	fewnf	21	*einundzwanzig*	ain·unt·tsvan·tsikh	
6	*sechs*	zeks	22	*zweiundzwanzig*	tsvai·unt·tsvan·tsikh	
7	*sieben*	zee·ben	30	*dreißig*	drai·tsikh	
8	*acht*	akht	40	*vierzig*	feer·tsikh	
9	*neun*	noyn	50	*fünfzig*	fewnf·tsikh	
10	*zehn*	tseyn	60	*sechzig*	zekh·tsikh	
11	*elf*	elf	70	*siebzig*	zeep·tsikh	
12	*zwölf*	zveulf	80	*achtzig*	akht·tsikh	
13	*dreizehn*	drai·tseyn	90	*neunzig*	noyn·tsikh	
14	*vierzehn*	feer·tseyn	100	*hundert*	hun·dert	
15	*fünfzehn*	fewnf·tseyn	1000	*tausend*	tow·sent	

time & dates

What time is it?	*Wie spät ist es?*	vee shpeyt ist es
It's one o'clock.	*Es ist ein Uhr.*	es ist ain oor
It's (10) o'clock.	*Es ist (zehn) Uhr.*	es ist (tseyn) oor
Quarter past (one).	*Viertel nach (eins).*	fir·tel naakh (ains)
Half past (one).	*Halb (zwei).* (lit: half two)	halp (tsvai)
Quarter to (one).	*Viertel vor (eins).*	fir·tel fawr (ains)
At what time ...?	*Um wie viel Uhr ...?*	um vee feel oor ...
At ...	*Um ...*	um ...
am	*vormittags*	fawr·mi·taaks
pm (midday–6pm)	*nachmittags*	naakh·mi·taaks
pm (6pm–midnight)	*abends*	aa·bents
Monday	*Montag*	mawn·taak
Tuesday	*Dienstag*	deens·taak
Wednesday	*Mittwoch*	mit·vokh
Thursday	*Donnerstag*	do·ners·taak
Friday	*Freitag*	frai·taak
Saturday	*Samstag*	zams·taak
Sunday	*Sonntag*	zon·taak

January	*Januar*	*yan*·u·aar
February	*Februar*	*fey*·bru·aar
March	*März*	merts
April	*April*	a·*pril*
May	*Mai*	mai
June	*Juni*	*yoo*·ni
July	*Juli*	*yoo*·li
August	*August*	ow·*gust*
September	*September*	zep·*tem*·ber
October	*Oktober*	ok·*taw*·ber
November	*November*	no·*vem*·ber
December	*Dezember*	de·*tsem*·ber

What date is it today?
   Der Wievielte ist heute?   dair vee·feel·te ist *hoy*·te

It's (18 October).
   Heute ist (der achtzehnte Oktober).   *hoy*·te ist dair (*akh*·tseyn·te ok·*taw*·ber)

| since (May) | *seit (Mai)* | zait (mai) |
| until (June) | *bis (Juni)* | bis (*yoo*·ni) |

yesterday	*gestern*	*ges*·tern
today	*heute*	*hoy*·te
tonight	*heute Abend*	*hoy*·te *aa*·bent
tomorrow	*morgen*	*mor*·gen

last ...
night	*vergangene Nacht*	fer·*gang*·e·ne nakht
week	*letzte Woche*	*lets*·te *vo*·khe
month	*letzten Monat*	*lets*·ten *maw*·nat
year	*letztes Jahr*	*lets*·tes yaar

next ...
week	*nächste Woche*	*neykhs*·te *vo*·khe
month	*nächsten Monat*	*neykhs*·ten *maw*·nat
year	*nächstes Jahr*	*neykhs*·tes yaar

yesterday/	*gestern/*	*ges*·tern/
tomorrow ...	*morgen ...*	*mor*·gen ...
morning	*Morgen*	*mor*·gen
afternoon	*Nachmittag*	*naakh*·mi·taak
evening	*Abend*	*aa*·bent

weather

What's the weather like?	*Wie ist das Wetter?*	vee ist das *ve*·ter

It's ...

cloudy	*Es ist wolkig.*	es ist *vol*·kikh
cold	*Es ist kalt.*	es ist kalt
hot	*Es ist heiß.*	es ist hais
raining	*Es regnet.*	es *reyg*·net
snowing	*Es schneit.*	es shnait
sunny	*Es ist sonnig.*	es ist *zo*·nikh
warm	*Es ist warm.*	es ist varm
windy	*Es ist windig.*	es ist *vin*·dikh

spring	*Frühling* m	*frew*·ling
summer	*Sommer* m	*zo*·mer
autumn	*Herbst* m	herpst
winter	*Winter* m	*vin*·ter

border crossing

I'm here ...	*Ich bin hier ...*	ikh bin heer ...
in transit	*auf der Durchreise*	owf dair *durkh*·rai·ze
on business	*auf Geschäftsreise*	owf ge·*shefts*·rai·ze
on holiday	*im Urlaub*	im *oor*·lowp

I'm here for ...	*Ich bin hier für ...*	ikh bin heer fewr ...
(10) days	*(zehn) Tage*	(tseyn) *taa*·ge
(three) weeks	*(drei) Wochen*	(drai) *vo*·khen
(two) months	*(zwei) Monate*	(tsvai) *maw*·na·te

I'm going to (Salzburg).
Ich gehe nach (Salzburg).   ikh *gey*·e nakh *zalts*·boorg

I'm staying at the (Hotel Park).
Ich wohne im (Hotel Park).   ikh *vaw*·ne im (ho·*tel* park)

I have nothing to declare.
Ich habe nichts zu verzollen.   ikh *haa*·be nikhts tsoo fer·*tso*·len

I have something to declare.
Ich habe etwas zu verzollen.   ikh *haa*·be *et*·vas tsoo fer·*tso*·len

That's (not) mine.
Das ist (nicht) meins.   das ist (nikht) mains

transport

tickets & luggage

Where can I buy a ticket?
Wo kann ich eine Fahrkarte kaufen?   vaw kan ikh *ai*·ne *faar*·kar·te *kow*·fen

Do I need to book a seat?
Muss ich einen Platz   mus ikh *ai*·nen plats
reservieren lassen?   re·zer·*vee*·ren *la*·sen

One ... ticket to	*Einen ... nach*	*ai*·nen ... naakh
(Berlin), please.	*(Berlin), bitte.*	(ber·*leen*) *bi*·te
one-way	*einfache Fahrkarte*	*ain*·fa·khe *faar*·kar·te
return	*Rückfahrkarte*	*rewk*·faar·kar·te

I'd like to ...	*Ich möchte meine*	ikh *meukh*·te *mai*·ne
my ticket, please.	*Fahrkarte bitte ...*	*faar*·kar·te *bi*·te ...
cancel	*zurückgeben*	tsu·*rewk*·gey·ben
change	*ändern lassen*	*en*·dern *la*·sen
collect	*abholen*	ab·*ho*·len
confirm	*bestätigen lassen*	be·*shtey*·ti·gen *la*·sen

I'd like a ...	*Ich hätte gern*	ikh *he*·te gern
seat, please.	*einen ...*	*ai*·nen ...
nonsmoking	*Nichtraucherplatz*	*nikht*·row·kher·plats
smoking	*Raucherplatz*	*row*·kher·plats

How much is it?
Was kostet das?   vas *kos*·tet das

Is there air conditioning?
Gibt es eine Klimaanlage?   gipt es *ai*·ne *klee*·ma·an·*laa*·ge

Is there a toilet?
Gibt es eine Toilette?   gipt es *ai*·ne to·a·*le*·te

How long does the trip take?
Wie lange dauert die Fahrt?   vee *lang*·e *dow*·ert dee faart

Is it a direct route?
Ist es eine direkte Verbindung?   ist es *ai*·ne di·*rek*·te fer·*bin*·dung

I'd like a luggage locker.
Ich hätte gern ein Gepäckschließfach.   ikh *he*·te gern ain ge·*pek*·shlees·fakh

My luggage has been ...	*Mein Gepäck ist ...*	main ge-*pek* ist ...
damaged	*beschädigt*	be-*shey*-dikht
lost	*verloren gegangen*	fer-*law*-ren ge-*gang*-en
stolen	*gestohlen worden*	ge-*shtaw*-len *vor*-den

getting around

Where does flight (D4) arrive?
Wo ist die Ankunft des Fluges (D4)? vaw ist dee *an*-kunft des *floo*-ges (de feer)

Where does flight (D4) depart?
Wo ist die der Abflug des Fluges (D4)? vaw ist dair *ab*-flug des *floo*-ges (de feer)

Where's the ...?	*Wo ist ...?*	vaw ist ...
arrivalls hall	*Ankunftshalle*	an-kunfts-*ha*-le
departures hall	*Abflughalle*	ab-flug-*ha*-le

Is this the ...	*Fährt ...*	fairt ...
to (Hamburg)?	*nach (Hamburg)?*	nakh (*ham*-burg)
boat	*das Boot*	das bawt
bus	*der Bus*	dair bus
plane	*das Flugzeug*	das *flook*-tsoyk
train	*der Zug*	dair tsook

What time's	*Wann fährt der*	van fairt dair
the ... bus?	*... Bus?*	... bus
first	*erste*	*ers*-te
last	*letzte*	*lets*-te
next	*nächste*	*neykhs*-te

At what time does it leave?
Wann fährt es ab? van fairt es ap

At what time does it arrive?
Wann kommt es an? van komt es an

How long will it be delayed?
Wie viel Verspätung wird es haben? vee feel fer-*shpey*-tung virt es *haa*-ben

What station/stop is this?
Welcher Bahnhof/Halt ist das? *vel*-kher *baan*-hawf/halt ist das

What's the next station/stop?
Welches ist der nächste *vel*-khes ist dair *neykhs*-te
Bahnhof/Halt? *baan*-hawf/halt

Does it stop at (Freiburg)?
Hält es in (Freiburg)?   helt *es* in (*frai*·boorg)

Please tell me when we get to (Kiel).
Könnten Sie mir bitte sagen,   *keun*·ten zee meer *bi*·te *zaa*·gen
wann wir in (Kiel) ankommen?   van veer in (keel) *an*·ko·men

How long do we stop here?
Wie lange halten wir hier?   vee *lan*·ge *hal*·ten veer heer

Is this seat available?
Ist dieser Platz frei?   ist *dee*·zer plats frai

That's my seat.
Dieses ist mein Platz.   *dee*·zes ist main plats

I'd like a taxi ...   *Ich hätte gern*   ikh *he*·te gern
               ein Taxi für ...   ain *tak*·si fewr ...
     at (9am)   *(neun Uhr vormittags)*   (noyn oor *fawr*·mi·taaks)
     now   *sofort*   zo·fort
     tomorrow   *morgen*   *mor*·gen

Is this taxi available?
Ist dieses Taxi frei?   ist *dee*·zes *tak*·si frai

How much is it to ...?
Was kostet es bis ...?   vas *kos*·tet es bis ...

Please put the meter on.
Schalten Sie bitte den Taxameter ein.   *shal*·ten zee *bi*·te deyn tak·sa·*mey*·ter ain

Please take me to (this address).
Bitte bringen Sie mich zu   *bi*·te *bring*·en zee mikh tsoo
(dieser Adresse).   (*dee*·zer a·*dre*·se)

Please ...   *Bitte ...*   *bi*·te ...
     slow down   *fahren Sie langsamer*   *faa*·ren zee *lang*·za·mer
     stop here   *halten Sie hier*   *hal*·ten zee heer
     wait here   *warten Sie hier*   *var*·ten zee heer

car, motorbike & bicycle hire

I'd like to hire a ...	Ich möchte ... mieten.	ikh *meukh*·te ... *mee*·ten
bicycle	ein Fahrrad	ain *faar*·raat
car	ein Auto	ain *ow*·to
motorbike	ein Motorrad	ain *maw*·tor·raat

with ...	mit ...	mit ...
a driver	Fahrer	*faa*·rer
air conditioning	Klimaanlage	*klee*·ma·an·*laa*·ge

How much for ... hire?	Wie viel kostet es pro ...?	vee feel *kos*·tet es praw ...
hourly	Stunde	*shtun*·de
daily	Tag	taak
weekly	Woche	*vo*·khe

air	Luft f	luft
oil	Öl n	eul
petrol	Benzin n	ben·*tseen*
tyres	Reifen m pl	*rai*·fen

I need a mechanic.
Ich brauche einen Mechaniker. ikh *brow*·khe *ai*·nen me·*khaa*·ni·ker

I've run out of petrol.
Ich habe kein Benzin mehr. ikh *haa*·be kain ben·*tseen* mair

I have a flat tyre.
Ich habe eine Reifenpanne. ikh *haa*·be *ai*·ne *rai*·fen·pa·ne

directions

Where's the ...?	Wo ist ...?	vaw ist ...
bank	die Bank	dee bangk
city centre	die Innenstadt	*i*·nen·shtat
hotel	das Hotel	das ho·*tel*
market	der Markt	dair markt
police station	das Polizeirevier	das po·li·*tsai*·re·veer
post office	das Postamt	das *post*·amt
public toilet	die öffentliche	dee *eu*·fent·li·khe
	Toilette	to·a·*le*·te
tourist office	das Fremden-	das *frem*·den-
	verkehrsbüro	fer·kairs·bew·raw

Is this the road to (Frankfurt)?
Führt diese Straße   fewrt dee·ze shtraa·se
nach (Frankfurt)?   naakh (frank·foort)

Can you show me (on the map)?
Können Sie es mir   keu·nen zee es meer
(auf der Karte) zeigen?   (owf dair kar·te) tsai·gen

What's the address?
Wie ist die Adresse?   vee ist dee a·dre·se

How far is it?
Wie weit ist es?   vee vait ist es

How do I get there?
Wie kann ich da hinkommen?   vee kan ikh daa hin·ko·men

Turn ...	*Biegen Sie ... ab.*	bee·gen zee ... ap
at the corner	*an der Ecke*	an dair e·ke
at the traffic lights	*bei der Ampel*	bai dair am·pel
left/right	*links/rechts*	lingks/rekhts

It's ...	*Es ist ...*	es ist ...
behind ...	*hinter ...*	hin·ter ...
far away	*weit weg*	vait vek
here	*hier*	heer
in front of ...	*vor ...*	fawr ...
left	*links*	lingks
near (to ...)	*nahe (zu ...)*	naa·e (zoo ...)
next to ...	*neben ...*	ney·ben ...
on the corner	*an der Ecke*	an dair e·ke
opposite ...	*gegenüber ...*	gey·gen·ew·ber ...
right	*rechts*	rekhts
straight ahead	*geradeaus*	ge·raa·de·ows
there	*dort*	dort

north	*Norden* m	nor·den
south	*Süden* m	zew·den
east	*Osten* m	os·ten
west	*Westen* m	ves·ten

by bus	*mit dem Bus*	mit deym bus
by taxi	*mit dem Taxi*	mit deym tak·si
by train	*mit dem Zug*	mit deym tsook
on foot	*zu Fuß*	tsoo foos

Eingang/Ausgang	*ain*-gang/*ows*-gang	**Entrance/Exit**
Offen/Geschlossen	*o*-fen/ge-*shlo*-sen	**Open/Closed**
Zimmer Frei	*tsi*-mer frai	**Rooms Available**
Ausgebucht	*ows*-ge-bukht	**No Vacancies**
Auskunft	*ows*-kunft	**Information**
Polizeirevier	po-li-*tsai*-re-veer	**Police Station**
Verboten	fer-*baw*-ten	**Prohibited**
Toiletten/WC	to-a-*le*-ten/vee-*tsee*	**Toilets**
Herren	*hair*-en	**Men**
Damen	*daa*-men	**Women**
Heiß/Kalt	hais/kalt	**Hot/Cold**

accommodation

finding accommodation

Where's a/an ...?	*Wo ist ...?*	vaw ist ...
camping ground	*ein Campingplatz*	ain *kem*-ping-plats
guesthouse	*eine Pension*	*ai*-ne paang-*zyawn*
hotel	*ein Hotel*	ain ho-*tel*
inn	*ein Gasthof*	ain *gast*-hawf
youth hostel	*eine Jugendherberge*	*ai*-ne yoo-gent-her-ber-ge

Can you recommend	*Können Sie etwas*	*keu*-nen zee et-vas
somewhere ...?	*... empfehlen?*	... emp-*fey*-len
cheap	*Billiges*	*bi*-li-ges
good	*Gutes*	*goo*-tes
luxurious	*Luxuriöses*	luk-su-ri-*eu*-ses
nearby	*in der Nähe*	in dair *ney*-e

I'd like to book a room, please.
Ich möchte bitte ein   ikh *meukh*-te *bi*-te ain
Zimmer reservieren.   *tsi*-mer re-zer-*vee*-ren

I have a reservation.
Ich habe eine Reservierung.   ikh *haa*-be *ai*-ne re-zer-*vee*-rung

My name's ...
Mein Name ist ...   main *naa*-me ist ...

Do you have a . . . room?	Haben Sie ein . . . ?	haa·ben zee ain . . .
single	Einzelzimmer	ain·tsel·tsi·mer
double	Doppelzimmer mit	do·pel·tsi·mer mit
	einem Doppelbett	ai·nem do·pel·bet
twin	Doppelzimmer mit	do·pel·tsi·mer mit
	zwei Einzelbetten	tsvai ain·tsel·be·ten

Can I pay by . . . ?	Nehmen Sie . . . ?	ney·men zee . . .
credit card	Kreditkarten	kre·deet·kar·ten
travellers cheque	Reiseschecks	rai·ze·sheks

How much is it per . . . ?	Wie viel kostet es pro . . . ?	vee feel kos·tet es praw . . .
night	Nacht	nakht
person	Person	per·zawn

I'd like to stay for (two) nights.
Ich möchte für (zwei)   ikh meukh·te fewr (tsvai)
Nächte bleiben.   nekh·te blai·ben

From (July 2) to (July 6).
Vom (zweiten Juli) bis zum   vom (tsvai·ten yoo·li) bis tsum
(sechsten Juli).   (zeks·ten yoo·li)

Can I see it?
Kann ich es sehen?   kan ikh es zey·en

Am I allowed to camp here?
Kann ich hier zelten?   kan ikh heer tsel·ten

Is there a camp site nearby?
Gibt es in der Nähe einen Zeltplatz?   gipt es in dair ney·e ai·nen tselt·plats

requests & queries

When/Where is breakfast served?
Wann/Wo gibt es Frühstück?   van/vaw gipt es frew·shtewk

Please wake me at (seven).
Bitte wecken Sie mich   bi·te ve·ken zee mikh
um (sieben) Uhr.   um (zee·ben) oor

Could I have my key, please?
Könnte ich bitte meinen Schlüssel   keun·te ikh bi·te mai·nen shlew·sel
haben?   haa·ben

Can I get another (blanket)?
Kann ich noch (eine Decke) bekommen?   kan ikh nokh (ai·ne de·ke) be·ko·men

Is there a/an ...?	Haben Sie ...?	haa·ben zee ...
elevator	einen Aufzug	ai·nen owf·tsook
safe	einen Safe	ai·nen sayf

The room is too ...	Es ist zu ...	es ist tsoo ...
expensive	teuer	toy·er
noisy	laut	lowt
small	klein	klain

The ... doesn't work.	... funktioniert nicht.	... fungk·tsyo·neert nikht
air conditioning	Die Klimaanlage	dee klee·ma·an·laa·ge
fan	Der Ventilator	dair ven·ti·laa·tor
toilet	Die Toilette	dee to·a·le·te

This ... isn't clean.	Dieses ... ist nicht sauber.	dee·zes ... ist nikht zow·ber
pillow	Kopfkissen	kopf·ki·sen
sheet	Bettlaken	bet·laa·ken
towel	Handtuch	hant·tookh

checking out

What time is checkout?
Wann muss ich auschecken?   van mus ikh *ows*·che·ken

Can I leave my luggage here?
Kann ich meine Taschen hier lassen?   kan ikh *mai*·ne *ta*·shen heer *la*·sen

Could I have my ..., please?	Könnte ich bitte ... haben?	keun·te ikh bi·te ... haa·ben
deposit	meine Anzahlung	mai·ne an·tsaa·lung
passport	meinen Pass	mai·nen pas
valuables	meine Wertsachen	mai·ne vert·za·khen

communications & banking

the internet

Where's the local Internet café?
Wo ist hier ein Internet-Café?   vaw ist heer ain *in*·ter·net·ka·fey

How much is it per hour?
Was kostet es pro Stunde?   vas *kos*·tet es praw *shtun*·de

I'd like to ...	Ich möchte ...	ikh *meukh*·te ...
check my email	meine E-Mails checken	*mai*·ne *ee*·mayls *che*·ken
get Internet access	Internetzugang haben	*in*·ter·net·tsoo·gang *haa*·ben
use a printer	einen Drucker benutzen	*ai*·nen *dru*·ker be·*nu*·tsen
use a scanner	einen Scanner benutzen	*ai*·nen *ske*·ner be·*nu*·tsen

mobile/cell phone

I'd like a ...	Ich hätte gern ...	ikh *he*·te gern ...
mobile/cell phone for hire	ein Miethandy	ain *meet*·hen·di
SIM card for your network	eine SIM-Karte für Ihr Netz	*ai*·ne *zim*·kar·te fewr eer nets

What are the rates?
Wie hoch sind die Gebühren? vee hawkh zint dee ge·*bew*·ren

telephone

What's your phone number?
Wie ist Ihre Telefonnummer? vee ist *ee*·re te·le·*fawn*·nu·mer

The number is ...
Die Nummer ist ... dee *nu*·mer ist ...

Where's the nearest public phone?
Wo ist das nächste öffentliche Telefon? vaw ist das *neykhs*·te *eu*·fent·li·khe te·le·*fawn*

I'd like to buy a phonecard.
Ich möchte eine Telefonkarte kaufen. ikh *meukh*·te *ai*·ne te·le·*fawn*·kar·te *kow*·fen

I want to ...	Ich möchte ...	ikh *meukh*·te ...
call (Singapore)	(nach Singapur) telefonieren	(naakh *zing*·a·poor) te·le·fo·*nee*·ren
make a local call	ein Ortsgespräch machen	ain *awrts*·ge·*shpreykh* *ma*·khen
reverse the charges	ein R-Gespräch führen	ain *air*·ge·shpreykh *few*·ren

How much does ... cost?	Wie viel kostet ...?	vee feel *kos*·tet ...
a (three)-minute	ein (drei)-minutiges	ain (*drai*)·mi·noo·ti·ges
call	Gespräch	ge·*shpreykh*
each extra	jede zusätzliche	*yey*·de tsoo·*zeyts*·li·khe
minute	Minute	mi·*noo*·te

| It's (one euro) per (minute). | | |
| *(Ein Euro) für (eine Minute).* | | (ain *oy*·ro) fewr (*ai*·ne mi·*noo*·te) |

post office

I want to send a ...	Ich möchte ... senden.	ikh *meukh*·te ... *zen*·den
fax	ein Fax	ain faks
letter	einen Brief	*ai*·nen breef
parcel	ein Paket	ain pa·*keyt*
postcard	eine Postkarte	*ai*·ne *post*·kar·te

I want to buy a/an ...	Ich möchte ... kaufen.	ikh *meukh*·te ... *kow*·fen
envelope	einen Umschlag	*ai*·nen *um*·shlaak
stamp	eine Briefmarke	*ai*·ne *breef*·mar·ke

Please send it	Bitte schicken Sie das	*bi*·te *shi*·ken zee das
(to Australia) by ...	(nach Australien) per ...	(nakh ows·*traa*·li·en) per ...
airmail	Luftpost	*luft*·post
express mail	Expresspost	eks·*pres*·post
registered mail	Einschreiben	*ain*·shrai·ben
surface mail	Landbeförderung	*lant*·be·feur·de·rung

| Is there any mail for me? | Ist Post für mich da? | ist post fewr mikh da |

bank

Where's a/an ...?	Wo ist ...?	vaw ist ...
ATM	der Geldautomat	dair *gelt*·ow·to·maat
foreign exchange office	die Geldwechselstube	dee *gelt*·vek·sel·shtoo·be

I'd like to ...	*Ich möchte ...*	ikh *meukh*·te ...
Where can I ...?	*Wo kann ich ...?*	vaw kan ikh ...
arrange a transfer	*einen Transfer tätigen*	*ai*·nen trans·*fer* tey·ti·gen
cash a cheque	*einen Scheck einlösen*	*ai*·nen shek *ain*·leu·zen
change a travellers cheque	*einen Reisescheck einlösen*	*ai*·nen *rai*·ze·shek *ain*·leu·zen
change money	*Geld umtauschen*	gelt *um*·tow·shen
get a cash advance	*eine Barauszahlung*	*ai*·ne *baar*·ows·tsaa·lung
withdraw money	*Geld abheben*	gelt *ap*·hey·ben

What's the ...?	*Wie ...?*	vee ...
charge for that	*hoch sind die Gebühren dafür*	hawkh zint dee ge·*bew*·ren da·*fewr*
exchange rate	*ist der Wechselkurs*	ist dair *vek*·sel·kurs

It's ...	*Das ...*	das ...
(12) euros	*kostet (zwölf) euro*	*kos*·tet (zveulf) *oy*·ro
free	*ist umsonst*	ist um·*zonst*

What time does the bank open?
Wann macht die Bank auf? van makht dee bangk owf

Has my money arrived yet?
Ist mein Geld schon angekommen? ist main gelt shawn *an*·ge·ko·men

sightseeing

getting in

What time does it open/close?
Wann macht es auf/zu? van makht es owf/tsoo

What's the admission charge?
Was kostet der Eintritt? vas *kos*·tet dair *ain*·trit

Is there a discount for children/students?
Gibt es eine Ermäßigung für Kinder/Studenten? gipt es *ai*·ne er·*mey*·si·gung fewr *kin*·der/shtu·*den*·ten

I'd like a …	Ich hätte gern …	ikh *he*·te gern …
catalogue	einen Katalog	*ai*·nen ka·ta·*lawg*
guide	einen Reiseführer	*ai*·nen *rai*·ze·few·rer
local map	eine Karte von hier	*ai*·ne *kar*·te fon heer

I'd like to see …	Ich möchte … sehen.	ikh *meukh*·te … *zey*·en
What's that?	Was ist das?	vas ist das
Can I take a photo?	Kann ich fotografieren?	kan ikh fo·to·gra·*fee*·ren

tours

When's the next …? m/f	Wann ist der/die nächste …? m/f	van ist dair/dee *neykhs*·te …
day trip	Tagesausflug m	*taa*·ges·ows·flook
tour	Tour f	toor

Is … included?	Ist … inbegriffen?	ist … *in*·be·gri·fen
accommodation	die Unterkunft	dee *un*·ter·kunft
the admission charge	der Eintritt	dair *ain*·trit
food	das Essen	das *e*·sen
transport	die Beförderung	dee be·*feur*·de·rung

How long is the tour?
Wie lange dauert die Führung? — vee *lang*·e *dow*·ert dee *few*·rung

What time should we be back?
Wann sollen wir zurück sein? — van *zo*·len veer tsu·*rewk* zain

sightseeing

castle	Burg f	burk
cathedral	Dom m	dawm
church	Kirche f	*kir*·khe
main square	Hauptplatz m	*howpt*·plats
monastery	Kloster n	*klaws*·ter
monument	Denkmal n	*dengk*·maal
museum	Museum n	mu·*zey*·um
old city	Altstadt f	*alt*·stat
palace	Schloss n	shlos
ruins	Ruinen f pl	ru·*ee*·nen
stadium	Stadion n	*shtaa*·di·on
statues	Statuen f pl	*shtaa*·tu·e

shopping

enquiries

Where's a ...?	Wo ist ...?	vaw ist ...
bank	die Bank	dee bangk
bookshop	die Buchhandlung	dee *bookh*·hand·lung
camera shop	das Fotogeschäft	das fo·to·ge·*sheft*
department store	das Warenhaus	das *vaa*·ren·hows
grocery store	der Lebensmittelladen	dair *ley*·bens·mi·tel·laa·den
market	der Markt	dair markt
newsagency	der Zeitungshändler	dair *tsai*·tungks·hen·dler
supermarket	der Supermarkt	dair *zoo*·per·markt

Where can I buy (a padlock)?
Wo kann ich (ein Vorhängeschloss) — vaw kan ikh (ain *fawr*·heng·e·shlos)
kaufen? — *kow*·fen

I'm looking for ...
Ich suche nach ... — ikh *zoo*·khe nakh ...

Can I look at it?
Können Sie es mir zeigen? — *keu*·nen zee es meer *tsai*·gen

Do you have any others?
Haben Sie noch andere? — *haa*·ben zee nokh *an*·de·re

Does it have a guarantee?
Gibt es darauf Garantie? — gipt es da·*rowf* ga·ran·*tee*

Can I have it sent overseas?
Kann ich es ins Ausland — kan ikh es ins *ows*·lant
verschicken lassen? — fer·*shi*·ken *la*·sen

Can I have my ... repaired?
Kann ich mein ... reparieren lassen? — kan ikh main ... re·pa·*ree*·ren *la*·sen

It's faulty.
Es ist fehlerhaft. — es ist *fey*·ler·haft

I'd like …, please.	Ich möchte bitte …	ikh *meukh*·te *bi*·te …
a bag	eine Tüte	*ai*·ne *tew*·te
a refund	mein Geld	main gelt
	zurückhaben	tsu·*rewk*·haa·ben
to return this	dieses zurückgeben	*dee*·zes tsu·*rewk*·gey·ben

paying

How much is it?
Wie viel kostet das?   vee feel *kos*·tet das

Can you write down the price?
Können Sie den Preis aufschreiben?   *keu*·nen zee deyn prais *owf*·shrai·ben

That's too expensive.
Das ist zu teuer.   das ist tsoo *toy*·er

Can you lower the price?
Können Sie mit dem Preis   *keu*·nen zee mit dem prais
heruntergehen?   he·*run*·ter·gey·en

I'll give you (five) euros.
Ich gebe Ihnen (fünf) euro.   ikh *gey*·be ee·nen (fewnf) *oy*·ro

There's a mistake in the bill.
Da ist ein Fehler in der Rechnung.   daa ist ain *fey*·ler in dair *rekh*·nung

Do you accept …?	Nehmen Sie …?	*ney*·men zee …
credit cards	Kreditkarten	kre·*deet*·kar·ten
debit cards	Debitkarten	*dey*·bit·kar·ten
travellers cheques	Reiseschecks	*rai*·ze·sheks

I'd like …, please.	Ich möchte bitte …	ikh *meukh*·te *bi*·te …
a receipt	eine Quittung	*ai*·ne *kvi*·tung
my change	mein Wechselgeld	main *vek*·sel·gelt

clothes & shoes

Can I try it on?	*Kann ich es anprobieren?*	kan ikh es *an*·pro·bee·ren
My size is (40).	*Ich habe Größe (vierzig).*	ikh *haa*·be *greu*·se (*feer*·tsikh)
It doesn't fit.	*Es passt nicht.*	es past nikht

small	klein	klain
medium	mittelgroß	*mi*·tel·graws
large	groß	graws

books & music

I'd like a ...	*Ich hätte gern ...*	ikh *he*·te gern ...
newspaper	*eine Zeitung*	*ai*·ne *tsai*·tung
(in English)	*(auf Englisch)*	(owf *eng*·lish)
pen	*einen Kugelschreiber*	*ai*·nen *koo*·gel·shrai·ber

Is there an English-language bookshop?
Gibt es einen Buchladen   gipt es *ai*·nen *bookh*·laa·den
für englische Bücher?   fewr *eng*·li·she *bew*·kher

I'm looking for something by (Herman Hesse).
Ich suche nach etwas von   ikh *zoo*·khe nakh *et*·vas fon
(Herman Hesse).   (*her*·man *he*·se)

Can I listen to this?
Kann ich mir das anhören?   kan ikh meer das *an*·heu·ren

photography

Can you ...?	*Können Sie ...?*	*keu*·nen zee ...
burn a CD from	*eine CD von meiner*	*ai*·ne tse de von *mai*·ner
my memory card	*Speicherkarte brennen*	*shpai*·kher·*kar*·te *bre*·nen
develop this film	*diesen Film entwickeln*	*dee*·zen film ent·*vi*·keln
load my film	*mir den Film einlegen*	meer deyn film *ain*·ley·gen

I need a ... film	*Ich brauche einen*	ikh *brow*·khe *ai*·nen
for this camera.	*... für diese Kamera.*	... fewr *dee*·ze *ka*·me·ra
APS	*APS-Film*	aa·pey·*es*·film
B&W	*Schwarzweißfilm*	shvarts·*vais*·film
colour	*Farbfilm*	*farp*·film
slide	*Diafilm*	*dee*·a·film
(200) speed	*(zweihundert)-*	(*tsvai*·hun·dert)·
	ASA-Film	*aa*·za·film

When will it be ready?	*Wann ist er fertig?*	van ist air *fer*·tikh

meeting people

greetings, goodbyes & introductions

Hello. (Austria)	Servus.	zer·vus
Hello. (Germany)	Guten Tag.	goo·ten taak
Hello. (Switzerland)	Grüezi.	grew·e·tsi
Hi.	Hallo.	ha·lo
Good night.	Gute Nacht.	goo·te nakht
Goodbye.	Auf Wiedersehen.	owf vee·der·zey·en
Bye.	Tschüss/Tschau.	chews/chow
See you later.	Bis später.	bis shpey·ter

Mr	Herr	her
Mrs	Frau	frow
Miss	Fräulein	froy·lain

How are you?	Wie geht es Ihnen?	vee geyt es ee·nen
Fine. And you?	Danke, gut. Und Ihnen?	dang·ke goot unt ee·nen
What's your name?	Wie ist Ihr Name?	vee ist eer naa·me
My name is ...	Mein Name ist ...	main naa·me ist ...
I'm pleased to meet you.	Angenehm.	an·ge·neym

This is my ...	Das ist mein/meine ... m/f	das ist main/mai·ne ...
brother	Bruder	broo·der
daughter	Tochter	tokh·ter
father	Vater	faa·ter
friend	Freund/Freundin m/f	froynt/froyn·din
husband	Mann	man
mother	Mutter	mu·ter
partner (intimate)	Partner/Partnerin m/f	part·ner/part·ne·rin
sister	Schwester	shves·ter
son	Sohn	zawn
wife	Frau	frow

Here's my ...	Hier ist meine ...	heer ist mai·ne ...
What's your ...?	Wie ist Ihre ...?	vee ist ee·re ...
address	Adresse	a·dre·se
email address	E-mail-Adresse	ee·mayl·a·dre·se
fax number	Faxnummer	faks·nu·mer
phone number	Telefonnummer	te·le·fawn·nu·mer

occupations

What's your occupation?	*Als was arbeiten Sie?* pol	als vas *ar*·bai·ten zee
	Als was arbeitest du? inf	als vas *ar*·bai·test doo
I'm a/an ...	*Ich bin ein/eine ...* m/f	ikh bin ain/*ai*·ne ...
artist	*Künstler/Künstlerin* m/f	*kewnst*·ler/*kewnst*·le·rin
business person	*Geschäftsmann* m	ge·*shefts*·man
	Geschäftsfrau f	ge·*shefts*·frow
farmer	*Bauer/Bäuerin* m/f	bow·er/*boy*·e·rin
manual worker	*Arbeiter/Arbeiterin* m/f	*ar*·bai·ter/*ar*·bai·te·rin
office worker	*Büroangestellte* m&f	bew·*raw*·an·ge·shtel·te
scientist	*Wissenschaftler* m	*vi*·sen·shaft·ler
	Wissenschaftlerin f	*vi*·sen·shaft·le·rin
student	*Student/Studentin* m/f	shtu·*dent*/shtu·*den*·tin

background

Where are you from?	*Woher kommen Sie?* pol	vaw·hair *ko*·men zee
	Woher kommst du? inf	vaw·hair komst doo
I'm from ...	*Ich komme aus ...*	ikh *ko*·me ows ...
Australia	*Australien*	ows·*traa*·li·en
Canada	*Kanada*	*ka*·na·daa
England	*England*	*eng*·lant
New Zealand	*Neuseeland*	noy·*zey*·lant
the USA	*den USA*	deyn oo·es·*aa*
Are you married?	*Sind Sie verheiratet?* pol	zint zee fer·*hai*·ra·tet
	Bist du verheiratet? inf	bist doo fer·*hai*·ra·tet
I'm married.	*Ich bin verheiratet.*	ikh bin fer·*hai*·ra·tet
I'm single.	*Ich bin ledig.*	ikh bin *ley*·dikh

age

How old ...?	*Wie alt ...?*	vee alt ...
are you	*sind Sie* pol	zint zee
	bist du inf	bist doo
is your daughter	*ist Ihre Tochter* pol	ist *ee*·re tokh·ter
is your son	*ist Ihr Sohn* pol	ist eer zawn
I'm ... years old.	*Ich bin ... Jahre alt.*	ikh bin ... *yaa*·re alt
He/She is ... years old.	*Er/Sie ist ... Jahre alt.*	air/zee ist ... *yaa*·re alt

feelings

I'm (not) ...	*Ich bin (nicht) ...*	ikh bin (nikht) ...
Are you ...?	*Sind Sie ...?* pol	zint zee ...
	Bist du ...? inf	bist doo ...
happy	*glücklich*	*glewk·likh*
sad	*traurig*	*trow·rikh*
I'm (not) ...	*Ich habe (kein) ...*	ikh *haa*·be (kain) ...
Are you ...?	*Haben Sie ...?* pol	*haa*·ben zee ...
	Hast du ...? inf	hast doo ...
hungry	*Hunger*	*hung*·er
thirsty	*Durst*	durst
I'm (not) ...	*Mir ist (nicht) ...*	meer ist (nikht) ...
Are you ...?	*Ist Ihnen/dir ...?* pol/inf	ist *ee*·nen/deer ...
cold	*kalt*	kalt
hot	*heiß*	hais

entertainment

going out

Where can I find ...?	*Wo sind die ...?*	vaw zint dee ...
clubs	*Klubs*	klups
gay venues	*Schwulen- und*	*shvoo*·len unt
	Lesbenkneipen	*les*·ben·knai·pen
pubs	*Kneipen*	*knai*·pen
I feel like going	*Ich hätte Lust,*	ikh *he*·te lust
to a/the ...	*... zu gehen.*	... tsoo *gey*·en
concert	*zum Konzert*	tsoom kon·*tsert*
movies	*ins Kino*	ins *kee*·no
party	*zu eine Party*	tsoo *ai*·ne *par*·ti
restaurant	*in ein Restaurant*	in ain res·to·*rang*
theatre	*ins Theater*	ins te·*aa*·ter

interests

Do you like ...?	*Magst du ...?* inf	maakst doo ...
I (don't) like ...	*Ich mag (keine/ keinen) ...* m/f	ikh maak (*kai*·ne/ *kai*·nen) ...
art	*Kunst* f	kunst
sport	*Sport* m	shport
I (don't) like ...	*Ich ... (nicht) gern.*	ikh ... (nikht) gern
cooking	*koche*	*ko*·khe
reading	*lese*	*ley*·ze
travelling	*reise*	*rai*·ze

Do you like to dance?
Tanzt du gern? inf   tantst doo gern

Do you like music?
Hörst du gern Musik? inf   heurst doo gern mu·*zeek*

food & drink

finding a place to eat

Can you recommend a ...?	*Können Sie ... empfehlen?*	*keu*·nen zee ... emp·*fey*·len
bar	*eine Kneipe*	*ai*·ne *knai*·pe
café	*ein Café*	ain ka·*fey*
restaurant	*ein Restaurant*	ain res·to·*rang*
I'd like ..., please.	*Ich hätte gern ..., bitte.*	ikh *he*·te gern ... *bi*·te
a table for (five)	*einen Tisch für (fünf) Personen*	*ai*·nen tish fewr (fewnf) per·*zaw*·nen
the (non)smoking section	*einen (Nicht-) rauchertisch*	*ai*·nen (nikht·) *row*·kher·tish

ordering food

breakfast	*Frühstück* n	*frew*·shtewk
lunch	*Mittagessen* n	*mi*·taak·e·sen
dinner	*Abendessen* n	*aa*·bent·e·sen
snack	*Snack* m	snek

What would you recommend?
Was empfehlen Sie? — vas emp·*fey*·len zee

I'd like (the) ..., please.	*Bitte bringen Sie ...*	*bi*·te *bring*·en zee ...
bill	*die Rechnung*	dee *rekh*·nung
drink list	*die Getränkekarte*	dee ge·*treng*·ke·kar·te
menu	*die Speisekarte*	dee *shpai*·ze·kar·te
that dish	*dieses Gericht*	*dee*·zes ge·*rikht*

drinks

(cup of) coffee ...	*(eine Tasse) Kaffee ...*	(*ai*·ne *ta*·se) *ka*·fey ...
(cup of) tea ...	*(eine Tasse) Tee ...*	(*ai*·ne *ta*·se) tey ...
with milk	*mit Milch*	mit milkh
without sugar	*ohne Zucker*	*aw*·ne *tsu*·ker
(orange) juice	*(Orangen)Saft* m	(o·*rang*·zhen·)zaft
mineral water	*Mineralwasser* n	mi·ne·*raal*·va·ser
soft drink	*Softdrink* m	*soft*·dringk
(boiled) water	*(heißes) Wasser* n	(*hai*·ses) *va*·ser

in the bar

I'll have ...	*Ich hätte gern ...*	ikh *he*·te gern ...
I'll buy you a drink.	*Ich gebe dir einen aus.* inf	ikh *gey*·be deer *ai*·nen ows
What would you like?	*Was möchtest du?* inf	vas *meukh*·test doo
Cheers!	*Prost!*	prawst
brandy	*Weinbrand* m	*vain*·brant
cognac	*Kognak* m	*ko*·nyak
cocktail	*Cocktail* m	*kok*·tayl
a shot of (whisky)	*einen (Whisky)*	*ai*·nen (*vis*·ki)
a bottle of ...	*eine Flasche ...*	*ai*·ne *fla*·she ...
a glass of ...	*ein Glas ...*	ain glaas ...
red wine	*Rotwein*	*rawt*·vain
sparkling wine	*Sekt*	zekt
white wine	*Weißwein*	*vais*·vain
a ... of beer	*... Bier*	... beer
bottle	*eine Flasche*	*ai*·ne *fla*·she
glass	*ein Glas*	ain glaas

self-catering

What's the local speciality?
Was ist eine örtliche Spezialität?   vas ist *ai*·ne *eurt*·li·khe shpe·tsya·li·*teyt*

What's that?
Was ist das?   vas ist das

How much is (a kilo of cheese)?
Was kostet (ein Kilo Käse)?   vas *kos*·tet (ain *kee*·lo *key*·ze)

I'd like ...	*Ich möchte ...*	ikh *meukh*·te ...
(100) grams	*(hundert) Gramm*	(hun·dert) gram
(two) kilos	*(zwei) Kilo*	(tsvai) *kee*·lo
(three) pieces	*(drei) Stück*	(drai) shtewk
(six) slices	*(sechs) Scheiben*	(zeks) *shai*·ben

Less.	*Weniger.*	*vey*·ni·ger
Enough.	*Genug.*	ge·*nook*
More.	*Mehr.*	mair

special diets & allergies

Is there a vegetarian restaurant near here?
Gibt es ein vegetarisches   gipt es ain vege·*tar*·ish·shes
Restaurant hier in der Nähe?   res·to·*rang* heer in dair *ney*·e

Do you have vegetarian food?
Haben Sie vegetarisches Essen?   *haa*·ben zee ve·ge·*taa*·ri·shes *e*·sen

Could you prepare	*Können Sie ein Gericht*	*keu*·nen zee ain ge·*rikht*
a meal without ...?	*ohne ... zubereiten?*	*aw*·ne ... *tsoo*·be·rai·ten
butter	*Butter*	*bu*·ter
eggs	*Eiern*	*ai*·ern
meat stock	*Fleischbrühe*	*flaish*·brew·e

I'm allergic to ...	*Ich bin allergisch*	ikh bin a·*lair*·gish
	gegen ...	*gey*·gen ...
dairy produce	*Milchprodukte*	*milkh*·pro·duk·te
gluten	*Gluten*	*gloo*·ten
MSG	*Natrium-glutamat*	*naa*·tri·um·glu·ta·maat
nuts	*Nüsse*	*new*·se
seafood	*Meeresfrüchte*	*mair*·res·frewkh·te

Bayrisch Kraut n	*bai*-rish krowt	shredded cabbage cooked with sliced apples, wine & sugar
Berliner m	ber-*lee*-ner	jam doughnut
Cervelatwurst f	ser-ve-*laat*-vurst	spicy pork & beef sausage
Erdäpfelgulasch n	ert-ep-fel-goo-lash	spicy sausage & potato stew
gekochter Schinken m	ge-*kokh*-ter *shing*-ken	cooked ham
Graupensuppe f	*grow*-pen-zu-pe	barley soup
Greyerzer m	*grai*-er-tser	a smooth, rich cheese
Grießklößchensuppe f	*grees*-kleus-khen-zu-pe	soup with semolina dumplings
Gröstl n	greustl	grated fried potatoes with meat
Grünkohl mit Pinkel m	*grewn*-kawl mit *ping*-kel	cabbage with sausages
Holsteiner Schnitzel n	*hol*-shtai-ner *shni*-tsel	veal schnitzel with fried egg & seafood
Husarenfleisch n	hu-*zaa*-ren-flaish	braised beef, veal & pork fillets with sweet peppers, onions & sour cream
Hutzelbrot n	*hu*-tsel-brawt	bread made of prunes & other dried fruit
Kaiserschmarren m	*kai*-zer-shmar-ren	pancakes with raisins, fruit compote or chocolate sauce
Kaisersemmeln f pl	*kai*-zer-ze-meln	Austrian bread rolls
Katenwurst f	*kaa*-ten-vurst	country-style smoked sausage
Königsuppe f	*keu*-ni-gin-zu-pe	creamy chicken soup
Königstorte f	*keu*-niks-tor-te	rum-flavoured fruit cake
Krautsalat m	*krowt*-za-laat	coleslaw
Leipziger Allerlei n	*laip*-tsi-ger *a*-ler-lai	mixed vegetable stew
Linzer Torte f	*lin*-tser tor-te	latticed tart with jam topping

Nudelauflauf m	noo-del-owf-lowf	pasta casserole
Obatzter m	aw-bats-ter	Bavarian soft cheese mousse
Ochsenschwanzsuppe f	ok-sen-shvants-zu-pe	oxtail soup
Palatschinken m	pa-lat-shing-ken	pancakes filled with jam or cheese
Rollmops m	rol-mops	pickled herring fillet rolled around chopped onions or gherkins
Sauerbraten m	zow-er-braa-ten	marinated roasted beef served with a sour cream sauce
Sauerkraut n	zow-er-krowt	pickled cabbage
Schafskäse m	shaafs-key-ze	sheep's milk feta
Schmorbraten m	shmawr-braa-ten	beef pot roast
Schnitzel n	shni-tsel	pork, veal or chicken breast rolled in breadcrumbs & fried
Strammer Max m	shtra-mer maks	ham, sausage or pork sandwich, served with fried eggs & onions
Streichkäse m	shtraikh-key-ze	any kind of soft cheese spread
Streuselkuchen m	shtroy-zel-koo-khen	coffee cake topped with cinnamon
Strudel m	shtroo-del	loaf-shaped pastry with a sweet or savoury filling
Tascherl n	ta-sherl	pastry with meat, cheese or jam
Voressen n	fawr-e-sen	meat stew
Weinkraut n	vain-krowt	white cabbage, braised with apples & simmered in wine
Wiener Schnitzel n	vee-ner shni-tsel	crumbed veal schnitzel
Wiener Würstchen n	vee-ner vewrst-khen	frankfurter (sausage)
Zwetschgendatschi m	tsvetsh-gen-dat-shi	damson plum tart
Zwiebelsuppe f	tsvee-bel-zu-pe	onion soup
Zwiebelwurst f	tsvee-bel-vurst	liver & onion sausage

emergencies

basics

Help!	Hilfe!	hil·fe
Stop!	Halt!	halt
Go away!	Gehen Sie weg!	gey·en zee vek
Thief!	Dieb!	deeb
Fire!	Feuer!	foy·er
Watch out!	Vorsicht!	for·zikht
Call ...!	Rufen Sie ...!	roo·fen zee ...
a doctor	einen Arzt	ai·nen artst
an ambulance	einen Krankenwagen	ai·nen krang·ken·vaa·gen
the police	die Polizei	dee po·li·tsai

It's an emergency!
Es ist ein Notfall!   es ist ain *nawt*·fal

Could you help me, please?
Könnten Sie mir bitte helfen?   *keun*·ten zee meer *bi*·te *hel*·fen

I have to use the telephone.
Ich muss das Telefon benutzen.   ikh mus das te·le·*fawn* be·*nu*·tsen

I'm lost.
Ich habe mich verirrt.   ikh *haa*·be mikh fer·*irt*

Where are the toilets?
Wo ist die Toilette?   vo ist dee to·a·*le*·te

police

Where's the police station?
Wo ist das Polizeirevier?   vaw ist das po·li·*tsai*·re·veer

I want to report an offence.
Ich möchte eine Straftat melden.   ikh *meukh*·te *ai*·ne *shtraaf*·taat *mel*·den

I have insurance.
Ich bin versichert.   ikh bin fer·*zi*·khert

I've been ...	Ich bin ... worden.	ikh bin ... *vor*·den
assaulted	angegriffen	*an*·ge·gri·fen
raped	vergewaltigt	fer·ge·*val*·tikht
robbed	bestohlen	be·*shtaw*·len

I've lost my...	Ich habe ... verloren.	ikh haa·be ... fer·law·ren
My ... was/	Man hat mir ...	man hat meer ...
were stolen.	gestohlen.	ge·shtaw·len
backpack	meinen Rucksack	mai·nen ruk·zak
bags	meine Reisetaschen	mai·ne rai·ze·ta·shen
credit card	meine Kreditkarte	mai·ne kre·deet·karte
handbag	meine Handtasche	mai·ne hant·ta·she
jewellery	meinen Schmuck	mai·nen shmuk
money	mein Geld	main gelt
passport	meinen Pass	mai·nen pas
travellers cheques	meine Reisechecks	mai·ne rai·ze·sheks
wallet	meine Brieftasche	mai·ne breef·ta·she

I want to contact	Ich möchte mich mit	ikh meukh·te mikh mit
my ...	... in Verbindung setzen.	... in fer·bin·dung ze·tsen
consulate	meinem Konsulat	mai·nem kon·zu·laat
embassy	meiner Botschaft	mai·ner bawt·shaft

health

medical needs

Where's the	Wo ist der/die/das	vaw ist dair/dee/das
nearest ...?	nächste ...? m/f/n	neykhs·te ...
dentist	Zahnarzt m	tsaan·artst
doctor	Arzt m	artst
hospital	Krankenhaus n	krang·ken·hows
(night) pharmacist	(Nacht)Apotheke f	(nakht·)a·po·tey·ke

I need a doctor (who speaks English).
Ich brauche einen Arzt   ikh brow·khe ai·nen artst
(der Englisch spricht).   (dair eng·lish shprikht)

Could I see a female doctor?
Könnte ich von einer   keun·te ikh fon ai·ner
Ärztin behandelt werden?   erts·tin be·han·delt ver·den

I've run out of my medication.
Ich habe keine   ikh haa·be kai·ne
Medikamente mehr.   me·di·ka·men·te mair

symptoms, conditions & allergies

| I'm sick. | Ich bin krank. | ikh bin krangk |
| It hurts here. | Es tut hier weh. | es toot heer *vey* |

I have (a) ...	Ich habe ...	ikh *haa*·be ...
asthma	Asthma	*ast*·ma
bronchitis	Bronchitis	bron·*khee*·tis
constipation	Verstopfung	fer·*shtop*·fung
cough	Husten	*hoos*·ten
diarrhoea	Durchfall	*durkh*·fal
fever	Fieber	*fee*·ber
headache	Kopfschmerzen	*kopf*·shmer·tsen
heart condition	Herzbeschwerden	*herts*·be·shver·den
nausea	Übelkeit	*ew*·bel·kait
pain	Schmerzen	*shmer*·tsen
sore throat	Halsschmerzen	*hals*·shmer·tsen
toothache	Zahnschmerzen	*tsaan*·shmer·tsen

I'm allergic to ...	Ich bin allergisch gegen ...	ikh bin a·*lair*·gish *gey*·gen ...
antibiotics	Antibiotika	an·ti·bi·*aw*·ti·ka
anti-inflammatories	entzündungs-hemmende Mittel	en·*tsewn*·dungks-he·men·de *mi*·tel
aspirin	Aspirin	as·pi·*reen*
bees	Bienen	*bee*·nen
codeine	Kodein	ko·de·*een*
penicillin	Penizillin	pe·ni·tsi·*leen*

antiseptic	Antiseptikum n	an·ti·*zep*·ti·kum
bandage	Verband m	fer·*bant*
condoms	Kondom n	kon·*dawm*
contraceptives	Verhütungsmittel n	fer·*hew*·tungks·mi·tel
diarrhoea medicine	Mittel gegen Durchfall n	*mi*·tel gey·gen durkh·fal
insect repellent	Insektenschutzmittel n	in·*zek*·ten·shuts·mi·tel
laxatives	Abführmittel n	*ap*·fewr·mi·tel
painkillers	Schmerzmittel n	*shmerts*·mi·tel
rehydration salts	Kochsalzlösung n	kokh·zalts·*leu*·zung
sleeping tablets	Schlaftabletten f pl	*shlaaf*·ta·ble·ten

english–german dictionary

German nouns in this dictionary have their gender indicated by ⓜ (masculine), ⓕ (feminine) or ⓝ (neuter). If it's a plural noun, you'll also see pl. Words are also marked as n (noun), a (adjective), v (verb), sg (singular), pl (plural), inf (informal) and pol (polite) where necessary.

A

A

accident *Unfall* ⓜ un-fal
accommodation *Unterkunft* ⓕ un-ter-kunft
adaptor *Adapter* ⓜ a-dap-ter
address *Adresse* ⓕ a-dre-se
after *nach* naakh
air-conditioned *mit Klimaanlage* ⓕ
   mit *klee-ma-an-laa-ge*
airplane *Flugzeug* ⓝ flook-tsoyk
airport *Flughafen* ⓜ flook-haa-fen
alcohol *Alkohol* ⓜ al-ko-hawl
all a *alle* a-le
allergy *Allergie* ⓕ a-lair-gee
ambulance *Krankenwagen* ⓜ krang-ken-vaa-gen
and *und* unt
ankle *Knöchel* ⓜ kneu-khel
arm *Arm* ⓜ arm
ashtray *Aschenbecher* ⓜ a-shen-be-kher
ATM *Geldautomat* ⓜ gelt-ow-to-maat
Austria *Österreich* ⓝ eus-ter-raikh

B

baby *Baby* ⓝ bay-bi
back (body) *Rücken* ⓜ rew-ken
backpack *Rucksack* ⓜ ruk-zak
bad *schlecht* shlekht
bag *Tasche* ⓕ ta-she
baggage claim *Gepäckausgabe* ⓕ ge-pek-ows-gaa-be
bank *Bank* ⓕ bangk
bar *Lokal* ⓝ lo-kaal
bathroom *Badezimmer* ⓝ baa-de-tsi-mer
battery *Batterie* ⓕ ba-te-ree
beautiful *schön* sheun
bed *Bett* ⓝ bet
beer *Bier* ⓝ beer
before *vor* fawr
behind *hinter* hin-ter
Belgium *Belgien* ⓝ bel-gi-en

bicycle *Fahrrad* ⓝ faar-raat
big *groß* graws
bill *Rechnung* ⓕ rekh-nung
black *schwarz* shvarts
blanket *Decke* ⓕ de-ke
blood group *Blutgruppe* ⓕ bloot-gru-pe
blue *blau* blow
book (make a reservation) v *buchen* boo-khen
bottle *Flasche* ⓕ fla-she
bottle opener *Flaschenöffner* ⓜ fla-shen-euf-ner
boy *Junge* ⓜ yung-e
brakes (car) *Bremsen* ⓕ pl brem-zen
breakfast *Frühstück* ⓝ frew-shtewk
broken (faulty) *kaputt* ka-put
bus *Bus* ⓜ bus
business *Geschäft* ⓝ ge-sheft
buy *kaufen* kow-fen

C

café *Café* ⓝ ka-fey
camera *Kamera* ⓕ ka-me-ra
camp site *Zeltplatz* ⓜ tselt-plats
can opener *Dosenöffner* ⓜ daw-zen-euf-ner
car *Auto* ⓝ ow-to
cash *Bargeld* ⓝ baar-gelt
cash (a cheque) v *(einen Scheck) einlösen*
   (ai-nen shek) ain-leu-zen
cell phone *Handy* ⓝ hen-di
centre *Zentrum* ⓝ tsen-trum
change (money) v *wechseln* vek-seln
cheap *billig* bi-likh
check (bill) *Rechnung* ⓕ rekh-nung
check-in *Abfertigungsschalter* ⓜ
   ap-fer-ti-gungks-shal-ter
chest *Brustkorb* ⓜ brust-korp
child *Kind* ⓝ kint
cigarette *Zigarette* ⓕ tsi-ga-re-te
city *Stadt* ⓕ shtat
clean a *sauber* zow-ber

closed *geschlossen* ge-*shlo*-sen
coffee *Kaffee* ⓜ *ka*-fey
coins *Münzen* ⓕ pl *mewn*-tsen
cold a *kalt* kalt
collect call *R-Gespräch* ⓝ *air*-ge-shpreykh
come *kommen* *ko*-men
computer *Computer* ⓜ kom-*pyoo*-ter
condom *Kondom* ⓝ kon-*dawm*
contact lenses *Kontaktlinsen* ⓕ pl kon-*takt*-lin-zen
cook v *kochen* *ko*-khen
cost *Preis* ⓜ prais
credit card *Kreditkarte* ⓕ kre-*deet*-kar-te
cup *Tasse* ⓕ *ta*-se
currency exchange *Geldwechsel* ⓜ *gelt*-vek-sel
customs (immigration) *Zoll* ⓜ tsol

D

dangerous *gefährlich* ge-*fair*-likh
date (time) *Datum* ⓝ *daa*-tum
day *Tag* ⓜ taak
delay n *Verspätung* ⓕ fer-*shpey*-tung
dentist *Zahnarzt/Zahnärztin* ⓜ/ⓕ tsaan-artst/tsaan-erts-tin
depart *abfahren* ap-faa-ren
diaper *Windel* ⓕ *vin*-del
dictionary *Wörterbuch* ⓝ *veur*-ter-bookh
dinner *Abendessen* ⓝ *aa*-bent-e-sen
direct *direkt* di-*rekt*
dirty *schmutzig* *shmu*-tsikh
disabled *behindert* be-*hin*-dert
discount n *Rabatt* ⓜ ra-*bat*
doctor *Arzt/Ärztin* ⓜ/ⓕ artst/erts-tin
double bed *Doppelbett* ⓝ *do*-pel-bet
double room *Doppelzimmer mit einem Doppelbett* ⓝ *do*-pel-tsi-mer mit ai-nem *do*-pel-bet
drink *Getränk* ⓝ ge-*trengk*
drive v *fahren* faa-ren
drivers licence *Führerschein* ⓜ *few*-rer-shain
drugs (illicit) *Droge* ⓕ *draw*-ge
dummy (pacifier) *Schnuller* ⓜ *shnu*-ler

E

ear *Ohr* ⓝ awr
east *Osten* ⓜ *os*-ten
eat *essen* e-sen
economy class *Touristenklasse* ⓕ tu-*ris*-ten-kla-se
electricity *Elektrizität* ⓕ e-lek-tri-tsi-*teyt*
elevator *Lift* ⓜ lift

email *E-Mail* e-*mayl*
embassy *Botschaft* ⓕ *bawt*-shaft
emergency *Notfall* ⓜ *nawt*-fal
English (language) *Englisch* ⓝ *eng*-lish
entrance *Eingang* ⓜ *ain*-gang
evening *Abend* ⓜ *aa*-bent
exchange rate *Wechselkurs* ⓜ *vek*-sel-kurs
exit *Ausgang* ⓜ *ows*-gang
expensive *teuer* *toy*-er
express mail *Expresspost* ⓕ eks-*pres*-post
eye *Auge* ⓝ *ow*-ge

F

far *weit* vait
fast *schnell* shnel
father *Vater* ⓜ *faa*-ter
film (camera) *Film* ⓜ film
finger *Finger* ⓜ *fing*-er
first-aid kit *Verbandskasten* ⓜ fer-*bants*-kas-ten
first class *erste Klasse* ⓕ ers-te *kla*-se
fish *Fisch* ⓜ fish
food *Essen* ⓝ e-sen
foot *Fuß* ⓜ foos
fork *Gabel* ⓕ *gaa*-bel
free (of charge) *gratis* *graa*-tis
friend *Freund/Freundin* ⓜ/ⓕ froynt/froyn-din
fruit *Frucht* ⓕ frukht
full *voll* fol
funny *lustig* *lus*-tikh

G

German (language) *Deutsch* ⓝ doytsh
Germany *Deutschland* ⓝ doytsh-lant
gift *Geschenk* ⓝ ge-*shengk*
girl *Mädchen* ⓝ *meyt*-khen
glass (drinking) *Glas* ⓝ glaas
glasses *Brille* ⓕ *bri*-le
go *gehen* *gey*-en
good *gut* goot
green *grün* grewn
guide *Führer* ⓜ *few*-rer

H

half *Hälfte* ⓕ *helf*-te
hand *Hand* ⓕ hant
handbag *Handtasche* ⓕ *hant*-ta-she
happy *glücklich* *glewk*-likh

have *haben* haa-ben
he *er* air
head *Kopf* ⓜ kopf
heart *Herz* ⓝ herts
heat n *Hitze* ⓕ hi-tse
heavy *schwer* shvair
help v *helfen* hel-fen
here *hier* heer
high *hoch* hawkh
highway *Autobahn* ⓕ ow-to-baan
hike v *wandern* van-dern
holiday *Urlaub* ⓜ oor-lowp
homosexual *homosexuell* haw-mo-zek-su-el
hospital *Krankenhaus* ⓝ krang-ken-hows
hot *heiß* hais
hotel *Hotel* ⓝ ho-tel
hungry *hungrig* hung-rikh
husband *Ehemann* ⓜ ey-e-man

I

I *ich* ikh
identification (card) *Personalausweis* ⓜ per-zo-naal-ows-vais
ill *krank* krangk
important *wichtig* vikh-tikh
included *inbegriffen* in-be-gri-fen
injury *Verletzung* ⓕ fer-le-tsung
insurance *Versicherung* ⓕ fer-zi-khe-rung
Internet *Internet* ⓝ in-ter-net
interpreter *Dolmetscher/Dolmetscherin* ⓜ/ⓕ dol-met-sher/dol-met-she-rin

J

jewellery *Schmuck* ⓜ shmuk
job *Arbeitsstelle* ⓕ ar-baits-shte-le

K

key *Schlüssel* ⓜ shlew-sel
kilogram *Kilogramm* ⓝ kee-lo-gram
kitchen *Küche* ⓕ kew-khe
knife *Messer* ⓝ me-ser

L

laundry (place) *Waschküche* ⓕ vash-kew-khe
lawyer *Rechtsanwalt/Rechtsanwältin* ⓜ/ⓕ rekhts-an-valt/rekhts-an-vel-tin

left (direction) *links* links
left-luggage office *Gepäckaufbewahrung* ⓕ ge-pek-owf-be-vaa-rung
leg *Bein* ⓝ bain
lesbian *Lesbierin* ⓕ les-bi-e-rin
less *weniger* vey-ni-ger
letter (mail) *Brief* ⓜ breef
lift (elevator) *Lift* ⓜ lift
light *Licht* ⓝ likht
like v *mögen* meu-gen
lock *Schloss* ⓝ shlos
long *lang* lang
lost *verloren* fer-law-ren
lost-property office *Fundbüro* ⓝ funt-bew-raw
love v *lieben* lee-ben
luggage *Gepäck* ⓝ ge-pek
lunch *Mittagessen* ⓝ mi-taak-e-sen

M

mail *Post* ⓕ post
man *Mann* ⓜ man
map *Karte* ⓕ kar-te
market *Markt* ⓜ markt
matches *Streichhölzer* ⓝ pl shtraikh-heul-tser
meat *Fleisch* ⓝ flaish
medicine *Medizin* ⓕ me-di-tseen
menu *Speisekarte* ⓕ shpai-ze-kar-te
message *Mitteilung* ⓕ mi-tai-lung
milk *Milch* ⓕ milkh
minute *Minute* ⓕ mi-noo-te
mobile phone *Handy* ⓝ hen-di
money *Geld* ⓝ gelt
month *Monat* ⓜ maw-nat
morning *Morgen* ⓜ mor-gen
mother *Mutter* ⓕ mu-ter
motorcycle *Motorrad* ⓝ maw-tor-raat
motorway *Autobahn* ⓕ ow-to-baan
mouth *Mund* ⓜ munt
music *Musik* ⓕ mu-zeek

N

name *Name* ⓜ naa-me
napkin *Serviette* ⓕ zer-vye-te
nappy *Windel* ⓕ vin-del
near *nahe* naa-e
neck *Hals* ⓜ hals
new *neu* noy
news *Nachrichten* ⓕ pl naakh-rikh-ten

newspaper *Zeitung* ① tsai-tung
night *Nacht* ① nakht
no *nein* nain
noisy *laut* lowt
nonsmoking *Nichtraucher* nikht-row-kher
north *Norden* ⓜ nor-den
nose *Nase* ① naa-ze
now *jetzt* yetst
number *Zahl* ① tsaal

O

oil (engine) *Öl* ⓝ eul
old *alt* alt
one-way ticket *einfache Fahrkarte* ①
ain-fa-khe faar-kar-te
open a *offen* o-fen
outside *draußen* drow-sen

P

package *Paket* ⓝ pa-keyt
paper *Papier* ⓝ pa-peer
park (car) v *parken* par-ken
passport *(Reise)Pass* ⓜ (rai-ze-)pas
pay *bezahlen* be-tsaa-len
pen *Kugelschreiber* ⓜ koo-gel-shrai-ber
petrol *Benzin* ⓝ ben-tseen
pharmacy *Apotheke* ① a-po-tey-ke
phonecard *Telefonkarte* ① te-le-fawn-kar-te
photo *Foto* ⓝ faw-to
plate *Teller* ⓜ te-ler
police *Polizei* ① po-li-tsai
postcard *Postkarte* ① post-kar-te
post office *Postamt* ⓝ post-amt
pregnant *schwanger* shvang-er
price *Preis* ⓜ prais

Q

quiet *ruhig* roo-ikh

R

rain n *Regen* ⓜ rey-gen
razor *Rasierer* ⓜ ra-zee-rer
receipt *Quittung* ① kvi-tung
red *rot* rawt
refund *Rückzahlung* ① rewk-tsaa-lung
registered mail *Einschreiben* ⓝ ain-shrai-ben

rent v *mieten* mee-ten
repair v *reparieren* re-pa-ree-ren
reservation *Reservierung* ① re-zer-vee-rung
restaurant *Restaurant* ⓝ res-to-raang
return v *zurückkommen* tsu-rewk-ko-men
return ticket *Rückfahrkarte* ① rewk-faar-kar-te
right (direction) *rechts* rekhts
road *Straße* ① shtraa-se
room *Zimmer* ⓝ tsi-mer

S

safe a *sicher* zi-kher
sanitary napkin *Damenbinden* ① pl daa-men-bin-den
seat *Platz* ⓜ plats
send *senden* zen-den
service station *Tankstelle* ① tangk-shte-le
sex *Sex* ⓜ seks
shampoo *Shampoo* ⓝ sham-poo
share (a dorm) *teilen (mit)* tai-len (mit)
shaving cream *Rasiercreme* ① ra-zeer-kreym
she *sie* zee
sheet (bed) *Bettlaken* ⓝ bet-laa-ken
shirt *Hemd* ⓝ hemt
shoes *Schuhe* ⓜ pl shoo-e
shop n *Geschäft* ⓝ ge-sheft
short *kurz* kurts
shower *Dusche* ① doo-she
single room *Einzelzimmer* ⓝ ain-tsel-tsi-mer
skin *Haut* ① howt
skirt *Rock* ⓜ rok
sleep v *schlafen* shlaa-fen
slowly *langsam* lang-zaam
small *klein* klain
smoke (cigarettes) v *rauchen* row-khen
soap *Seife* ① zai-fe
some *einige* ai-ni-ge
soon *bald* balt
south *Süden* ⓜ zew-den
souvenir shop *Souvenirladen* ⓜ zu-ve-neer-laa-den
speak *sprechen* shpre-khen
spoon *Löffel* ⓜ leu-fel
stamp *Briefmarke* ① breef-mar-ke
stand-by ticket *Standby-Ticket* ⓝ stend-bai-ti-ket
station (train) *Bahnhof* ⓜ baan-hawf
stomach *Magen* ⓜ maa-gen
stop v *anhalten* an-hal-ten
stop (bus) *Bushaltestelle* ① bus-hal-te-shte-le
street *Straße* ① shtraa-se

student *Student/Studentin* ⓜ/ⓕ
  shtu-*dent*/shtu-*den*-tin
sun *Sonne* ⓕ *zo*-ne
sunscreen *Sonnencreme* ⓕ *zo*-nen-kreym
swim v *schwimmen* *shvi*-men
Switzerland *Schweiz* ⓕ shvaits

T

tampons *Tampons* ⓜ pl *tam*-pons
taxi *Taxi* ⓝ *tak*-si
teaspoon *Teelöffel* ⓜ *tey*-leu-fel
teeth *Zähne* ⓜ pl *tsey*-ne
telephone *Telefon* ⓝ te-le-*fawn*
television *Fernseher* ⓜ *fern*-zey-er
temperature (weather) *Temperatur* ⓕ tem-pe-ra-*toor*
tent *Zelt* ⓝ tselt
that (one) *jene* *yey*-ne
they *sie* zee
thirsty *durstig* *durs*-tikh
this (one) *diese* *dee*-ze
throat *Kehle* ⓕ *key*-le
ticket (transport) *Fahrkarte* ⓕ *faar*-kar-te
ticket (sightseeing) *Eintrittskarte* ⓕ *ain*-trits-kar-te
time *Zeit* ⓕ tsait
tired *müde* *mew*-de
tissues *Papiertaschentücher* ⓜ pl
  pa-*peer*-ta-shen-tew-kher
today *heute* *hoy*-te
toilet *Toilette* ⓕ to-a-*le*-te
tomorrow *morgen* *mor*-gen
tonight *heute Abend* *hoy*-te aa-*bent*
toothbrush *Zahnbürste* ⓕ *tsaan*-bewrs-te
toothpaste *Zahnpasta* ⓕ *tsaan*-pas-ta
torch (flashlight) *Taschenlampe* ⓕ *ta*-shen-lam-pe
tour *Tour* ⓕ toor
tourist office *Fremdenverkehrsbüro* ⓝ
  frem-den-fer-kairs-bew-raw
towel *Handtuch* ⓝ *hant*-tookh
train *Zug* ⓜ tsook
translate *übersetzen* ew-ber-*ze*-tsen
travel agency *Reisebüro* ⓝ *rai*-ze-bew-raw
travellers cheque *Reisescheck* ⓜ *rai*-ze-shek
trousers *Hose* ⓕ *haw*-ze
twin beds *zwei Einzelbetten* ⓜ pl tsvai *ain*-tsel-be-ten
tyre *Reifen* ⓜ *rai*-fen

U

underwear *Unterwäsche* ⓕ *un*-ter-ve-she
urgent *dringend* *dring*-ent

V

vacant *frei* frai
vacation *Ferien* pl *fair*-i-en
vegetable *Gemüse* ⓝ ge-*mew*-ze
vegetarian a *vegetarisch* ve-ge-*taa*-rish
visa *Visum* ⓝ *vee*-zum

W

waiter *Kellner/Kellnerin* ⓜ/ⓕ *kel*-ner/*kel*-ne-rin
walk v *gehen* *gey*-en
wallet *Brieftasche* ⓕ *breef*-ta-she
warm a *warm* varm
wash (something) *waschen* *va*-shen
watch *Uhr* ⓕ oor
water *Wasser* ⓝ *va*-ser
we *wir* veer
weekend *Wochenende* ⓝ *vo*-khen-en-de
west *Westen* ⓜ *ves*-ten
wheelchair *Rollstuhl* ⓜ *rol*-shtool
when *wann* van
where *wo* vaw
white *weiß* vais
who *wer* vair
why *warum* va-*rum*
wife *Ehefrau* ⓕ *ey*-e-frow
window *Fenster* ⓝ *fens*-ter
wine *Wein* ⓝ vain
with *mit* mit
without *ohne* *aw*-ne
woman *Frau* ⓕ frow
write *schreiben* *shrai*-ben

Y

yellow *gelb* gelp
yes *ja* yaa
yesterday *gestern* *ges*-tern
you sg inf *du* doo
you sg pol *Sie* zee
you pl *Sie* zee

Hungarian

hungarian alphabet

A a o	*Á á* a	*B b* bey	*C c* tsey	*Cs cs* chey	*D d* dey	*Dz dz* dzey	*Dzs dzs* jey
E e e	*É é* ey	*F f* ef	*G g* gey	*Gy gy* dyey	*H h* ha	*I i* i	*Í í* ee
J j yey	*K k* ka	*L l* el	*Ly ly* ey	*M m* em	*N n* en	*Ny ny* en'	*O o* aw
Ó ó âw	*Ö ö* eu	*Ő ő* eũ	*P p* pey	*Q q* ku	*R r* er	*S s* esh	*Sz sz* es
T t tey	*Ty ty* tyey	*U u* u	*Ú ú* û	*Ü ü* ew	*Ű ű* êw	*V v* vey	*W w* *du*-plo-vey
X x iks	*Y y* *ip*·sil-awn	*Z z* zey	*Zs zs* zhey				

hungarian

MAGYAR

introduction

Hungarian (*magyar* mo·dyor) is a unique language. Though distantly related to Finnish, it has no significant similarities to any other language in the world. If you have some background in European languages you'll be surprised at just how different Hungarian is. English actually has more in common with Russian and Sinhala (from Sri Lanka) than it does with Hungarian – even though words like *goulash*, *paprika* and *vampire* came to English from this language.

So how did such an unusual language end up in the heart of the European continent? The answer lies somewhere beyond the Ural mountains in western Siberia, where the nomadic ancestors of today's Hungarian speakers began a slow migration west about 2000 years ago. At some point in the journey the group began to split. One group turned towards Finland, while the other continued towards the Carpathian Basin, arriving in the late 9th century. Calling themselves Magyars (derived from the Finno-Ugric words for 'speak' and 'man') they cultivated and developed the occupied lands. By AD 1000 the Kingdom of Hungary was officially established. Along the way Hungarian acquired words from languages like Latin, Persian, Turkish and Bulgarian, yet overall changed remarkably little.

With more than 14.5 million speakers worldwide, Hungarian is nowadays the official language of Hungary and a minority language in the parts of Eastern Europe which belonged to the Austro-Hungarian Empire before World War I – Slovakia, Croatia, the northern Serbian province of Vojvodina and parts of Austria, Romania and the Ukraine.

Hungarian is a language rich in grammar and expression. These characteristics can be both alluring and intimidating. Word order in Hungarian is fairly free, and it has been argued that this stimulates creative or experimental thinking. Some believe that the flexibility of the tongue, combined with Hungary's linguistic isolation, has encouraged the culture's strong tradition of poetry and literature. For the same reason, however, the language is resistant to translation and much of the nation's literary heritage is still unavailable to English speakers. Another theory holds that Hungary's extraordinary number of great scientists is also attributable to the language's versatile nature. Still, Hungarian needn't be intimidating and you won't need to look very far to discover the beauty of the language. You may even find yourself unlocking the poet or scientist within!

pronunciation

The Hungarian language may seem daunting with its long words and many accent marks, but it's surprisingly easy to pronounce. Like English, Hungarian isn't always written the way it's pronounced, but just stick to the coloured phonetic guides that accompany each phrase or word and you can't go wrong.

vowel sounds

Hungarian vowels sounds are similar to those found in the English words listed in the table below. The symbol ¯ over a vowel, like ā, means you say it as a long vowel sound. The letter y is always pronounced as in 'yes'.

symbol	english equivalent	hungarian example	transliteration
a	father	*hátizsák*	*ha*·ti·zhak
aw	law (but short)	*kor*	kawr
e	bet	*zsebkés*	*zheb*·keysh
ee	see	*cím*	tseem
eu	her	*zöld*	zeuld
ew	ee pronounced with rounded lips	*csütörtök*	*chew*·teur·teuk
ey	hey	*én*	eyn
i	bit	*rizs*	rizh
o	pot	*gazda*	*goz*·do
oy	toy	*megfojt, komoly*	*meg*·foyt, *kaw*·moy
u	put	*utas*	*u*·tosh

word stress

Accent marks over vowels don't influence word stress, which always falls on the first syllable of the word. The stressed syllables in our coloured pronunciation guides are always in italics.

consonant sounds

Always pronounce y like the 'y' in 'yes'. We've also used the ' symbol to show this
y sound when it's attached to n, d, and t and at the end of a syllable. You'll also see
double consonants like bb, dd or tt – draw them out a little longer than you would
in English.

symbol	english equivalent	hungarian example	transliteration
b	bed	*bajusz*	*bo*-yus
ch	cheat	*család*	*cho*-lad
d	dog	*dervis*	*der*-vish
dy	during	*magyar*	*mo*-dyor
f	fat	*farok*	*fo*-rawk
g	go	*gallér, igen*	*gol*-leyr, *i*-gen
h	hat	*hát*	hat
j	joke	*dzsem, hogy*	jem, hawj
k	kit	*kacsa*	*ko*-cho
l	lot	*lakat*	*lo*-kot
m	man	*most*	mawsht
n	not	*nem*	nem
p	pet	*pamut*	*po*-mut
r	run (rolled)	*piros*	*pi*-rawsh
s	sun	*kolbász*	*kawl*-bas
sh	shot	*tojást*	*taw*-yasht
t	top	*tag*	tog
ty	tutor	*kártya*	*kar*-tyo
ts	hats	*koncert*	*kawn*-tsert
v	very	*vajon*	*vo*-yawn
y	yes	*hajó, melyik*	ho-*yāw*, *me*-yik
z	zero	*zab*	zob
zh	pleasure	*zsemle*	*zhem*-le
'	a slight y sound	*poggyász, hány*	*pawd'*-dyas, han'

tools

language difficulties

Do you speak English?
Beszél/Beszélsz angolul? pol/inf   be·seyl/be·seyls on·gaw·lul

Do you understand?
Érti/Érted? pol/inf   eyr·ti/eyr·ted

I (don't) understand.
(Nem) Értem.   (nem) eyr·tem

What does (lángos) mean?
Mit jelent az, hogy (lángos)?   mit ye·lent oz hawj (lan·gawsh)

How do you ...?	*Hogyan ...?*	haw·dyon ...
pronounce this	*mondja ki ezt*	mawnd·yo ki ezt
write (útlevél)	*írja azt, hogy*	eer·yo ozt hawj
	(útlevél)	(üt·le·veyl)

Could you please ...?	*..., kérem.*	... key·rem
repeat that	*Megismételné ezt*	meg·ish·mey·tel·ney ezt
speak more	*Tudna lassabban*	tud·no losh·shob·bon
slowly	*beszélni*	be·seyl·ni
write it down	*Leírná*	le·eer·na

essentials

Yes.	*Igen.*	i·gen
No.	*Nem.*	nem
Please.	*Kérem/Kérlek.* pol/inf	key·rem/keyr·lek
Thank you	*(Nagyon)*	(no·dyawn)
(very much).	*Köszönöm.*	keu·seu·neum
You're welcome.	*Szívesen.*	see·ve·shen
Excuse me.	*Elnézést kérek.*	el·ney·zeysht key·rek
Sorry.	*Sajnálom.*	shoy·na·lawm

numbers

0	*nulla*	nul·lo	16	*tizenhat*	*ti*·zen·hot
1	*egy*	ej	17	*tizenhét*	*ti*·zen·heyt
2	*kettő*	ket·tēū	18	*tizennyolc*	*ti*·zen·nyawlts
3	*három*	ha·rawm	19	*tizenkilenc*	*ti*·zen·ki·lents
4	*négy*	neyj	20	*húsz*	hüs
5	*öt*	eut	21	*huszonegy*	hu·sawn·ej
6	*hat*	hot	22	*huszonkettő*	hu·sawn·ket·tēū
7	*hét*	heyt	30	*harminc*	hor·mints
8	*nyolc*	nyawlts	40	*negyven*	*nej*·ven
9	*kilenc*	ki·lents	50	*ötven*	eut·ven
10	*tíz*	teez	60	*hatvan*	hot·von
11	*tizenegy*	*ti*·zen·ej	70	*hetven*	het·ven
12	*tizenkettő*	*ti*·zen·ket·tēū	80	*nyolcvan*	nyawlts·von
13	*tizenhárom*	*ti*·zen·ha·rawm	90	*kilencven*	*ki*·lents·ven
14	*tizennégy*	*ti*·zen·neyj	100	*száz*	saz
15	*tizenöt*	*ti*·zen·eut	1000	*ezer*	e·zer

time & dates

What time is it?	*Hány óra?*	han' *āw*·ra
It's one o'clock.	*(Egy) óra van.*	(ej) *āw*·ra von
It's (10) o'clock.	*(Tíz) óra van.*	(teez) *āw*·ra von
Quarter past (10).	*Negyed (tizenegy).*	ne·dyed (*ti*·zen·ej)
Half past (10).	*Fél (tizenegy).*	feyl (*ti*·zen·ej)
Quarter to (11).	*Háromnegyed (tizenegy).*	ha·rawm·ne·dyed (*ti*·zen·ej)
At what time ...?	*Hány órakor ...?*	han' *āw*·ro·kawr ...
At ...	*...kor.*	...kawr
am (morning)	*délelőtt*	deyl·e·lēütt
pm (afternoon)	*délután*	deyl·u·tan
pm (evening)	*este*	esh·te
Monday	*hétfő*	heyt·fēū
Tuesday	*kedd*	kedd
Wednesday	*szerda*	ser·do
Thursday	*csütörtök*	chew·teur·teuk
Friday	*péntek*	peyn·tek
Saturday	*szombat*	sawm·bot
Sunday	*vasárnap*	vo·shar·nop

January	január	yo·nu·ar
February	február	feb·ru·ar
March	március	mar·tsi·ush
April	április	ap·ri·lish
May	május	ma·yush
June	június	yū·ni·ush
July	július	yū·li·ush
August	augusztus	o·u·gus·tush
September	szeptember	sep·tem·ber
October	október	awk·tāw·ber
November	november	naw·vem·ber
December	december	de·tsem·ber

What date is it today?
  Hányadika van ma?   ha·nyo·di·ko von mo
It's (18 October).
  (Október tizennyolcadika) van.   (awk·tāw·ber ti·zen·nyawl·tso·di·ko) von

since (May)	(május) óta	(ma·yush) āw·to
until (June)	(június)ig	(yū·ni·ush)·ig
yesterday	tegnap	teg·nop
last night	tegnap éjjel	hawl·nop ey·yel
today	ma	mo
tonight	ma este	mo esh·te
tomorrow	holnap	hawl·nop
last/next ...	a múlt/a jövő ...	o mült/o yeu·vēū ...
week	héten	hey·ten
month	hónapban	hāw·nop·bon
year	évben	eyv·ben
yesterday/tomorrow ...	tegnap/holnap ...	teg·nop/hawl·nop ...
morning	reggel	reg·gel
afternoon	délután	deyl·u·tan
evening	este	esh·te

weather

What's the weather like?	Milyen az idő?	*mi*·yen oz *i*·dēü

It's ...

cloudy	Az idő felhős.	oz *i*·dēü *fel*·hēüsh
cold	Az idő hideg.	oz *i*·dēü *hi*·deg
hot	Az idő nagyon meleg.	oz *i*·dēü *no*·dyawn *me*·leg
raining	Esik az eső.	e·shik oz e·shēü
snowing	Esik a hó.	e·shik o hāw
sunny	Az idő napos.	oz *i*·dēü *no*·pawsh
warm	Az idő meleg.	oz *i*·dēü *me*·leg
windy	Az idő szeles.	oz *i*·dēü *se*·lesh

spring	tavasz	*to*·vos
summer	nyár	nyar
autumn	ősz	ēüs
winter	tél	teyl

border crossing

I'm ...	... vagyok.	... *vo*·dyawk
in transit	Átutazóban	*at*·u·to·zāw·bon
on business	Üzleti úton	*ewz*·le·ti *ū*·tawn
on holiday	Szabadságon	so·bod·sha·gawn

I'm here for ...	... vagyok itt.	... *vo*·dyawk itt
(10) days	(Tíz) napig	(teez) *no*·pig
(two) months	(Két) hónapig	(keyt) *hāw*·no·pig
(three) weeks	(Három) hétig	(*ha*·rawm) *hey*·tig

I'm going to (Szeged).
(Szeged)re megyek.   (*se*·ged)·re *me*·dyek

I'm staying at (the Gellért Hotel).
A (Gellért)ben fogok lakni.   o (*gel*·leyrt)·ben *faw*·gawk *lok*·ni

I have nothing to declare.
Nincs elvámolnivalóm.   ninch *el*·va·mawl·ni·vo·lāwm

I have something to declare.
Van valami elvámolnivalóm.   von *vo*·lo·mi *el*·va·mawl·ni·vo·lāwm

That's (not) mine.
Az (nem) az enyém.   oz (nem) oz e·nyeym

transport

tickets & luggage

Where can I buy a ticket?
Hol kapok jegyet? hawl *ko*·pawk *ye*·dyet

Do I need to book a seat?
Kell helyjegyet váltanom? kell *he*·ye·dyet *val*·ta·nawm

One ... ticket	*Egy ... jegy*	ej ... yej
to (Eger), please.	*(Eger)be.*	(e·ger)·be
one-way	*csak oda*	chok *aw*·do
return	*oda-vissza*	*aw*·do·*vis*·so

I'd like to ... my	*Szeretném ...*	se·ret·neym ...
ticket, please.	*a jegyemet.*	o *ye*·dye·met
cancel	*törölni*	*teu*·reul·ni
change	*megváltoztatni*	*meg*·val·tawz·tot·ni
collect	*átvenni*	*at*·ven·ni
confirm	*megerősíteni*	*meg*·e·rēū·shee·te·ni

I'd like a ... seat,	*... helyet*	... *he*·yet
please.	*szeretnék.*	se·ret·neyk
nonsmoking	*Nemdohányzó*	nem·daw·han'·zāw
smoking	*Dohányzó*	daw·han'·zāw

How much is it?
Mennyibe kerül? men'·nyi·be *ke*·rewl

Is there air conditioning?
Van légkondicionálás? von *leyg*·kawn·di·tsi·aw·na·lash

Is there a toilet?
Van vécé? von *vey*·tsey

How long does the trip take?
Mennyi ideig tart az út? men'·nyi *i*·de·ig tort oz üt

Is it a direct route?
Ez közvetlen járat? ez *keuz*·vet·len *ya*·rot

My luggage has been ...	*A poggyászom ...*	o *pawd'*·dya·sawm ...
damaged	*megsérült*	*meg*·shey·rewlt
lost	*elveszett*	*el*·ve·sett

My luggage has been stolen.
  Ellopták a poggyászomat.   *el*·lawp·tak o *pawd*′·dya·saw·mot

Where can I find a luggage locker?
  Hol találok egy poggyász-   hawl *to*·la·lawk ej *pawd*′·dyas·
  megőrző automatát?   meg·eür·zēū o·u·taw·mo·tat

getting around

Where does flight (BA15) arrive?
  Hova érkezik a (BA tizenötös)   *haw*·vo eyr·ke·zik a (bey o *ti*·zen·eu·teush)
  számú járat?   sa·mū *ya*·rot

Where does flight (BA26) depart?
  Honnan indul a (BA huszonhatos)   *hawn*·non *in*·dul a (bey o *hu*·sawn·ho·tawsh)
  számú járat?   sa·mū *ya*·rot

Where's (the) ...?	*Hol van ...?*	hawl von ...
arrivals hall	*az érkezési csarnok*	oz eyr·ke·zey·shi *chor*·nawk
departures hall	*az indulási csarnok*	oz in·du·la·shi *chor*·nawk
duty-free shop	*a vámmentes üzlet*	o *vam*·men·tesh *ewz*·let
gate (five)	*az (ötös) kapu*	oz (*eu*·teush) *ko*·pu

Which ... goes	*Melyik ... megy*	*me*·yik ... mej
to (Budapest)?	*(Budapest)re?*	(*bu*·do·pesht)·re
boat	*hajó*	*ho*·yāw
bus	*busz*	bus
plane	*repülőgép*	re·pew·lēū·geyp
train	*vonat*	*vaw*·not

What time's the	*Mikor megy ... (busz)?*	*mi*·kawr mej ... (bus)
... (bus)?		
first	*az első*	oz *el*·shēū
last	*az utolsó*	oz u·tawl·shāw
next	*a következő*	o *keu*·vet·ke·zēū

At what time does it arrive/leave?
  Mikor érkezik/indul?   *mi*·kawr eyr·kez·ik/*in*·dul

How long will it be delayed?
  Mennyit késik?   men′·nyit *key*·shik

What station/stop is this?
  Ez milyen állomás/megálló?   ez *mi*·yen *al*·law·mash/*meg*·al·lāw

What's the next station/stop?
Mi a következő állomás/megálló?   mi o *keu*·vet·ke·zēū *al*·law·mash/*meg*·al·lāw

Does it stop at (Visegrád)?
Megáll (Visegrád)on?   *meg*·all (*vi*·she·grad)·on

Please tell me when we get to (Eger).
Kérem, szóljon, amikor   *key*·rem *sāwl*·yawn *o*·mi·kawr
(Eger)be érünk.   (*e*·ger)·be *ey*·rewnk

How long do we stop here?
Mennyi ideig állunk itt?   *men*'·nyi *i*·de·ig *al*·lunk itt

Is this seat available?
Szabad ez a hely?   so·bod ez o *he*·y

That's my seat.
Az az én helyem.   oz oz eyn *he*·yem

I'd like a taxi ...   *Szeretnék egy taxit ...*   se·ret·neyk ej *tok*·sit ...
   at (9am)   *(reggel kilenc)re*   (*reg*·gel *ki*·lents)·re
   now   *most*   mawsht
   tomorrow   *holnapra*   *hawl*·nop·ro

Is this taxi available?
Szabad ez a taxi?   so·bod ez o *tok*·si

How much is it to ...?
Mennyibe kerül ...ba?   *men*'·nyi·be *ke*·rewl ...·bo

Please put the meter on.
Kérem, kapcsolja be az órát.   *key*·rem *kop*·chawl·yo be oz *āw*·rat

Please take me to (this address).
Kérem, vigyen el (erre a címre).   *kay*·re *vi*·dyen el (*er*·re o *tseem*·re)

Please ...   *Kérem, ...*   *key*·rem ...
   slow down   *lassítson*   *losh*·sheet·shawn
   stop here   *álljon meg itt*   *all*·yawn meg itt
   here   *várjon itt*   *var*·yawn itt

car, motorbike & bicycle hire

I'd like to hire a ...   *Szeretnék egy ... bérelni.*   se·ret·neyk ej ... *bey*·rel·ni
   bicycle   *biciklit*   *bi*·tsik·lit
   car   *autót*   *o*·u·tāwt
   motorbike   *motort*   *maw*·tawrt

with a driver	soförrel	shaw·feür·rel
with air conditioning	lég-kondicionálóval	leyg·kawn·di·tsi·aw·na·läw·vol
with antifreeze	fagyállóval	fod'·al·läw·vol
with snow chains	hólánccal	häw·lant'·tsol

How much	Mennyibe kerül	men'·nyi·be ke·rewl
for ... hire?	a kölcsönzés ...?	o keul·cheun·zeysh ...
hourly	óránként	äw·ran·keynt
daily	egy napra	ej nop·ro
weekly	egy hétre	ej heyt·re

air	levegő	le·ve·gêü
oil	olaj	aw·lo·y
petrol	benzin	ben·zin
tyres	gumi	gu·mi

I need a mechanic.
Szükségem van egy
autószerelőre.
sewk·shey·gem von ej
o·u·täw·se·re·lêü·re

I've run out of petrol.
Kifogyott a benzinem.
ki·faw·dyawtt o ben·zi·nem

I have a flat tyre.
Defektem van.
de·fek·tem von

directions

Where's the ...?	Hol van a ...?	hawl von o ...
bank	bank	bonk
city centre	városközpont	va·rawsh·keuz·pawnt
hotel	szálloda	sal·law·do
market	piac	pi·ots
police station	rendőrség	rend·êür·sheyg
post office	postahivatal	pawsh·to·hi·vo·tol
public toilet	nyilvános vécé	nyil·va·nawsh vey·tsey
tourist office	turistairoda	tu·rish·to·i·raw·do

Is this the road to (Sopron)?
Ez az út vezet (Sopron)ba?
ez oz üt ve·zet (shawp·rawn)·bo

Can you show me (on the map)?
Meg tudja mutatni nekem
(a térképen)?
meg tud·yo mu·tot·ni ne·kem
(o teyr·key·pen)

What's the address?
Mi a cím?   mi o tseem

How far is it?
Milyen messze van?   *mi*-yen *mes*-se von

How do I get there?
Hogyan jutok oda?   *haw*-dyon *yu*-tawk *aw*-do

Turn ...	*Forduljon ...*	*fawr*-dul-yawn ...
at the corner	*a saroknál*	o *sho*-rawk-nal
at the traffic lights	*a közlekedési lámpánál*	o *keuz*-le-ke-dey-shi *lam*-pa-nal
left/right	*balra/jobbra*	*bol*-ro/*yawbb*-ro

It's ...	*... van.*	*... von*
behind ...	*... mögött*	... *meu*-geutt
far away	*Messze*	*mes*-se
here	*Itt*	itt
in front of ...	*... előtt*	... e-*lëütt*
left	*Balra*	*bol*-ro
near ...	*... közelében*	... *keu*-ze-ley-ben
next to ...	*... mellett*	... *mel*-lett
on the corner	*A sarkon*	o *shor*-kawn
opposite ...	*...val szemben*	...vol *sem*-ben
right	*Jobbra*	*yawbb*-ro
straight ahead	*Egyenesen előttünk*	e-*dye*-ne-shen e-*lëüt*-tewnk
there	*Ott*	ott

by bus	*busszal*	*bus*-sol
by taxi	*taxival*	*tok*-si-vol
by train	*vonattal*	*vaw*-not-tol
on foot	*gyalog*	*dyo*-lawg

north	*észak*	*ey*-sok
south	*dél*	deyl
east	*kelet*	*ke*-let
west	*nyugat*	*nyu*-got

Bejárat/Kijárat	be·ya·rot/ki·ya·rot	Entrance/Exit
Nyitva/Zárva	nyit·vo/zar·vo	Open/Closed
Van Üres Szoba	von ew·resh saw·bo	Rooms Available
Minden Szoba Foglalt	min·den saw·bo fawg·lolt	No Vacancies
Információ	in·fawr·ma·tsi·āw	Information
Rendőrség	rend·ēūr·sheyg	Police Station
Tilos	ti·lawsh	Prohibited
Mosdó	mawsh·dāw	Toilets
Férfiak	feyr·fi·ok	Men
Nők	nēūk	Women
Meleg/Hideg	me·leg/hi·deg	Hot/Cold

accommodation

finding accommodation

Where's a ...?	Hol van egy ...?	hawl von ej ...
camping ground	kemping	kem·ping
guesthouse	panzió	pon·zi·āw
hotel	szálloda	sal·law·do
youth hostel	ifjúsági szálló	if·yū·sha·gi sal·lāw
Can you recommend	Tud ajánlani	tud o·yan·lo·ni
somewhere ...?	egy ... helyet?	ej ... he·yet
cheap	olcsó	awl·chāw
good	jó	yāw
nearby	közeli	keu·ze·li
I'd like to book a	Szeretnék egy	se·ret·neyk ej
room, please.	szobát foglalni.	saw·bat fawg·lol·ni
I have a reservation.	Van foglalásom.	von fawg·lo·la·shawm
My name's ...	A nevem ...	o ne·vem ...
Do you have	Van Önnek kiadó	von eun·nek ki·o·dāw
a ... room?	egy ... szobája?	ed' ... saw·ba·yo
single	egyágyas	ej·a·dyosh
double	duplaágyas	dup·lo·a·dyosh
twin	kétágyas	keyt·a·dyosh

How much is it per ...?	Mennyibe kerül egy ...?	men'·nyi·be ke·rewl ej ...
night	éjszakára	ey·so·ka·ro
person	főre	feü·re

Can I pay by ...?	Fizethetek ...?	fi·zet·he·tek ...
credit card	hitelkártyával	hi·tel·kar·tya·vol
travellers cheque	utazási csekkel	u·to·za·shi chek·kel

I'd like to stay for (three) nights.
(Három) éjszakára.   (ha·rawm) ey·so·ka·ro

From (July 2) to (July 6).
(Július kettő)től (július hat)ig.   (yū·li·ush ket·tēü)·tēül (yū·li·ush hot)·ig

Can I see it?
Megnézhetem?   meg·neyz·he·tem

Am I allowed to camp here?
Táborozhatok itt?   ta·baw·rawz·ho·tawk itt

Where can I find the camping ground?
Hol találom a kempinget?   hawl to·la·lawm o kem·pin·get

requests & queries

When/Where is breakfast served?
Mikor/Hol van a reggeli?   mi·kawr/hawl von o reg·ge·li

Please wake me at (seven).
Kérem, ébresszen fel (hét)kor.   key·rem eyb·res·sen fel (heyt)·kawr

Could I have my key, please?
Megkaphatnám a kulcsomat, kérem?   meg·kop·hot·nam o kul·chaw·mot key·rem

Can I get another (blanket)?
Kaphatok egy másik (takaró)t?   kop·ho·tawk ej ma·shik (to·ko·rāw)t

Is there a/an ...?	Van Önöknél ...?	von eu·neuk·neyl ...
elevator	lift	lift
safe	széf	seyf

The room is too ...	Túl ...	tül ...
expensive	drága	dra·go
noisy	zajos	zo·yawsh
small	kicsi	ki·chi

The ... doesn't work.	A ... nem működik.	o ... nem mēw·keu·dik
air conditioning	légkondicionáló	leyg·kawn·di·tsi·aw·na·lāw
fan	ventilátor	ven·ti·la·tawr
toilet	vécé	vey·tsey

This ... isn't clean.	Ez a ... nem tiszta.	ez o ... nem tis·to
sheet	lepedő	le·pe·dēü
towel	törülköző	teu·rewl·keu·zēü

checking out

What time is checkout?
Mikor kell kijelentkezni? mi·kawr kell ki·ye·lent·kez·ni

Can I leave my luggage here?
Itt hagyhatom a csomagjaimat? itt hoj·ho·tawm o chaw·mog·yo·i·mot

Could I have my ..., please?	Visszakaphatnám ..., kérem?	vis·so·kop·hot·nam ... key·rem
deposit	a letétemet	o le·tey·te·met
passport	az útlevelemet	oz üt·le·ve·le·met
valuables	az értékeimet	oz eyr·tey·ke·i·met

communications & banking

the internet

Where's the local Internet café?
Hol van a legközelebbi internet kávézó? hawl von o leg·keu·ze·leb·bi in·ter·net ka·vey·zāw

How much is it per hour?
Mennyibe kerül óránként? men'·nyi·be ke·rewl āw·ran·keynt

I'd like to check my email.
Szeretném megnézni az e-mailjeimet. se·ret·neym meg·neyz·ni oz ee·meyl·ye·i·met

I'd like to ...	Szeretnék ...	se·ret·neyk ...
get Internet access	rámenni az internetre	ra·men·ni oz in·ter·net·re
use a printer	használni egy nyomtatót	hos·nal·ni ej nyawm·to·täwt
use a scanner	használni egy szkennert	hos·nal·ni ej sken·nert

mobile/cell phone

I'd like a ...	Szeretnék egy ...	se·ret·neyk ej ...
mobile/cell phone	mobiltelefont	maw·bil·te·le·fawnt
for hire	bérelni	bey·rel·ni
SIM card	SIM-kártyát	sim·kar·tyat
for your network	ennek a hálózatnak	en·nek o ha·law·zot·nok
What are the rates?	Milyen díjak vannak?	mi·yen dee·yok von·nok

telephone

What's your phone number?
Mi a telefonszáma/   mi o te·le·fawn·sa·ma/
telefonszámod? pol/inf   te·le·fawn·sa·mawd

The number is ...
A szám ...   o sam ...

Where's the nearest public phone?
Hol a legközelebbi   hawl o leg·keu·ze·leb·bi
nyilvános telefon?   nyil·va·nawsh te·le·fawn

I'd like to buy a phonecard.
Szeretnék telefonkártyát venni.   se·ret·neyk te·le·fawn·kar·tyat ven·ni

I want to make a reverse-charge call.
'R' beszélgetést szeretnék kérni.   er·be·seyl·ge·teysht se·ret·neyk keyr·ni

I want to ...	Szeretnék ...	se·ret·neyk ...
call (Singapore)	(Szingapúr)ba	(sin·go·pür)·bo
	telefonálni	te·le·faw·nal·ni
make a local call	helyi telefon-	he·yi te·le·fawn·
	beszélgetést	be·seyl·ge·teysht
	folytatni	faw·y·tot·ni

How much	Mennyibe	men'·nyi·be
does ... cost?	kerül ...?	ke·rewl ...
a (three)-minute	egy (három)perces	ej (ha·rawm)·per·tsesh
call	beszélgetés	be·seyl·ge·teysh
each extra minute	minden további perc	min·den taw·vab·bi perts

(30) forints per (30) seconds.
(Harminc) másodpercenként   (hor·mints) ma·shawd·per·tsen·keynt
(harminc) forint.   (hor·mints) faw·rint.

post office

I want to send a ...	... szeretnék küldeni.	... se·ret·neyk kewl·de·ni
fax	Faxot	fok·sawt
letter	Levelet	le·ve·let
parcel	Csomagot	chaw·mo·gawt
postcard	Képeslapot	key·pesh·lo·pawt

I want to buy a/an...	... szeretnék venni.	... se·ret·neyk ven·ni
envelope	Borítékot	baw·ree·tey·kawt
stamp	Bélyeget	bey·ye·get

Please send it to (Australia) by ...	Kérem, küldje ... (Ausztráliá)ba.	key·rem kewld·ye ... (o·ust·ra·li·a)·bo
airmail	légipostán	ley·gi·pawsh·tan
express mail	expresszel	eks·press·zel
registered mail	ajánlottan	o·yan·law·tton
surface mail	simán	shi·man

Is there any mail for me?	Van levelem?	von le·ve·lem

bank

Where's a/an ...?	Hol van egy ...?	hawl von ej ...
ATM	bankautomata	bonk·o·u·taw·mo·to
foreign exchange office	valutaváltó ügynökség	vo·lu·to·val·tāw ewj·neuk·sheyg

I'd like to ...	Szeretnék ...	se·ret·neyk ...
Where can I ...?	Hol tudok ...?	hawl tu·dawk ...
arrange a transfer	pénzt átutalni	peynzt at·u·tol·ni
cash a cheque	beváltani egy csekket	be·val·to·ni ej chek·ket
change a travellers cheque	beváltani egy utazási csekket	be·val·to·ni ej u·to·za·shi chek·ket
change money	pénzt váltani	peynzt val·to·ni
get a cash advance	készpénzelőleget felvenni	keys·peynz·e·lēū·le·get fel·ven·ni
withdraw money	pénzt kivenni	peynzt ki·ven·ni

What's the ...?	Mennyi ...?	*men'·nyi ...*
charge for that	a díj	o *dee·y*
exchange rate	a valutaárfolyam	o *vo·lu·to·ar·faw·yom*

It's (100) euros.	(Száz) euró.	*(saz) e·u·raw*
It's (500) forints.	(Ötszáz) forint.	*(eut·saz) faw·rint*
It's free.	Ingyen van.	*in·dyen von*

What time does the bank open?
Mikor nyit a bank?   *mi·kawr nyit o bonk*

Has my money arrived yet?
Megérkezett már a pénzem?   *meg·eyr·ke·zett mar o peyn·zem*

sightseeing

getting in

What time does it open/close?
Mikor nyit/zár?   *mi·kawr nyit/zar*

What's the admission charge?
Mennyibe kerül a belépőjegy?   *men'·nyi·be ke·rewl o be·ley·pēū·yej*

Is there a discount for students/children?
Van kedvezmény diákok/   *von ked·vez·meyn' di·a·kawk/*
gyerekek számára?   *dye·re·kek sa·ma·ro*

I'd like a ...	Szeretnék egy ...	*se·ret·neyk ej ...*
catalogue	katalógust	*ko·to·lāw·gusht*
guide	idegenvezetőt	*i·de·gen·ve·ze·tēūt*
local map	itteni térképet	*it·te·ni teyr·key·pet*

I'd like to see ...	Szeretnék látni ...	*se·ret·neyk lat·ni ...*
What's that?	Az mi?	*oz mi*
Can I take a photo?	Fényképezhetek?	*feyn'·key·pez·he·tek*

tours

When's the	Mikor van a	*mi·kawr von o*
next ...?	következő ...?	*keu·vet·ke·zēū ...*
day trip	egynapos kirándulás	*ej·no·pawsh ki·ran·du·lash*
tour	túra	*tū·ro*

sightseeing

castle	*vár*	var
cathedral	*székesegyház*	sey·kesh·ej·haz
church	*templom*	temp·lawm
main square	*fő tér*	fëü ter
monastery	*kolostor*	kaw·lawsh·tawr
monument	*emlékmű*	em·leyk·mëw
museum	*múzeum*	mü·ze·um
old city	*óváros*	āw·va·rawsh
palace	*palota*	po·law·to
ruins	*romok*	raw·mawk
stadium	*stadion*	shto·di·awn
statues	*szobrok*	saw·brawk

Is ... included?	*Benne van az árban ...?*	ben·ne von oz ar·bon ...
accommodation	*a szállás*	o sal·lash
the admission charge	*a belépőjegy*	o be·ley·pëü·yej
food	*az ennivaló*	oz en·ni·vo·lāw
transport	*a közlekedés*	o keuz·le·ke·deysh

How long is the tour?
Mennyi ideig tart a túra?   men'·nyi i·de·ig tort o tü·ra

What time should we be back?
Mikorra érünk vissza?   mi·kawr·ro ey·rewnk vis·so

shopping

enquiries

Where's a ...?	*Hol van egy ...?*	hawl von ej ...
bank	*bank*	bonk
bookshop	*könyvesbolt*	keun'·vesh·bawlt
camera shop	*fényképezőgép-bolt*	feyn'·key·pe·zëü·geyp·bawlt
department store	*áruház*	a·ru·haz
grocery store	*élelmiszerbolt*	ey·lel·mi·ser·bawlt
market	*piac*	pi·ots
newsagency	*újságárus*	ü·y·shag·a·rush
supermarket	*élelmiszeráruház*	ey·lel·mi·ser·a·ru·haz

Where can I buy (a padlock)?
   Hol tudok venni (egy lakatot)?   hawl *tu*-dawk *ven*-ni (ej *lo*-ko-tawt)

I'm looking for ...
   Keresem a ...   *ke*-re-shem o ...

Can I look at it?
   Megnézhetem?   *meg*-neyz-he-tem

Do you have any others?
   Van másmilyen is?   von *mash*-mi-yen ish

Does it have a guarantee?
   Van rajta garancia?   von *ro*-y-to *go*-ron-tsi-o

Can I have it sent overseas?
   El lehet küldetni külföldre?   el *le*-het *kewl*-det-ni *kewl*-feuld-re

Can I have my ... repaired?
   Megjavíttathatnám itt ...?   *meg*-yo-veet-tot-hot-nam itt ...

It's faulty.
   Hibás.   *hi*-bash

I'd like ..., please.	*..., kérem.*	... *key*-rem
a bag	*Kaphatnék egy zacskót*	*kop*-hot-neyk ej *zoch*-kãwt
a refund	*Vissza szeretném*	*vis*-so se-ret-neym
	kapni a pénzemet	*kop*-ni o *peyn*-ze-met
to return this	*Szeretném*	*se*-ret-neym
	visszaadni ezt	*vis*-so-od-ni ezt

paying

How much is it?
   Mennyibe kerül?   *men*'-nyi-be *ke*-rewl

Could you write down the price?
   Le tudná írni az árat?   le *tud*-na *eer*-ni oz *a*-rot

That's too expensive.
   Ez túl drága.   ez *túl dra*-go

Do you have something cheaper?
   Van valami olcsóbb?   von *vo*-lo-mi *awl*-chãwbb

I'll give you (500 forints).
   Adok Önnek (ötszáz forintot).   *o*-dawk *eun*-nek (*eut*-saz *faw*-rin-tawt)

There's a mistake in the bill.
   Valami nem stimmel a számlával.   *vo*-lo-mi nem *shtim*-mel o *sam*-la-vol

Do you accept ...?	Elfogadnak ...?	el-faw-god-nok ...
credit cards	hitelkártyát	hi-tel-kar-tyat
debit cards	bankkártyát	bonk-kar-tyat
travellers cheques	utazási csekket	u-to-za-shi chek-ket

I'd like ..., please.	..., kérem.	... key-rem
a receipt	Kaphatnék egy nyugtát	kop-hot-neyk ej nyug-tat
my change	Szeretném megkapni	se-ret-neym meg-kop-ni
	a visszajáró pénzt	o vis-so-ya-rāw peynzt

clothes & shoes

Can I try it on?	Felpróbálhatom?	fel-präw-bal-ho-tawm
My size is (40).	A méretem	o mey-re-tem
	(negyvenes).	(nej-ve-nesh)
It doesn't fit.	Nem jó.	nem yāw

small	kicsi	ki-chi
medium	közepes	keu-ze-pesh
large	nagy	noj

books & music

I'd like a ...	Szeretnék egy ...	se-ret-neyk ej ...
newspaper	(angol)	(on-gawl)
(in English)	újságot	ūy-sha-gawt
pen	tollat	tawl-lot

Is there an English-language bookshop?

| Van valahol egy angol | von vo-lo-hawl ej on-gawl |
| nyelvű könyvesbolt? | nyel-vēw keun'-vesh-bawlt |

I'm looking for something by (Zsuzsa Koncz).

| (Koncz Zsuzsá)tól | (konts zhu-zha)-tāwl |
| keresek valamit. | ke-re-shek vo-lo-mit |

Can I listen to this?

| Meghallgathatom ezt? | meg-holl-got-ho-tawm ezt |

photography

Can you transfer photos from my camera to CD?
Át tudják vinni a képeket   at·tud·yak vin·ni o key·pe·ket
a fényképezőgépemről CD-re?   o feyn'·key·pe·zēū·gey·pem·rēūl tsey·dey·re

Can you develop this film?
Elő tudják hívni ezt a filmet?   e·lēū tud·yak heev·ni ezt o fil·met

Can you load my film?
Bele tudják tenni a filmet   be·le tud·yak ten·ni o fil·met
a gépembe?   o gey·pem·be

I need a ... film for this camera.	... filmet szeretnék.	... fil·met se·ret·neyk
B&W	Fekete-fehér	fe·ke·te·fe·heyr
colour	Színes	see·nesh
slide	Dia	di·o
(200) speed	(Kétszáz)as fényérzékenységű	(keyt·saz)·osh feyn'·eyr·zey·ken'·shey·gēw

When will it be ready? *Mikor lesz kész?*   mi·kawr les keys

meeting people

greetings, goodbyes & introductions

Hello.	Szervusz/Szervusztok. sg/pl	ser·vus/ser·vus·tawk
Hi.	Szia/Sziasztok. sg/pl	si·o/si·os·tawk
Good night.	Jó éjszakát.	yāw ey·y·so·kat
Goodbye.	Viszlát.	vis·lat
Bye.	Szia/Sziasztok. sg/pl	si·o/si·os·tawk

Mr	Úr	ūr
Mrs	Asszony	os·sawn'
Miss	Kisasszony	kish·os·sawn'

How are you?	Hogy van/vagy? pol/inf	hawj von/voj
Fine. And you?	Jól. És Ön/te? pol/inf	yāwl eysh eun/te
What's your name?	Mi a neve/neved? pol/inf	mi o ne·ve/ne·ved
My name is ...	A nevem ...	o ne·vem ...
I'm pleased to meet you.	Örvendek.	eur·ven·dek

This is my ...	Ez ...	ez ...
boyfriend	a barátom	o bo·ra·tawm
brother (older)	a bátyám	o ba·tyam
brother (younger)	az öcsém	oz eu·cheym
daughter	a lányom	o la·nyawm
father	az apám	oz o·pam
friend	a barátom/barátnőm m/f	o bo·ra·tawm/bo·rat·nēūm
girlfriend	a barátnőm	o bo·rat·nēūm
husband	a férjem	o feyr·yem
mother	az anyám	oz o·nyam
partner (intimate)	a barátom/barátnőm m/f	o bo·ra·tawm/bo·rat·nēūm
sister (older)	a nővérem	o nēū·vey·rem
sister (younger)	a húgom	o hū·gawm
son	a fiam	o fi·om
wife	a feleségem	o fe·le·shey·gem

Here's my ...	Itt van ...	itt von ...
address	a címem	o tsee·mem
email address	az e-mail címem	oz ee·meyl tsee·mem
fax number	a faxszámom	o foks·sa·mawm
phone number	a telefonszámom	o te·le·fawn·sa·mawm

What's your ...?	Mi ...?	mi ...
address	a címe	o tsee·me
email address	az e-mail címe	oz ee·meyl tsee·me
fax number	a faxszáma	o foks·sa·ma
phone number	a telefonszáma	o te·le·fawn·sa·ma

occupations

What's your occupation?	Mi a foglalkozása/ foglalkozásod? pol/inf	mi o fawg·lol·kaw·za·sho/ fawg·lol·kaw·za·shawd
I'm a/an ...	... vagyok.	... vo·dyawk
artist	Művész	mēw·veys
businessperson	Üzletember m	ewz·let·em·ber
	Üzletasszony f	ewz·let·os·sawn'
farmer	Gazda	goz·do
office worker	Irodai dolgozó	i·raw·do·i dawl·gaw·zāw
scientist	Természettudós	ter·mey·set·tu·dāwsh
student	Diák	di·ak
tradesperson	Kereskedő	ke·resh·ke·dēū

background

Where are you from?	Ön honnan jön? pol	eun *hawn*·non yeun
	Te honnan jössz? inf	te *hawn*·non yeuss
I'm from ...	Én ... jövök.	eyn ... *yeu*·veuk
Australia	Ausztráliából	o·ust·ra·li·a·bāwl
Canada	Kanadából	ko·no·da·bāwl
England	Angliából	ong·li·a·bāwl
New Zealand	Új-Zélandból	ü·y·zey·lond·bāwl
the USA	USAból	u·sho·bāwl
Are you married? m	Nős?	nēūsh
Are you married? f	Férjnél van?	feyr·y·neyl von
I'm ...	... vagyok.	... vo·dyawk
married	Nős/Férjnél m/f	nēūsh/feyr·y·neyl
single	Egyedülálló	e·dye·dewl·al·lāw

age

How old are you?	Hány éves? pol	han' ey·vesh
	Hány éves vagy? inf	han' ey·vesh voj
How old are your children?	Hány évesek a gyerekei/gyerekeid? pol/inf	han' ey·ve·shek o dye·re·ke·i/dye·re·ke·id
I'm ... years old.	... éves vagyok.	... ey·vesh vo·dyawk
He/She is ... years old.	... éves.	... ey·vesh

feelings

Are you ...?	... vagy?	... voj
happy	Boldog	bawl·dawg
hungry	Éhes	ey·hesh
sad	Szomorú	saw·maw·rü
thirsty	Szomjas	sawm·yosh
I'm ...	... vagyok.	... vo·dyawk
I'm not ...	Nem vagyok ...	nem vo·dyawk ...
happy	boldog	bawl·dawg
hungry	éhes	ey·hesh
sad	szomorú	saw·maw·rü
thirsty	szomjas	sawm·yosh

Are you cold?	*Fázik/Fázol?* pol/inf	*fa*·zik/*fa*·zawl
I'm (not) cold.	*(Nem) Fázom.*	(nem) *fa*·zawm
Are you hot?	*Melege/Meleged van?* pol/inf	*me*·le·ge/*me*·le·ged von
I'm hot.	*Melegem van.*	*me*·le·gem von
I'm not hot.	*Nincs melegem.*	ninch *me*·le·gem

entertainment

going out

Where can I find ...?	*Hol találok ...?*	hawl *to*·la·lawk ...
clubs	*klubokat*	*klu*·baw·kot
gay venues	*meleg*	*me*·leg
	szórakozóhelyeket	*säw*·ro·kaw·zäw·he·ye·ket
pubs	*pubokat*	*po*·baw·kot
I feel like going	*Szeretnék*	se·ret·neyk
to a/the ...	*elmenni egy ...*	*el*·men·ni ej ...
concert	*koncertre*	*kawn*·tsert·re
movies	*moziba*	*maw*·zi·bo
party	*partira*	*por*·ti·ro
restaurant	*étterembe*	*eyt*·te·rem·be
theatre	*színházba*	*seen*·haz·bo

interests

Do you like ...?	*Szeret ...?*	se·re·ted ...
I (don't) like ...	*(Nem) Szeretem ...*	(nem) se·re·tem ...
art	*a művészetet*	o *mēw*·vey·ve·se·tet
movies	*a filmeket*	o *fil*·me·ket
sport	*a sportot*	o *shpawr*·tawt
Do you like ...?	*Szeretsz ...?*	se·rets ...
I (don't) like ...	*(Nem) Szeretek ...*	(nem) se·re·tek ...
cooking	*főzni*	*fēūz*·ni
nightclubs	*diszkóba járni*	*dis*·käw·bo *yar*·ni
reading	*olvasni*	*awl*·vosh·ni
shopping	*vásárolni*	*va*·sha·rawl·ni
travelling	*utazni*	*u*·toz·ni

Do you ...?		
dance	*Táncolsz?*	*tan·tsawls*
go to concerts	*Jársz koncertre?*	*yars kawn·tsert·re*
listen to music	*Hallgatsz zenét?*	*holl·gots ze·neyt*

food & drink

finding a place to eat

Can you recommend	*Tud/Tudsz ajánlani*	*tud/tuds o·yan·lo·ni*
a ...?	*egy ...?* pol/inf	*ej ...*
bar	*bárt*	*bart*
café	*kávézót*	*ka·vey·zāwt*
restaurant	*éttermet*	*eyt·ter·met*
I'd like ...	*Szeretnék ...*	*se·ret·neyk ...*
a table for (five)	*egy asztalt (öt)*	*ej os·tolt (eut)*
	személyre	*se·mey·re*
the (non)smoking	*a (nem)dohányzó*	*o (nem·)daw·han'·zāw*
section	*részben ülni*	*reys·ben ewl·ni*

ordering food

breakfast	*reggeli*	*reg·ge·li*
lunch	*ebéd*	*e·beyd*
dinner	*vacsora*	*vo·chaw·ro*
snack	*snack*	*snekk*
today's special	*napi ajánlat*	*no·pi oy·an·lot*

How long is the wait?
Mennyi ideig kell várni?   *men'·nyi i·de·ig kell vaar·ni*

What would you recommend?
Mit ajánlana?   *mit o·yan·lo·no*

I'd like (the) ...	*... szeretném.*	*... se·ret·neym*
bill	*A számlát*	*o sam·lat*
drink list	*Az itallapot*	*oz i·tol·lo·pawt*
menu	*Az étlapot*	*oz eyt·lo·pawt*
that dish	*Azt az ételt*	*ozt oz ey·telt*

drinks

(cup of) coffee ...	*(csésze) kávé ...*	*(chey·se) ka·vey ...*
(cup of) tea ...	*(csésze) tea ...*	*(chey·se) te·o ...*
with milk	*tejjel*	*ey·yel*
without sugar	*cukor nélkül*	*tsu·kawr neyl·kewl*
... mineral water	*... ásványvíz*	*... ash·van'·veez*
sparkling	*szénsavas*	*seyn·sho·vosh*
still	*szénsavmentes*	*seyn·shov·men·tesh*
orange juice	*narancslé*	*no·ronch·ley*
soft drink	*üdítőital*	*ew·dee·teű·i·tal*
(boiled) water	*(forralt) víz*	*(fawr·rolt) veez*

in the bar

I'll have ...	*... kérek.*	*... key·rek*
I'll buy you a drink.	*Fizetek neked egy italt.*	*fi·ze·tek ne·ked ej i·tolt*
What would you like?	*Mit kérsz?*	*mit keyrs*
Cheers! (to one person)	*Egészségedre!*	*e·geys·shey·ged·re*
Cheers! (to more than one person)	*Egészségetekre!*	*e·geys·shey·ge·tek·re*
brandy	*brandy*	*bren·di*
champagne	*pezsgő*	*pezh·gēū*
cocktail	*koktél*	*kawk·teyl*
a bottle/glass of (beer)	*egy üveg/pohár (sör)*	*ej ew·veg/paw·har (sheur)*
a shot of (whisky)	*egy kupica (whisky)*	*ej ku·pi·tso (vis·ki)*
a bottle/glass of ... wine	*egy üveg/pohár ... bor*	*ej ew·veg/paw·har ... bawr*
red	*vörös*	*veu·reush*
sparkling	*pezsgő*	*pezh·gēū*
white	*fehér*	*fe·heyr*

What's the local speciality?
Mi az itteni specialitás?   mi oz it·te·ni shpe·tsi·o·li·tash

What's that?
Az mi?   oz mi

How much is (a kilo of cheese)?
Mennyibe kerül (egy kiló sajt)?   men'·nyi·be ke·rewl (ej ki·läw shoyt)

I'd like ...	*Kérek ...*	key·rek ...
200 grams	*húsz dekát*	hüs de·kat
a kilo	*egy kilót*	ej ki·läwt
a piece	*egy darabot*	ej do·ro·bawt
a slice	*egy szeletet*	ej se·le·tet
Less.	*Kevésbé.*	ke·veysh·bey
Enough.	*Elég.*	e·leyg
More.	*Több.*	teubb

Is there a vegetarian restaurant near here?
Van a közelben   von o keu·zel·ben
vegetáriánus étterem?   ve·ge·ta·ri·a·nush eyt·te·rem

Do you have vegetarian food?
Vannak Önöknél   von·nok eu·neuk·neyl
vegetáriánus ételek?   ve·ge·ta·ri·a·nush ey·te·lek

Could you prepare	*Tudna készíteni*	tud·no key·see·te·ni
a meal without ...?	*egy ételt ... nélkül?*	ej ey·telt ... neyl·kewl
butter	*vaj*	vo·y
eggs	*tojás*	taw·yash
meat stock	*húsleveskocka*	hüsh·le·vesh·kawts·ko
I'm allergic to ...	*Allergiás vagyok a ...*	ol·ler·gi·ash vo·dyawk o ...
dairy produce	*tejtermékekre*	te·y·ter·mey·kek·re
gluten	*sikérre*	shi·keyr·re
MSG	*monoszódium*	maw·naw·säw·di·um
	glutamátra	glu·to·mat·ro
nuts	*diófélékre*	di·äw·fey·leyk·re
seafood	*tenger gyümölcseire*	ten·ger yew·meul·che·i·re

bableves csülökkel	*bob*-le-vesh *chew*-leuk-kel	*bean soup with smoked pork*
csúsztatott palacsinta	*chūs*-to-tawtt *po*-lo-chin-to	*pancakes in a stack sprinkled with chocolate*
dobostorta	*daw*-bawsh-tawr-to	*sponge cake with chocolate cream, with a glazed sponge layer on top*
gombaleves	*gom*-bo-le-vesh	*mushroom & onion soup seasoned with paprika*
grenadírmas	*gre*-no-deer-morsh	*potatoes with sweet paprika, onion & pasta, served with sour gherkins*
gulyásleves	*gu*-yash-le-vesh	*beef soup with vegetables & pasta*
halászlé vegyes halból	*ho*-las-ley *ve*-dyesh *hol*-bāwl	*fish soup with onion, tomato & a dose of paprika*
hortobágyi ürügulyás	*hawr*-taw-ba-dyi *ew*-rew-gu-yash	*mutton stew*
kacsapecsenye	*ko*-cho-pe-che-nye	*roasted duck with apples, quinces & marjoram*
korhelyleves	*kawr*-he-y-le-vesh	*stew of smoked ham, sauerkraut & sliced sausage*
kürtőskalács	*kewr*-tēush-ko-lach	*dough wrapped around a roller, coated with honey & almonds or walnuts & roasted on a spit*
lángos	*lan*-gawsh	*deep-fried potato cakes topped with cabbage, ham, cheese or sour cream*
lecsó	*le*-chāw	*stewed tomatoes, peppers, onions & paprika*
lekváros szelet	*lek*-va-rawsh *se*-let	*sponge cake layered with strawberry jam*

májgaluska	*ma·y·go·lush·ko*	fried egg dumplings made from chicken, veal or pork livers
mákos tészta	*ma·kawsh teys·to*	sweet pasta with poppy seeds
meggyes rétes	*mej·dyesh rey·tesh*	cherry & walnut strudel
meggyleves	*mejj·le·vesh*	chilled soup with cherries, sour cream & red wine
palóc leves	*po·lāwts le·vesh*	soup made from cubed leg of mutton or beef & vegetables
paprikás	*pop·ri·kash*	veal, chicken or rabbit stew
pörkölt	*peur·keult*	diced meat stew with a paprika gravy
sonkás kocka	*shawn·kash kots·ko*	chopped ham mixed with sour cream & pasta, then baked
sonkával töltött gomba	*shawn·ka·vol teul·teutt gawm·bo*	mushrooms stuffed with smoked ham in cheese sauce & grilled
székely gulyás	*sey·ke·y gu·yash*	stew of sautéed pork, bacon, sauerkraut & sour cream
szilvás gombóc	*sil·vash gawm·bāwts*	boiled potato-based dumplings filled with pitted plums
tokány	*taw·kan'*	meat stewed in white wine, tomato paste & seasonings
töltött káposzta	*teul·teutt ka·paws·to*	cabbage leaves stuffed with rice & ground pork
töltött paprika	*teul·teutt pop·ri·ko*	capsicums stuffed with rice & ground pork
tűzdelt fácán	*tēwz·delt fa·tsan*	pheasant larded with smoked bacon & roasted in red wine gravy
vargabéles	*vor·go·bey·lesh*	layered pasta & dough topped with a custard-like mixture
zöldbabfőzelék	*zeuld·bob·fēū·ze·leyk*	cooked green beans with sour cream & seasonings

emergencies

basics

Help!	Segítség!	she-geet-sheyg
Stop!	Álljon meg!	all-yawn meg
Go away!	Menjen innen!	men-yen in-nen
Thief!	Tolvaj!	tawl-voy
Fire!	Tűz!	tēwz
Watch out!	Vigyázzon!	vi-dyaz-zawn
Call a doctor!	Hívjon orvost!	heev-yawn awr-vawsht
Call an ambulance!	Hívja a mentőket!	heev-yo o men-tēū-ket
Call the police!	Hívja a rendőrséget!	heev-yo o rend-ēūr-shey-get

It's an emergency!
Sürgős esetről van szó.   shewr-gēūsh e-shet-rēūl von sāw

Could you help me, please?
Tudna segíteni?   tud-no she-gee-te-ni

Can I use your phone?
Használhatom a telefonját?   hos-nal-ho-tawm o te-le-fawn-yat

I'm lost.
Eltévedtem.   el-tey-ved-tem

Where are the toilets?
Hol a vécé?   hawl o vey-tsey

police

Where's the police station?
Hol a rendőrség?   hawl o rend-ēūr-sheyg

I want to report an offence.
Bűncselekményt szeretnék   bēwn-che-lek-meynyt se-ret-neyk
bejelenteni.   be-ye-len-te-ni

I have insurance.
Van biztosításom.   von biz-taw-shee-ta-shawm

I've been ...

assaulted	Megtámadtak.	meg-ta-mod-tok
raped	Megerőszakoltak.	meg-e-rēū-so-kawl-tok
robbed	Kiraboltak.	ki-ro-bawl-tok

I've lost my ...	Elvesztettem ...	el-ves-tet-tem ...
My ... was/were stolen.	Ellopták ...	el-lawp-tak ...
backpack	a hátizsákomat	o ha-ti-zha-kaw-mot
bags	a csomagjaimat	o chaw-mog-yo-i-mot
credit card	a hitelkártyámat	o hi-tel-kar-tya-mot
handbag	a kézitáskámat	o key-zi-tash-ka-mot
jewellery	az ékszereimet	oz eyk-se-re-i-met
money	a pénzemet	o peyn-ze-met
passport	az útlevelemet	oz üt-le-ve-le-met
travellers cheques	az utazási csekkjeimet	oz u-to-za-shi chekk-ye-i-met
wallet	a tárcámat	o tar-tsa-mot

I want to contact my embassy/consulate.

Kapcsolatba akarok lépni a követségemmel/ konzulátusommal.

kop-chaw-lot-bo o-ko-rawk leyp-ni o keu-vet-shey-gem-mel/ kawn-zu-la-tu-shawm-mol

health

medical needs

Where's the nearest ...?	Hol a legközelebbi ...?	hawl o leg-keu-ze-leb-bi ...
dentist	fogorvos	fawg-awr-vawsh
doctor	orvos	awr-vawsh
hospital	kórház	kāwr-haz
(night) pharmacist	(éjszaka nyitvatartó) gyógyszertár	(ey-so-ko nyit-vo-tor-tāw) dyāwj-ser-tar

I need a doctor (who speaks English).

(Angolul beszélő) Orvosra van szükségem.

(on-gaw-lul be-sey-leū) awr-vawsh-ro von sewk-shey-gem

Could I see a female doctor?

Beszélhetnék egy orvosnővel?

be-seyl-het-neyk ej awr-vawsh-neū-vel

I've run out of my medication.

Elfogyott az orvosságom.

el-faw-dyawtt oz awr-vawsh-sha-gawm

symptoms, conditions & allergies

| I'm sick. | Rosszul vagyok. | raws·sul vo·dyawk |
| It hurts here. | Itt fáj. | itt fa·y |

I have a ...		
cough	Köhögök.	keu·heu·geuk
headache	Fáj a fejem.	fa·y o fe·yem
sore throat	Fáj a torkom.	fa·y o tawr·kawm
toothache	Fáj a fogam.	fa·y o faw·gom

I have (a) ...	... van.	... von
asthma	Asztmám	ost·mam
bronchitis	Hörghurutom	heurg·hu·rut·awm
constipation	Székrekedésem	seyk·re·ke·dey·shem
diarrhoea	Hasmenésem	hosh·me·ney·shem
fever	Lázam	la·zom
heart condition	Szívbetegségem	seev·be·teg·sheyg·em
nausea	Hányingerem	han'·in·ge·rem
pain	Fájdalmam	fay·dol·mom

I'm allergic to ...	Allergiás vagyok ...	ol·ler·gi·ash vo·dyawk ...
antibiotics	az antibiotikumokra	oz on·ti·bi·aw·ti·ku·mawk·ro
anti-inflammatories	a gyulladásgátlókra	o dyul·lo·dash·gat·lawk·ro
aspirin	az aszpirinre	oz os·pi·rin·re
bees	a méhekre	o mey·hek·re
codeine	a kodeinre	o ko·de·in·re
penicillin	a penicillinre	o pe·ni·tsil·lin·re

antiseptic n	fertőzésgátló	fer·teü·zeysh·gat·law
bandage	kötés	keu·teysh
condoms	óvszer	awv·ser
contraceptives	fogamzásgátló	faw·gom·zash·gat·law
diarrhoea medicine	hasmenés gyógyszer	hosh·men·eysh dyáwd'·ser
insect repellent	rovarirtó	raw·vor·ir·taw
laxatives	hashajtó	hosh·ho·y·taw
painkillers	fájdalomcsillapító	fa·y·do·lawm·chil·lo·pee·taw
rehydration salts	folyadékpótló sók	faw·yo·deyk·pawt·law shawk
sleeping tablets	altató	ol·to·taw

english–hungarian dictionary

In this dictionary, words are marked as n (noun), a (adjective), v (verb), sg (singular), pl (plural), inf (informal) or pol (polite) where necessary.

A

accident *baleset* bol-e-shet
accommodation *szállás* sal-lash
adaptor *adapter* o-dop-ter
address n *cím* tseem
after *után* u-tan
air-conditioned *légkondicionált* leyg-kawn-di-tsi-aw-nalt
airplane *repülőgép* re-pew-lêü-geyp
airport *repülőtér* re-pew-lêü-teyr
alcohol *alkohol* ol-kaw-hawl
all *minden* min-den
allergy *allergia* ol-ler-gi-o
ambulance *mentő* men-têü
and *és* eysh
ankle *boka* baw-ko
arm *kar* kor
ashtray *hamutartó* ho-mu-tor-tāw
ATM *bankautomata* bonk-o-u-taw-mo-to

B

baby *baba* bo-bo
back (body) *hát* hat
backpack *hátizsák* ha-ti-zhak
bad *rossz* rawss
bag *táska* tash-ko
baggage claim *poggyászkiadó* pawd'-dyas-ki-o-dāw
bank *bank* bonk
bar *bár* bar
bathroom *fürdőszoba* fewr-dêü-saw-bo
battery *elem* e-lem
beautiful *szép* seyp
bed *ágy* aj
beer *sör* sheur
before *előtt* e-lêütt
behind *mögött* meu-geutt
bicycle *bicikli* bi-tsik-li
big *nagy* noj
bill *számla* sam-lo
black *fekete* fe-ke-te

blanket *takaró* to-ko-rāw
blood group *vércsoport* veyr-chaw-pawrt
blue *kék* keyk
boat (big) *hajó* ho-yāw
boat (small) *csónak* chāw-nok
book (make a reservation) v *lefoglal* le-fawg-lol
bottle *üveg* ew-veg
bottle opener *sörnyitó* sheur-nyi-tāw
boy *fiú* fi-ū
brake (car) *fék* feyk
breakfast *reggeli* reg-ge-li
broken (faulty) *hibás* hi-bash
bus *busz* bus
business *üzlet* ewz-let
buy *vesz* ves

C

café *kávézó* ka-vey-zāw
camera *fényképezőgép* feyn'-key-pe-zêü-geyp
camp site *táborhely* ta-bawr-he-y
cancel *töröl* teu-reul
can opener *konzervnyitó* kawn-zerv-nyi-tāw
car *autó* o-u-tāw
cash n *készpénz* keys-peynz
cash (a cheque) v *bevált csekket* be-valt chek-ket
cell phone *mobil telefon* maw-bil te-le-fawn
centre n *központ* keuz-pawnt
change (money) v *pénzt vált* peynzt valt
cheap *olcsó* owl-chāw
check (bill) *számla* sam-lo
check-in n *bejelentkezés* be-ye-lent-ke-zeysh
chest *mellkas* mell-kosh
child *gyerek* dye-rek
cigarette *cigaretta* tsi-go-ret-to
city *város* va-rawsh
clean a *tiszta* tis-to
closed *zárva* zar-vo
coffee *kávé* ka-vey
coins *pénzérmék* peynz-eyr-meyk
cold a *hideg* hi-deg
collect call *'R' beszélgetés* er-be-seyl-ge-teysh
come *jön* yeun

computer *számítógép* sa-mee-täw-geyp
condom *óvszer* awv-ser
contact lenses *kontaktlencse* kawn-tokt-len-che
cook v *főz* feüz
cost n *ár* ar
credit card *hitelkártya* hi-tel-kar-tyo
cup *csésze* chey-se
currency exchange *valutaátváltás* vo-lu-to-at-val-tash
customs (immigration) *vám* vam

D

dangerous *veszélyes* ve-sey-yesh
date (time) *dátum* da-tum
day *nap* nop
delay n *késés* key-sheysh
dentist *fogorvos* fawg-awr-vawsh
depart *elutazik* el-u-to-zik
diaper *pelenka* pe-len-ko
dictionary *szótár* sáw-tar
dinner *vacsora* vo-chaw-ro
direct *közvetlen* keuz-vet-len
dirty *piszkos* pis-kawsh
disabled *mozgássérült* mawz-gash-shey-rewlt
discount n *árengedmény* ar-en-ged-meyn'
doctor *orvos* awr-vawsh
double bed *dupla ágy* dup-lo aj
double room *dupla ágyas szoba* dup-lo-a-dyosh saw-bo
drink n *ital* i-tol
drive v *vezet* ve-zet
drivers licence *jogosítvány* yaw-gaw-sheet-van'
drug (illicit) *kábítószerek* ka-bee-täw-se-rek
dummy (pacifier) *cumi* tsu-mi

E

ear *fül* fewl
east *kelet* ke-let
eat *eszik* e-sik
economy class *turistaosztály* tu-rish-to-aws-ta-y
electricity *villany* vil-lon'
elevator *lift* lift
email *e-mail* ee-meyl
embassy *nagykövetség* noj-keu-vet-sheyg
emergency *vészhelyzet* veys-he-y-zet
English (language) *angol* on-gawl
entrance *bejárat* be-ya-rot
evening *este* esh-te
exchange rate *átváltási árfolyam*
at-val-ta-shi ar-faw-yom

exit n *kijárat* ki-ya-rot
expensive *drága* dra-go
express mail *expressz posta* eks-press pawsh-to
eye *szem* sem

F

far *messze* mes-se
fast *gyors* dyawrsh
father *apa* o-po
film (camera) *film* film
finger *ujj* u-y
first-aid kit *elsősegély-láda* el-shëü-she-gey-la-do
first class *első osztály* el-shëü aws-ta-y
fish n *hal* hol
food *ennivaló* en-ni-vo-láw
foot *lábfej* lab-fe-y
fork *villa* vil-lo
free (of charge) *ingyenes* in-dye-nesh
friend (female) *barátnő* bo-rat-nëü
friend (male) *barát* bo-rat
fruit *gyümölcs* dyew-meulch
full *tele* te-le
funny *mulatságos* mu-lot-sha-gawsh

G

gift *ajándék* o-yan-deyk
girl *lány* lan'
glass (drinking) *üveg* ew-veg
glasses *szemüveg* sem-ew-veg
go *megy* mej
good *jó* yäw
green *zöld* zeuld
guide n *idegenvezető* i-de-gen-ve-ze-tëü

H

half n *fél* feyl
hand *kéz* keyz
handbag *kézitáska* key-zi-tash-ko
happy *boldog* bawl-dawg
have *van neki* von ne-ki
he *ő* ëü
head *fej* fe-y
heart *szív* seev
heat n *forróság* fawr-räw-shag
heavy *nehéz* ne-heyz
help v *segít* she-geet
here *itt* itt

high *magas* mo·gosh
highway *országút* awr·sag·üt
hike v *kirándul* ki·ran·dul
holiday *szabadság* so·bod·shag
homosexual n *homoszexuális* haw·maw·sek·su·a·lish
hospital *kórház* kawr·haz
hot *forró* fawr·raw
hotel *szálloda* sal·law·do
Hungarian (language) *magyar* mo·dyor
Hungary *Magyarország* mo·dyor·awr·sag
hungry *éhes* ey·hesh
husband *férj* feyr·y

I

I *én* eyn
identification (card) *személyi igazolvány*
 se·mey·yi i·go·zawl·van'
ill *beteg* be·teg
important *fontos* fawn·tawsh
included *beleértve* be·le·eyrt·ve
injury *sérülés* shey·rew·leysh
insurance *biztosítás* biz·taw·shee·tash
Internet *Internet* in·ter·net
interpreter *tolmács* tawl·mach

J

jewellery *ékszerek* eyk·se·rek
job *állás* al·lash

K

key *kulcs* kulch
kilogram *kilogramm* ki·läw·gromm
kitchen *konyha* kawn'·ho
knife *kés* keysh

L

laundry (place) *mosoda* maw·shaw·do
lawyer *jogász* yaw·gas
left (direction) *balra* bol·ro
left-luggage office *csomagmegőrző*
 chaw·mog·meg·eūr·zēū
leg *láb* lab
lesbian n *leszbikus* les·bi·kush
less *kevésbé* ke·veysh·bey
letter (mail) *levél* le·veyl
lift (elevator) *lift* lift

light n *fény* feyn'
like v *szeret* se·ret
lock n *zár* zar
long *hosszú* haws·sü
lost *elveszett* el·ve·sett
lost-property office *talált tárgyak hivatala*
 to·lalt tar·dyok hi·vo·to·lo
love v *szeret* se·ret
luggage *poggyász* pawd'·dyas
lunch *ebéd* e·beyd

M

mail n *posta* pawsh·to
man *férfi* feyr·fi
map *térkép* teyr·keyp
market *piac* pi·ots
matches *gyufa* dyu·fo
meat *hús* hüsh
medicine *orvosság* awr·vawsh·shag
menu *étlap* eyt·lop
message *üzenet* ew·ze·net
milk *tej* te·y
minute *perc* perts
mobile phone *mobil telefon* maw·bil te·le·fawn
money *pénz* peynz
month *hónap* häw·nop
morning *reggel* reg·gel
mother *anya* o·nyo
motorcycle *motorbicikli* maw·tawr·bi·tsik·li
motorway *autópálya* o·u·täw·pa·yo
mouth *száj* sa·y
music *zene* ze·ne

N

name *keresztnév* ke·rest·neyv
napkin *szalvéta* sol·vey·to
nappy *pelenka* pe·len·ko
near *közelében* keu·ze·ley·ben
neck *nyak* nyok
new *új* ü·y
news *hírek* hee·rek
newspaper *újság* ü·y·shag
night *éjszaka* ey·so·ko
no *nem* nem
noisy *zajos* zo·yawsh
nonsmoking *nemdohányzó* nem·daw·han'·zäw
north *észak* ey·sok
nose *orr* awrr
now *most* mawsht
number *szám* sam

O

oil (engine) *olaj aw*-lo-y
old (person/thing) *öreg/régi eu-*reg/*rey*-gi
one-way ticket *csak oda jegy* chok aw-do yej
open a *nyitva nyit*-vo
outside *kint* kint

P

package *csomag chaw*-mog
paper *papír* po-peer
park (a car) v *parkol por*-kawl
passport *útlevél üt*-le-veyl
pay *fizet* fi-zet
pen *golyóstoll gaw*-yäwsh-tawll
petrol *benzin* ben-zin
pharmacy *gyógyszertár* dyäwj-ser-tar
phonecard *telefonkártya* te-le-fawn-kar-tyo
photo *fénykép feyn'*-keyp
plate *tányér* ta-nyeyr
police *rendőrség* rend-ēür-sheyg
postcard *levelezőlap* le-ve-le-zēü-lop
post office *postahivatal pawsh*-to-hi-vo-tol
pregnant *terhes* ter-hesh
price *ár* ar

Q

quiet *csendes* chen-desh

R

rain n *eső* e-shēü
razor *borotva baw*-rawt-vo
receipt n *nyugta* nyug-to
red *piros* pi-rawsh
refund n *visszatérítés vis*-so-tey-ree-teysh
registered mail *ajánlott levél* o-yan-lawtt le-veyl
rent v *bérel* bey-rel
repair v *megjavít* meg-yo-veet
reservation *foglalás* fawg-lo-lash
restaurant *étterem* eyt-te-rem
return v *visszatér* vis-so-teyr
return ticket *oda-vissza jegy* aw-do-vis-so yej
right (direction) *jobbra* yawbb-ro
road *út* üt
room *szoba* saw-bo

S

safe a *biztonságos* biz-tawn-sha-gawsh
sanitary napkin *egészségügyi törlőkendő*
e-geys-sheyg-ew-dyi teur-lēü-ken-dēü
seat *ülés* ew-leysh
send *küld* kewld
service station *benzinkút* ben-zin-küt
sex *szex* seks
shampoo *sampon* shom-pawn
share (a dorm) *ben/ban lakik* -ben/-ban lo-kik
shaving cream *borotvakrém* baw-rawt-vo-kreym
she *ő* ēü
sheet (bed) *lepedő* le-pe-dēü
shirt *ing* ing
shoes *cipők* tsi-pēük
shop n *üzlet* ewz-let
short *alacsony* o-lo-chawn'
shower *zuhany* zu-hon'
single room *egyágyas szoba* ej-a-dyosh saw-bo
skin *bőr* bēür
skirt *szoknya* sawk-nyo
sleep v *alszik* ol-sik
slowly *lassan* losh-shon
small *kicsi* ki-chi
smoke (cigarettes) v *dohányzik* daw-han'-zik
soap *szappan* sop-pon
some *néhány* ney-han'
soon *hamarosan* ho-mo-raw-shon
south *dél* deyl
souvenir shop *ajándékbolt* o-yan-deyk-bawlt
speak *beszél* be-seyl
spoon *kanál* ko-nal
stamp n *bélyeg* bey-yeg
stand-by ticket *készenléti jegy* key-sen-ley-ti yej
station (train) *állomás* al-law-mash
stomach *gyomor* dyaw-mawr
stop v *abbahagy* ob-bo-hoj
stop (bus) n *megálló* meg-al-läw
street *utca* ut-tso
student *diák* di-ak
sun *nap* nop
sunscreen *napolaj* nop-aw-lo-y
swim v *úszik* ü-sik

T

tampons *tampon* tom-pawn
taxi *taxi* tok-si
teaspoon *teáskanál* te-ash-ko-nal
teeth *fogak* faw-gok
telephone n *telefon* te-le-fawn

television *televízió* te-le-vee-zi-äw
temperature (weather) *hőmérséklet*
    hëü-meyr-sheyk-let
tent *sátor* sha-tawr
that (one) *az* oz
they *ők* ëük
thirsty *szomjas* sawm-yosh
this (one) *ez* ez
throat *torok* taw-rawk
ticket *jegy* yej
time *idő* i-dëü
tired *fáradt* fa-rott
tissues *szövetek* seu-ve-tek
today *ma* mo
toilet *vécé* vey-tsey
tomorrow *holnap* hawl-nop
tonight *ma este* mo esh-te
toothbrush *fogkefe* fawg-ke-fe
toothpaste *fogkrém* fawg-kreym
torch (flashlight) *zseblámpa* zheb-lam-po
tour n *túra* tü-ro
tourist office *turistairoda* tu-rish-to-i-raw-do
towel *törülköző* teu-rewl-keu-zëü
train *vonat* vaw-not
translate *fordít* fawr-deet
travel agency *utazási iroda* u-to-za-shi i-raw-do
travellers cheque *utazási csekk* u-to-za-shi chekk
trousers *nadrág* nod-rag
twin beds *két ágy* keyt aj
tyre *autógumi* o-u-täw-gu-mi

underwear *alsónemű* ol-shäw-ne-mëw
urgent *sürgős* shewr-gëüsh

vacant *üres* ew-resh
vacation *vakáció* vo-ka-tsi-äw

vegetable n *zöldség* zeuld-sheyg
vegetarian a *vegetáriánus* ve-ge-ta-ri-a-nush
visa *vízum* vee-zum

waiter *pincér* pin-tseyr
walk v *sétál* shey-tal
wallet *tárcá* tar-tsa-mot
warm a *meleg* me-leg
wash (something) *megmos* meg-mawsh
watch n *óra* äw-ro
water *víz* veez
we *mi* mi
weekend *hétvége* heyt-vey-ge
west *nyugat* nyu-got
wheelchair *rokkantkocsi* rawk-kont-kaw-chi
when *mikor* mi-kawr
where *hol* hawl
white *fehér* fe-heyr
who *ki* ki
why *miért* mi-eyrt
wife *feleség* fe-le-sheyg
window *ablak* ob-lok
wine *bor* bawr
with *-val/-vel* -vol/-vel
without *nélkül* neyl-kewl
woman *nő* nëü
write *ír* eer

yellow *sárga* shar-go
yes *igen* i-gen
yesterday *tegnap* teg-nop
you sg inf *te* te
you pl inf *ti* ti
you sg pol *Ön* eun
you pl pol *Önök* eu-neuk

Polish

polish alphabet

Aa a	*Ą ą* om/on	*Bb* be	*Cc* tse	*Ćć* che	*Dd* de
Ee e	*Ęę* em/en	*Ff* ef	*Gg* gye	*Hh* kha	*Ii* ee
Jj yot	*Kk* ka	*Ll* el	*Łł* ew	*Mm* em	*Nn* en
Ńń en'	*Oo* o	*Óó* oo	*Pp* pe	*Rr* er	*Ss* es
Śś esh	*Tt* te	*Uu* oo	*Ww* woo	*Yy* i	*Zz* zet
Żż zhet	*Żż* zhyet				

polish

POLSKI

introduction

Ask most English speakers what they know about Polish (*polski* pol-skee), the language which donated the words *horde, mazurka* and *vodka* to English, and they will most likely dismiss it as an unpronounceable language. Who could pronounce an apparently vowel-less word like *szczyt* shchit (peak), for example? To be put off by this unfairly gained reputation, however, would be to miss out on a rich and rewarding language. The mother tongue of Copernicus, Chopin, Marie Curie and Pope John Paul II has a fascinating and turbulent past and symbolises the resilience of the Polish people in the face of domination and adversity.

The Polish tribes who occupied the basins of the Oder and Vistula rivers in the 6th century AD spoke a range of West Slavic dialects, which over time evolved into Polish. The closest living relatives of Polish are Czech and Slovak which also belong to the wider West Slavic family of languages. The language reached the apex of its influence during the era of the Polish Lithuanian Commonwealth (1569–1795). The Commonwealth covered a swath of territory from what are now Poland and Lithuania through Belarus, Ukraine and Latvia and part of Western Russia. Polish became a lingua franca throughout much of Central and Eastern Europe at this time due to the political, cultural, scientific and military might of this power.

When Poland was wiped off the map of Europe from 1795 to 1918 after three successive partitions in the second half of the 18th century (when it was carved up between Russia, Austria and Prussia), the language suffered attempts at both Germanisation and Russification. Later, after WWII, Poland became a satellite state of the Soviet Union and the language came under the renewed influence of Russian. Polish showed impressive resistance in the face of this oppression. The language not only survived these onslaughts but enriched itself by borrowing many words from both Russian and German. The works of Poland's greatest literary figures who wrote in exile – the Romantic poet Adam Mickiewicz and, during Communist rule, the Nobel Prize winner Czesław Miłosz – are testament to this fact.

Today, Poland is linguistically one of the most homogenous countries in Europe – over 95% of the population speaks Polish as their first language. There are significant Polish-speaking minorities in the western border areas of Ukraine, Belarus and in southern Lithuania, with smaller populations in other neighbouring countries.

pronunciation

vowel sounds

Polish vowels are generally prounounced short, giving them a 'clipped' quality.

symbol	english equivalent	polish example	transliteration
a	run	*tak*	tak
ai	aisle	*tutaj*	*too*-tai
e	bet	*bez*	bes
ee	see	*wino*	*vee*-no
ey	hey	*kolejka*	ko-*ley*-ka
i	bit	*czy*	chi
o	pot	*woda*	*vo*-da
oo	zoo	*zakupy, mój*	za-*koo*-pi, mooy
ow	how	*migdał*	*meeg*-dow
oy	toy	*ojciec*	*oy*-chets

Polish also has nasal vowels, pronounced as though you're trying to force the air out of your nose rather than your mouth. Nasal vowels are indicated in written Polish by the letters *ą* and *ę*. Depending upon the letters that follow these vowels, they're pronounced with either an 'm' or an 'n' sound following the vowel.

symbol	english equivalent	polish example	transliteration
em	like the 'e' in 'get' plus	*wstęp*	fstemp
en	nasal consonant sound	*mięso*	*myen*-so
om	like the 'o' in 'not' plus	*kąpiel*	*kom*-pyel
on	nasal consonant sound	*wąsy*	*von*-si

word stress

In Polish, stress almost always falls on the second-last syllable. In our coloured pronunciation guides, the stressed syllable is italicised.

consonant sounds

Most Polish consonant sounds are also found in English, with the exception of the kh sound (pronounced as in the Scottish word *loch*) and the rolled r sound.

symbol	english equivalent	polish example	transliteration
b	bed	*babka*	*bap*·ka
ch	cheat	*cień, czas, ćma*	chen', chas, chma
d	dog	*drobne*	*drob*·ne
f	fat	*fala*	*fa*·la
g	go	*garnek*	*gar*·nek
j	joke	*dzieci*	*je*·chee
k	kit	*kac*	kats
kh	loch	*chata, hałas*	*kha*·ta, *kha*·was
l	lot	*lato*	*la*·to
m	man	*malarz*	*ma*·lash
n	not	*nagle*	*na*·gle
p	pet	*palec*	*pa*·lets
r	run (rolled)	*róg*	roog
s	sun	*samolot*	*sa*·*mo*·lot
sh	shot	*siedem, śnieg, szlak*	*shye*·dem, shnyek, shlak
t	top	*targ*	tark
v	very	*widok*	*vee*·dok
w	win	*złoto*	*zwo*·to
y	yes	*zajęty*	za·*yen*·ti
z	zero	*zachód*	*za*·khoot
zh	pleasure	*zima, żart, rzeźba*	*zhee*·ma, zhart, *zhezh*·ba
'	a slight y sound	*kwiecień*	*kfye*·chen'

tools

language difficulties

Do you speak English?
Czy pan/pani mówi   chi pan/*pa*·nee *moo*·vee
po angielsku? m/f pol   po an·*gyel*·skoo

Do you understand?
Czy pan/pani rozumie? m/f pol   chi pan/*pa*·nee ro·*zoo*·mye

I (don't) understand.
(Nie) Rozumiem.   (nye) ro·*zoo*·myem

What does (*nieczynne*) mean?
Co to znaczy (nieczynne)?   tso to *zna*·chi (nye·*chi*·ne)

How do you ...?	*Jak się ...?*	yak shye ...
pronounce this	*to wymawia*	to vi·*mav*·ya
write (*pierogi*)	*pisze (pierogi)*	*pee*·she (pye·*ro*·gee)

Could you please ...?	*Proszę ...*	*pro*·she ...
repeat that	*to powtórzyć*	to po v·*too*·zhich
speak more	*mówić trochę*	*moo*·veech tro·khe
slowly	*wolniej*	*vol*·nyey
write it down	*to napisać*	to na·*pee*·sach

essentials

Yes.	*Tak.*	tak
No.	*Nie.*	nye
Please.	*Proszę.*	*pro*·she
Thank you (very much).	*Dziękuję (bardzo).*	jyen·*koo*·ye (*bar*·dzo)
You're welcome.	*Proszę.*	*pro*·she
Excuse me.	*Przepraszam.*	pshe·*pra*·sham
Sorry.	*Przepraszam.*	pshe·*pra*·sham

0	zero	ze·ro		15	piętnaście	pyent·nash·chye
1	jeden m	ye·den		16	szesnaście	shes·nash·chye
	jedna f	yed·na		17	siedemnaście	shye·dem·nash·chye
	jedno n	yed·no		18	osiemnaście	o·shem·nash·chye
2	dwa m	dva		19	dziewiętnaście	jye·vyet·nash·chye
	dwie f	dvye		20	dwadzieścia	dva·jyesh·chya
	dwoje n	dvo·ye		21	dwadzieścia	dva·jyesh·chya
3	trzy	tshi			jeden	ye·den
4	cztery	chte·ri		22	dwadzieścia	dva·jyesh·chya
5	pięć	pyench			dwa	dva
6	sześć	sheshch		30	trzydzieści	tshi·jyesh·chee
7	siedem	shye·dem		40	czterdzieści	chter·jyesh·chee
8	osiem	o·shyem		50	pięćdziesiąt	pyen·jye·shont
9	dziewięć	jye·vyench		60	sześćdziesiąt	shesh·jye·shont
10	dziesięć	jye·shench		70	siedemdziesiąt	shye·dem·jye·shont
11	jedenaście	ye·de·nash·chye		80	osiemdziesiąt	o·shem·jye·shont
12	dwanaście	dva·nash·chye		90	dziewięćdziesiąt	jye·vyen·jye·shont
13	trzynaście	tshi·nash·chye		100	sto	sto
14	czternaście	chter·nash·chye		1000	tysiąc	ti·shonts

time & dates

What time is it?	Która jest godzina?	ktoo·ra yest go·jee·na
It's one o'clock.	Pierwsza.	pyerf·sha
It's (10) o'clock.	Jest (dziesiąta).	yest (jye·shon·ta)
Quarter past (10).	Piętnaście po (dziesiątej).	pyent·nash·chye po (jye·shon·tey)
Half past (10).	Wpół do (jedenastej).	fpoow do (ye·de·nas·tey)
Quarter to (11).	Za piętnaście (jedenasta).	za pyent·nash·chye (ye·de·nas·ta)
At what time ...?	O której godzinie ...?	o ktoo·rey go·jee·nye ...
At ...	O ...	o ...
in the morning	rano	ra·no
in the afternoon	po południu	po po·wood·nyoo
in the evening (6pm–10pm)	wieczorem	vye·cho·rem
at night (11pm–3am)	w nocy	v no·tsi

Monday	*poniedziałek*	po-nye-*jya*-wek
Tuesday	*wtorek*	*fto*-rek
Wednesday	*środa*	*shro*-da
Thursday	*czwartek*	*chfar*-tek
Friday	*piątek*	*pyon*-tek
Saturday	*sobota*	so-*bo*-ta
Sunday	*niedziela*	nye-*jye*-la

January	*styczeń*	*sti*-chen'
February	*luty*	*loo*-ti
March	*marzec*	*ma*-zhets
April	*kwiecień*	*kfye*-chyen'
May	*maj*	mai
June	*czerwiec*	*cher*-vyets
July	*lipiec*	*lee*-pyets
August	*sierpień*	*shyer*-pyen'
September	*wrzesień*	*vzhe*-shyen'
October	*październik*	*pazh*-jyer-neek
November	*listopad*	*lees*-to-pat
December	*grudzień*	*groo*-jyen'

What date is it today?	*Którego jest dzisiaj?*	ktoo-*re*-go yest *jee*-shai
It's (18 October).	*Jest (osiemnastego*	yest (o-shem-nas-*te*-go
	października).	pazh-jyer-*nee*-ka)
last night	*wczoraj wieczorem*	*fcho*-rai vye-*cho*-rem
last/next ...	*w zeszłym/przyszłym ...*	v *zesh*-wim/*pshish*-wim ...
week	*tygodniu*	ti-*god*-nyoo
month	*miesiącu*	mye-*shon*-tsoo
year	*roku*	*ro*-koo
yesterday/	*wczoraj/*	*fcho*-rai/
tomorrow ...	*jutro ...*	*yoo*-tro ...
morning	*rano*	*ra*-no
afternoon	*po południu*	po po-*wood*-nyoo
evening	*wieczorem*	vye-*cho*-rem

weather

What's the weather like?	*Jaka jest pogoda?*	*ya*-ka yest po-*go*-da
It's ...		
cloudy	*Jest pochmurnie.*	yest pokh-*moor*-nye
cold	*Jest zimno.*	yest *zheem*-no
hot	*Jest gorąco.*	yest go-*ron*-tso
raining	*Pada deszcz.*	*pa*-da deshch
snowing	*Pada śnieg.*	*pa*-da shnyeg
sunny	*Jest słonecznie.*	yest swo-*nech*-nye
warm	*Jest ciepło.*	yest *chyep*-wo
windy	*Jest wietrznie.*	yest *vyetzh*-nye
spring	*wiosna* f	*vyos*-na
summer	*lato* n	*la*-to
autumn	*jesień* f	*ye*-shyen'
winter	*zima* f	*zhee*-ma

border crossing

I'm ...	*Jestem ...*	*yes*-tem ...
in transit	*w tranzycie*	v tran-*zi*-chye
on business	*służbowo*	swoozh-*bo*-vo
on holiday	*na wakacjach*	na va-*kats*-yakh
I'm here for ...	*Będę tu przez ...*	*ben*-de too pshes ...
(10) days	*(dziesięć) dni*	(*jye*-shench) dnee
(three) weeks	*(trzy) tygodnie*	(tshi) ti-*god*-nye
(two) months	*(dwa) miesiące*	(dva) mye-*shon*-tse

I'm going to (Kraków).
Jadę do (Krakowa).   *ya*-de do (kra-*ko*-va)

I'm staying at the (Pod Różą Hotel).
Zatrzymuję się w (hotelu 'pod Różą').   za-tshi-*moo*-ye shye v (ho-*te*-loo pod *roo*-zhom)

I have nothing to declare.
Nie mam nic do zgłoszenia.   nye mam neets do zgwo-*she*-nya

I have something to declare.
Mam coś do zgłoszenia.   mam tsosh do zgwo-*she*-nya

That's (not) mine.
To (nie) jest moje.   to (nye) yest *mo*-ye

transport

tickets & luggage

Where can I buy a ticket?
Gdzie mogę kupić bilet?   gjye mo·ge koo·peech bee·let

Do I need to book a seat?
Czy muszę rezerwować?   chi moo·she re·zer·vo·vach

One ... ticket	*Proszę bilet ...*	pro·she bee·let ...
(to Katowice), please.	*(do Katowic).*	do (ka·to·veets)
one-way	*w jedną stronę*	v yed·nom stro·ne
return	*powrotny*	po·vro·tni

I'd like to ...	*Chcę ... mój bilet.*	khtse ... mooy bee·let
my ticket, please.		
cancel	*odwołać*	od·vo·wach
change	*zmienić*	zmye·neech
collect	*odebrać*	o·de·brach
confirm	*potwierdzić*	po·tvyer·jyeech

I'd like a ... seat,	*Proszę miejsce ...*	pro·she myeys·tse ...
please.		
nonsmoking	*dla niepalących*	dla nye·pa·lon·tsikh
smoking	*dla palących*	dla pa·lon·tsikh

How much is it?
Ile kosztuje?   ee·le kosh·too·ye

Is there air conditioning?
Czy jest tam klimatyzacja?   chi yest tam klee·ma·ti·za·tsya

Is there a toilet?
Czy jest tam toaleta?   chi yest tam to·a·le·ta

How long does the trip take?
Ile trwa podróż?   ee·le trfa po·droosh

Is it a direct route?
Czy to jest bezpośrednie połączenie?   chi to yest bes·po·shred·nye po·won·che·nye

Where can I find a luggage locker?
Gdzie jest schowek na bagaż?   gjye yest skho·vek na ba·gazh

My luggage	Mój bagaż	mooy ba·gazh
has been ...	został ...	zos·tow ...
damaged	uszkodzony	oosh·ko·dzo·ni
lost	zagubiony	za·goo·byo·ni
stolen	skradziony	skra·jyo·ni

getting around

Where does flight (LO125) arrive/depart?

Skąd przylatuje/odlatuje
lot (LO125)?

skont pshi·la·too·ye/od·la·too·ye
lot (el o sto dva·jyesh·chya pyench)

Where's (the) ...?	Gdzie jest ...?	gjye yest ...
arrivals hall	hala przylotów	kha·la pshi·lo·toof
departures hall	hala odlotów	kha·la od·lo·toof
duty-free shop	sklep wolnocłowy	sklep vol·no·tswo·vi
gate (five)	wejście	veysh·chye
	(numer pięć)	(noo·mer pyench)

Is this the ...	Czy to jest ...	chi to yest ...
to (Wrocław)?	do (Wrocławia)?	do (vrots·wa·vya)
bus	autobus	ow·to·boos
plane	samolot	sa·mo·lot
train	pociąg	po·chonk

When's the ... bus?	Kiedy jest ... autobus?	kye·di yest ... ow·to·boos
first	pierwszy	pyerf·shi
last	ostatni	os·tat·nee
next	następny	nas·temp·ni

At what time does it arrive/leave?

O której godzinie przyjeżdża/
odjeżdża?

o ktoo·rey go·jee·nye pshi·yezh·ja/
ot·yezh·ja

How long will it be delayed?

Jakie będzie opóźnienie?

ya·kye ben·jye o·poozh·nye·nye

What's the next station?

Jaka jest następna stacja?

ya·ka yest nas·temp·na sta·tsya

What's the next stop?

Jaki jest następny przystanek?

ya·kee yest nas·tem·pni pshi·sta·nek

Does it stop at (Kalisz)?
Czy on się zatrzymuje w (Kaliszu)?   chi on shye za·tshi·*moo*·ye f (ka·*lee*·shoo)

Please tell me when we get to (Krynica).
Proszę mi powiedzieć gdy   *pro*·she mee po·*vye*·jyech gdi
dojedziemy do (Krynicy).   do·ye·*jye*·mi do (kri·*nee*·tsi)

How long do we stop here?
Na jak długo się tu zatrzymamy?   na yak *dwoo*·go shye too za·tshi·*ma*·mi

Is this seat available?
Czy to miejsce jest wolne?   chi to *myeys*·tse yest *vol*·ne

That's my seat.
To jest moje miejsce.   to yest *mo*·ye *myeys*·tse

I'd like a taxi ...	*Chcę zamówić*	khtse za·*moo*·veech
	taksówę na ...	tak·*soof*·ke na ...
now	*teraz*	*te*·ras
tomorrow	*jutro*	*yoo*·tro
at (9am)	*(dziewiątą rano)*	(jye·*vyon*·tom *ra*·no)

Is this taxi available?
Czy ta taksówka jest wolna?   chi ta tak·*soof*·ka yest *vol*·na

How much is it to (Szczecin)?
Ile kosztuje do (Szczecina)?   ee·le kosh·*too*·ye (do shche·*chee*·na)

Please put the meter on.
Proszę włączyć taksometr.   *pro*·she *vwon*·chich tak·*so*·metr

Please take me to (this address).
Proszę mnie zawieźć pod (ten adres).   *pro*·she mnye *za*·vyeshch pod (ten *ad*·res)

Please ...	*Proszę ...*	*pro*·she ...
slow down	*zwolnić*	*zvol*·neech
stop here	*się tu zatrzymać*	shye too za·*tshi*·mach
wait here	*tu zaczekać*	too za·*che*·kach

car, motorbike & bicycle hire

I'd like to hire a ...	*Chcę wypożyczyć ...*	khtse vi·po·*zhi*·chich ...
bicycle	*rower*	*ro*·ver
car	*samochód*	sa·*mo*·khoot
motorbike	*motocykl*	mo·*to*·tsikl

with …	z …	z …
air conditioning	*klimatyzacją*	klee-ma-ti-*za*-tsyom
a driver	*kierowcą*	kye-*rof*-tsom
antifreeze	*płynem nie*	*pwi*-nem nye
	zamarzającym	za-mar-za-*yon*-tsim
snow chains	*łańcuchami*	wan'-tsoo-*kha*-mee
	śnieżnymi	shnezh-*ni*-mee

How much for	*Ile kosztuje*	ee-le kosh-*too*-ye
… hire?	*wypożyczenie na …?*	vi-po-zhi-*che*-nye na …
hourly	*godzinę*	go-*jee*-ne
daily	*dzień*	jyen'
weekly	*tydzień*	ti-jyen'

air	*powietrze* n	po-*vye*-tshe
oil	*olej* m	*o*-ley
petrol	*benzyna* f	ben-*zi*-na
tyre	*opona* f	o-*po*-na

I need a mechanic.
Potrzebuję mechanika.   po-tshe-*boo*-ye me-kha-*nee*-ka

I've run out of petrol.
Zabrakło mi benzyny.   za-*bra*-kwo mee ben-*zi*-ni

I have a flat tyre.
Złapałem/Złapałam gumę. m/f   zwa-*pa*-wem/zwa-*pa*-wam *goo*-me

directions

Where's the …?	*Gdzie jest …?*	gjye yest …
bank	*bank*	bank
city centre	*centrum miasta*	*tsen*-troom *myas*-ta
hotel	*hotel*	*ho*-tel
market	*targ*	tark
police station	*komisariat*	ko-mee-*sar*-yat
	policji	po-*leets*-yee
post office	*urząd pocztowy*	*oo*-zhond poch-*to*-vi
public toilet	*toaleta publiczna*	to-a-*le*-ta poo-*bleech*-na
tourist office	*biuro turystyczne*	*byoo*-ro too-ris-*tich*-ne

Is this the road to (Malbork)?
Czy to jest droga do (Malborka)?   chi to yest *dro*-ga do (mal-*bor*-ka)

Can you show me (on the map)?
Czy może pan/pani
mi pokazać (na mapie)? m/f

chi *mo*·zhe pan/*pa*·nee
mee po·*ka*·zach (na *ma*·pye)

What's the address?
Jaki jest adres?

ya·kee yest *ad*·res

How far is it?
Jak daleko to jest?

yak da·*le*·ko to yest

How do I get there?
Jak tam mogę się dostać?

yak tam *mo*·ge shye *dos*·tach

Turn ...	*Proszę skręcić ...*	*pro*·she *skren*·cheech ...
at the corner	*na rogu*	na *ro*·goo
at the traffic lights	*na światłach*	na *shfyat*·wakh
left/right	*w lewo/prawo*	v *le*·vo/*pra*·vo

It's ...	*To jest ...*	to yest ...
behind ...	*za ...*	za ...
far away	*daleko*	da·*le*·ko
here	*tu*	too
in front of ...	*przed ...*	pshet ...
left	*po lewej*	po *le*·vey
near	*blisko*	*blees*·ko
next to ...	*obok ...*	*o*·bok ...
on the corner	*na rogu*	na *ro*·goo
opposite ...	*naprzeciwko ...*	nap·she·*cheef*·ko ...
right	*po prawej*	po *pra*·vey
straight ahead	*na wprost*	na fprost
there	*tam*	tam

by bus	*autobusem*	ow·to·*boo*·sem
by taxi	*taksówką*	tak·*soof*·kom
by train	*pociągiem*	po·*chon*·gyem
on foot	*pieszo*	*pye*·sho

north	*północ*	*poow*·nots
south	*południe*	po·*wood*·nye
east	*wschód*	fskhoot
west	*zachód*	*za*·khoot

Wjazd/Wyjazd	vyazd/*vi*·yazd	**Entrance/Exit**
Otwarte/Zamknięte	ot·*far*·te/zamk·*nyen*·te	**Open/Closed**
Wolne pokoje	*vol*·ne po·*ko*·ye	**Rooms Available**
Brak wolnych miejsc	brak *vol*·nikh myeysts	**No Vacancies**
Informacja	een·for·*ma*·tsya	**Information**
Komisariat policji	ko·mee·*sar*·yat po·*lee*·tsyee	**Police Station**
Zabroniony	za·bro·*nyo*·ni	**Prohibited**
Toalety	to·a·*le*·ti	**Toilets**
Męskie	mens·kye	**Men**
Damskie	dams·kye	**Women**
Zimna/Gorąca	*zheem*·na/go·*ron*·tsa	**Hot/Cold**

accommodation

finding accommodation

Where's a ...?	*Gdzie jest ...?*	gjye yest ...
camping ground	*kamping*	*kam*·peeng
guesthouse	*pokoje gościnne*	po·*ko*·ye gosh·*chee*·ne
hotel	*hotel*	*ho*·tel
youth hostel	*schronisko*	skhro·*nees*·ko
	młodzieżowe	mwo·jye·*zho*·ve

Can you recommend	*Czy może pan/pani*	chi *mo*·zhe pan/*pa*·nee
somewhere ...?	*polecić coś ...? m/f*	po·*le*·cheech tsosh ...
cheap	*taniego*	ta·*nye*·go
good	*dobrego*	do·*bre*·go
nearby	*coś w pobliżu*	tsosh f po·*blee*·zhoo

I'd like to book a room, please.
Chcę zarezerwować pokój.   khtse za·re·zer·*vo*·vach *po*·kooy

I have a reservation.
Mam rezerwację.   mam re·zer·*va*·tsye

My name's ...
Nazywam się ...   na·*zi*·vam shye ...

Do you have a ... room?	Czy jest pokój ...?	chi yest *po*·kooy ...
single	jednoosobowy	yed·no·o·so·*bo*·vi
double	z podwójnym	z pod·*vooy*·nim
	łóżkiem	*woozh*·kyem
twin	z dwoma łożkami	z *dvo*·ma wozh·*ka*·mee

How much is it per ...?	Ile kosztuje za ...?	*ee*·le kosh·*too*·ye za ...
night	noc	nots
person	osobę	o·*so*·be

Can I pay ...?	Czy mogę zapłacić ...?	chi *mo*·ge za·*pwa*·cheech ...
by credit card	kartą kredytową	*kar*·tom kre·di·*to*·vom
with a travellers	czekami	che·*ka*·mee
cheque	podróżnymi	po·*droozh*·ni·mee

For (three) nights/weeks.
Na (trzy) noce/tygodnie. na (tshi) *no*·tse/ti·*god*·nye

From (2 July) to (6 July).
Od (drugiego lipca) do od (droo·*gye*·go *leep*·tsa) do
(szóstego lipca). (shoos·*te*·go *leep*·tsa)

Can I see it?
Czy mogę go zobaczyć? chi *mo*·ge go zo·*ba*·chich

Am I allowed to I camp here?
Czy mogę się tutaj rozbić? chi *mo*·ge shye *too*·tai *roz*·beech

Where can I find the camping ground?
Gdzie jest pole kampingowe? gjye yest *po*·le kam·peen·*go*·ve

requests & queries

When's breakfast served?
O której jest śniadanie? o *ktoo*·rey yest shnya·*da*·nye

Where's breakfast served?
Gdzie jest śniadanie? gjye yest shnya·*da*·nye

Please wake me at (seven).
Proszę obudzić mnie o (siódmej). *pro*·she o·*boo*·jeech mnye o (*shyood*·mey)

Could I have my key, please?
Czy mogę prosić o klucz? chi *mo*·ge *pro*·sheech o klooch

Can I get another (blanket)?
Czy mogę prosić o jeszcze chi *mo*·ge *pro*·sheech o *yesh*·che
jeden (koc)? *ye*·den (kots)

Is there an elevator/a safe?
Czy jest winda/sejf?   chi yest *veen*·da/seyf

This (towel) isn't clean.
Ten (ręcznik) nie jest czysty.   ten (*rench*·neek) nye yest *chis*·ti

It's too ...	*Jest zbyt ...*	yest zbit ...
expensive	*drogi*	*dro*·gee
noisy	*głośny*	*gwosh*·ni
small	*mały*	*ma*·wi

The ... doesn't work.	*... nie działa.*	... nye *jya*·wa
air conditioner	*Klimatyzator*	klee·ma·ti·*za*·tor
fan	*Wentylator*	ven·ti·*la*·tor
toilet	*Ubikacja*	oo·bee·*kats*·ya

checking out

What time is checkout?
O której godzinie   o *ktoo*·rey go·*jye*·nye
muszę się wymeldować?   *moo*·she shye vi·mel·*do*·vach

Can I leave my luggage here?
Czy mogę tu zostawić   chi *mo*·ge too zo·*sta*·veech
moje bagaże?   *mo*·ye ba·*ga*·zhe

Could I have	*Czy mogę prosić*	chi *mo*·ge *pro*·sheech
my ..., please?	*o mój/moje ...?* sg/pl	o mooy/*mo*·ye ...
deposit	*depozyt* sg	de·*po*·zit
passport	*paszport* sg	*pash*·port
valuables	*kosztowności* pl	kosh·tov·*nosh*·chee

communications & banking

the internet

Where's the local Internet café?
Gdzie jest kawiarnia internetowa?   gjye yest ka·*vyar*·nya een·ter·ne·*to*·va

How much is it per hour?
Ile kosztuje za godzinę?   *ee*·le kosh·*too*·ye za go·*jee*·ne

I'd like to ...	Chciałem/Chciałam ... m/f	khchow-em/khchow-am ...
check my email	sprawdzić mój email	sprav-jeech mooy ee-mayl
get Internet	podłączyć się	pod-won-chich shye
access	do internetu	do een-ter-ne-too
use a printer	użyć drukarki	oo-zhich droo-kar-kee
use a scanner	użyć skaner	oo-zhich ska-ner

mobile/cell phone

I'd like a ...	Chciałem/Chciałam ... m/f	khchow-em/khchow-am ...
mobile/cell	wypożyczyć	vi-po-zhi-chich
phone for hire	telefon komórkowy	te-le-fon ko-moor-ko-vi
SIM card for	kartę SIM	kar-te seem
your network	na waszą sieć	na va-shom shyech
What are the rates?	Jakie są stawki	ya-kye som staf-kee
	za rozmowy?	za roz-mo-vi

telephone

What's your phone number?
Jaki jest pana/pani   ya-kee yest pa-na/pa-nee
numer telefonu? m/f pol   noo-mer te-le-fo-noo

The number is ...
Numer jest ...   noo-mer yest ...

Where's the nearest public phone?
Gdzie jest najbliższy telefon?   gjye yest nai-bleezh-shi te-le-fon

I'd like to buy a chip phonecard.
Chciałem/Chciałam kupić   khchow-em/khchow-am koo-peech
czipową kartę telefoniczną. m/f   chee-po-vom kar-te te-le-fo-neech-nom

I want to ...	Chciałem/Chciałam ... m/f	khchow-em/khchow-am ...
call (Singapore)	zadzwonić do	zad-zvo-neech do
	(Singapuru)	(seen-ga-poo-roo)
make a local	zadzwonić pod	zad-zvo-neech pod
call	lokalny numer	lo-kal-ni noo-mer
reverse the	zamówić	za-moo-veech
charges	rozmowę na koszt	roz-mo-ve na kosht
	odbiorcy	od-byor-tsi

How much does ... cost?	Ile kosztuje ...?	ee·le kosh·too·ye ...
a (three)-minute call	rozmowa (trzy) minutowa	roz·mo·va (tshi) mee·noo·to·va
each extra minute	każda dodatkowa minuta	kazh·da do·dat·ko·va mee·noo·ta
(Two złotys) per (30) seconds.	(Dwa złote) za (trzydzieści) sekund.	(dva zwo·te) za (tshi·jyesh·chee) se·koond

post office

I want to send a ...	Chciałem/Chciałam wysłać ... m/f	khchow·em/khchow·am vis·wach ...
fax	faks	faks
letter	list	leest
parcel	paczkę	pach·ke
postcard	pocztówkę	poch·toof·ke

I want to buy a/an ...	Chciałem/Chciałam kupić ... m/f	khchow·em/khchow·am koo·peech ...
envelope	kopertę	ko·per·te
stamp	znaczek	zna·chek

Please send it (to Australia) by ...	Proszę wysłać to ... (do Australii).	pro·she vis·wach to ... (do ows·tra·lyee)
airmail	pocztą lotniczą	poch·tom lot·nee·chom
express mail	pocztą ekspresową	poch·tom eks·pre·so·vom
registered mail	pocztą poleconą	poch·tom po·le·tso·nom
surface mail	pocztą lądową	poch·tom lon·do·vom

Is there any mail for me?	Czy jest dla mnie jakaś korespondencja?	chi yest dla mnye ya·kash ko·res·pon·den·tsya

bank

Where's a/an ...?	Gdzie jest ...?	gjye yest ...
ATM	bankomat	ban·ko·mat
foreign exchange office	kantor walut	kan·tor va·loot

I'd like to ...	Chciałem/Chciałam ... m/f	khchow·em/khchow·am ...
Where can I ...?	Gdzie mogę ...?	gjye mo·ge ...
cash a cheque	wymienić czek	vi·mye·neech chek
	na gotówkę	na go·toof·ke
change a travellers	wymienić czek	vi·mye·neech chek
cheque	podróżny	po·droozh·ni
change money	wymienić	vi·mye·neech
	pieniądze	pye·nyon·dze
get a cash	dostać zaliczkę	dos·tach za·leech·ke
advance	na moją kartę	na mo·yom kar·te
	kredytową	kre·di·to·vom
withdraw money	wypłacić	vi·pwa·cheech
	pieniądze	pye·nyon·dze

What's the ...?	Jaki/Jaka jest ...? m/f	ya·kee/ya·ka yest ...
charge for that	prowizja f	pro·veez·ya
exchange rate	kurs wymiany m	koors vi·mya·ni

It's (12) złotys.
To kosztuje (dwanaście) złotych. to kosh·too·ye (dva·nash·chye) zwo·tikh

It's free.
Jest bezpłatny. yest bes·pwat·ni

What time does the bank open?
W jakich godzinach v ya·keekh go·jee·nakh
jest bank otwarty? yest bank ot·far·ti

Has my money arrived yet?
Czy doszły już moje pieniądze? chi dosh·wi yoosh mo·ye pye·nyon·dze

sightseeing

getting in

What time does it open/close?
O której godzinie jest o ktoo·rey go·jee·nye yest
otwarte/zamknięte? ot·far·te/zam·knyen·te

What's the admission charge?
Ile kosztuje wstęp? ee·le kosh·too·ye fstemp

Is there a discount for students/children?

*Czy jest zniżka dla
studentów/dzieci?*

chi yest *zneezh*·ka dla
stoo·*den*·toof/*jye*·chee

I'd like to see ...

Chciałem/Chciałam obejrzeć ... m/f

khchow·em/khchow·am o·*bey*·zhech ...

What's that?

Co to jest?

tso to yest

Can I take a photo?

Czy mogę zrobić zdjęcie?

chi *mo*·ge *zro*·beech *zdyen*·chye

I'd like a ...

Chciałem/Chciałam ... m/f

khchow·em/khchow·am ...

catalogue	*broszurę*	bro·*shoo*·re
guide	*przewodnik*	pshe·*vod*·neek
local map	*mapę okolic*	*ma*·pe o·*ko*·leets

tours

When's the next ...?

Kiedy jest następna ...?

kye·di yest nas·*temp*·na ...

day trip	*wycieczka jednodniowa*	vi·*chyech*·ka yed·no·*dnyo*·va
tour	*tura*	*too*·ra

Is ... included?

Czy ... wliczone/a? n&pl/f

chi ... vlee·*cho*·ne/na

accommodation	*noclegi są* pl	nots·*le*·gee som
the admission charge	*opłata za wstęp jest* f	o·*pwa*·ta za fstemp yest
food	*wyżywienie jest* n	vi·zhi·*vye*·nye yest

Is transport included?

Czy transport jest wliczony?

chi *trans*·port yest vlee·*cho*·ne

How long is the tour?

Jak długo trwa wycieczka?

yak *dwoo*·go trfa vi·*chyech*·ka

What time should we be back?

*O której godzinie
powinniśmy wrócić?*

o *ktoo*·rey go·*jee*·nye
po·vee·*neesh*·mi *vroo*·cheech

sightseeing		
castle	*zamek* m	*za*·mek
cathedral	*katedra* f	ka·*te*·dra
church	*kościół* m	*kosh*·chyoow'
main square	*rynek główny* m	*ri*·nek *gwoov*·ni
monastery	*klasztor* m	*klash*·tor
monument	*pomnik* m	*pom*·neek
museum	*muzeum* n	moo·*ze*·oom
old city	*stare miasto* n	*sta*·re *myas*·to
palace	*pałac* m	*pa*·wats
ruins	*ruiny* f pl	roo·*ee*·ni
stadium	*stadion* m	*sta*·dyon
statue	*pomnik* m	*pom*·neek

shopping

enquiries

Where's a …?	*Gdzie jest …?*	gjye yest …
bank	*bank*	bank
bookshop	*księgarnia*	kshyen·*gar*·nya
camera shop	*sklep fotograficzny*	sklep fo·to·gra·*feech*·ni
department store	*dom towarowy*	dom to·va·*ro*·vi
grocery store	*sklep spożywczy*	sklep spo·*zhiv*·chi
market	*targ*	tark
newsagency	*kiosk*	kyosk
supermarket	*supermarket*	soo·per·*mar*·ket

Where can I buy (a padlock)?
Gdzie mogę kupić (kłódkę)?   gjye *mo*·ge *koo*·peech (*kwoot*·ke)

I'm looking for …
Szukam …   *shoo*·kam

Can I look at it?
Czy mogę to zobaczyć?   chi *mo*·ge to zo·*ba*·chich

Do you have any others?
Czy są jakieś inne?   chi som *ya*·kyesh *ee*·ne

Does it have a guarantee?
Czy to ma gwarancję?   chi to ma gva·*ran*·tsye

Can I have it sent overseas?
Czy mogę to wysłać za granicę?   chi *mo*·ge to *vis*·wach za gra·*nee*·tse

Can I have my ... repaired?
Czy mogę tu oddać ... do naprawy?   chi *mo*·ge too *ot*·dach ... do na·*pra*·vi

It's faulty.
To jest wadliwe.   to yest vad·*lee*·ve

I'd like to return this, please.
Chciałem/Chciałam to zwrócić. m/f   khchow·em/khchow·am to zvroo·cheech

I'd like a ..., please.	*Proszę o ...*	pro·she o ...
bag	*torbę*	*tor*·be
refund	*zwrot pieniędzy*	zvrot pye·*nyen*·dzi

paying

How much is it?
Ile to kosztuje?   ee·le to kosh·*too*·ye

Can you write down the price?
Proszę napisać cenę.   pro·she na·*pee*·sach *tse*·ne

That's too expensive.
To jest za drogie.   to yest za *dro*·gye

What's your final price?
Jaka jest pana/pani   *ya*·ka yest *pa*·na/*pa*·nee
ostateczna cena? m/f   os·ta·*tech*·na *tse*·na

I'll give you (10 złotys).
Dam panu/pani (dziesięć złotych). m/f   dam *pa*·noo/*pa*·nee (*jye*·shench *zwo*·tikh)

There's a mistake in the bill.
Na czeku jest pomyłka.   na *che*·koo yest po·*miw*·ka

Do you accept ...?	*Czy mogę zapłacić ...?*	chi *mo*·ge za·*pwa*·cheech ...
credit cards	*kartą kredytową*	*kar*·tom kre·di·*to*·vom
debit cards	*kartą debetową*	*kar*·tom de·be·*to*·vom
travellers	*czekami*	che·*ka*·mee
cheques	*podróżnymi*	pod·roozh·*ni*·mee
I'd like ..., please.	*Proszę o ...*	pro·she o ...
a receipt	*rachunek*	ra·*khoo*·nek
my change	*moją resztę*	*mo*·yom *resh*·te

clothes & shoes

Can I try it on?	*Czy mogę przymierzyć?*	chi *mo*·ge pshi·*mye*·zhich
My size is (40).	*Noszę rozmiar (czterdzieści).*	*no*·she *roz*·myar (chter·*jyesh*·chee)
It doesn't fit.	*Nie pasuje.*	nye pa·*soo*·ye
large/medium/small	*L/M/S*	*el*·ke/*em*·ke/*es*·ke

books & music

I'd like a ...	*Chciałem/Chciałam ...* m/f	khchow·em/khchow·am ...
newspaper	*gazetę (w języku*	ga·*ze*·te (v yen·*zi*·koo
(in English)	*angielskim)*	an·*gyel*·skeem)
pen	*długopis*	dwoo·*go*·pees

Is there an English-language bookshop?
Czy jest tu księgarnia angielska? chi yest too kshyen·*gar*·nya an·*gyel*·ska

I'm looking for something by (Górecki).
Szukam czegoś (Góreckiego). shoo·kam *che*·gosh (goo·rets·*kye*·go)

Can I listen to this?
Czy mogę tego posłuchać? chi *mo*·ge *te*·go pos·*woo*·khach

photography

Can you ...?	*Czy może pan/pani ...?* m/f	chi *mo*·zhe pan/*pa*·nee ...
develop this film	*wywołać ten film*	vi·*vo*·wach ten film
load my film	*założyć film*	za·*wo*·zhich film
transfer photos	*skopiować zdjęcia*	sko·*pyo*·vach zdyen·chya
from my camera	*z mojego aparatu*	z mo·ye·go a·pa·*ra*·too
to CD	*na płytę kompaktową*	na *pwi*·te kom·pak·*to*·vom
I need a/an ... film	*Potrzebuję film ...*	po·tshe·*boo*·ye film ...
for this camera.	*do tego aparatu.*	do *te*·go a·pa·*ra*·too
APS	*APS*	a pe es
B&W	*panchromatyczny*	pan·khro·ma·*tich*·ni
colour	*kolorowy*	ko·lo·*ro*·vi
slide	*do slajdów*	do *slai*·doof
(200) speed	*(dwieście) ASA*	(*dvyesh*·chye) *a*·sa

When will it be ready? *Na kiedy będzie gotowe?* na *kye*·di *ben*·jye go·*to*·ve

meeting people

greetings, goodbyes & introductions

Hello/Hi.	*Cześć.*	cheshch
Good night.	*Dobranoc.*	do·*bra*·nots
Goodbye.	*Do widzenia.*	do vee·*dze*·nya
Bye.	*Pa.*	pa
See you later.	*Do zobaczenia.*	do zo·ba·*che*·nya
Mr/Mrs/Miss	*Pan/Pani/Panna*	pan/*pa*·nee/*pa*·na
How are you?	*Jak pan/pani*	yak pan/*pa*·nee
	się miewa? m/f pol	shye *mye*·va
	Jak się masz? inf	yak shye mash
Fine. And you?	*Dobrze. A pan/pani?* m/f pol	*dob*·zhe a pan/*pa*·nee
	Dobrze. A ty? inf	*dob*·zhe a ti
What's your name?	*Jak się pan/pani*	yak shye pan/*pa*·nee
	nazywa? m/f pol	na·*zi*·va
	Jakie się nazywasz? inf	yak shye na·*zi*·vash
My name is ...	*Nazywam się ...*	na·*zi*·vam shye ...
I'm pleased to	*Miło mi pana/panią*	*mee*·wo mee *pa*·na/*pa*·nyom
meet you.	*poznać.* m/f pol	*po*·znach
	Miło mi ciebie poznać. inf	*mee*·wo mee *chye*·bye *po*·znach

This is my ...	*To jest mój/moja ...* m/f	to yest mooy/*mo*·ya ...
boyfriend	*chłopak*	*khwo*·pak
brother	*brat*	brat
daughter	*córka*	*tsoor*·ka
father	*ojciec*	*oy*·chyets
friend	*przyjaciel* m	pzhi·*ya*·chyel
	przyjaciółka f	pzhi·*ya*·chyoow·ka
girlfriend	*dziewczyna*	jyev·*chi*·na
husband	*mąż*	monzh
mother	*matka*	*mat*·ka
partner (intimate)	*partner/partnerka* m/f	*part*·ner/part·*ner*·ka
sister	*siostra*	*shyos*·tra
son	*syn*	sin
wife	*żona*	*zho*·na

Here's my ...	*Tu jest mój ...*	too yest mooy ...
What's your ...?	*Jaki jest pana/*	ya·kee yest pa·na/
	pani ...? m/f pol	pa·nee ...
(email) address	*adres (emailowy)*	ad·res (e·mai·lo·vi)
fax number	*numer faksu*	noo·mer fak·soo
phone number	*numer telefonu*	noo·mer te·le·fo·noo

occupations

What's your	*Jaki jest pana/pani*	ya·kee yest pa·na/pa·nee
occupation?	*zawód?* m/f pol	za·vood
I'm a/an ...	*Jestem ...*	yes·tem ...
artist	*artystą/artystką* m/f	ar·tis·tom/ar·tist·kom
farmer	*rolnikiem* m&f	rol·nee·kyem
manual worker	*pracownikiem*	pra·tsov·nee·kyem
	fizycznym m&f	fee·zich·nim
office worker	*pracownikiem*	pra·tsov·nee·kyem
	biurowym m&f	byoo·ro·vim
scientist	*naukowcem* m&f	now·kov·tsem
tradesperson	*rzemieślnikiem* m&f	zhe·mye·shlnee·kyem

background

Where are you from?	*Skąd pan/pani jest?* m/f pol	skont pan/pa·nee yest
I'm from ...	*Jestem z ...*	yes·tem z ...
Australia	*Australii*	ow·stra·lyee
Canada	*Kanady*	ka·na·di
England	*Anglii*	ang·lee
New Zealand	*Nowej Zelandii*	no·vey ze·lan·dyee
the USA	*USA*	oo es a

Are you married? (to a man)
Czy jest pan żonaty? pol — chi yest pan zho·na·ti

Are you married? (to a woman)
Czy jest pani zamężna? pol — chi yest pa·nee za·menzh·na

I'm married.
Jestem żonaty/zamężna. m/f — yes·tem zho·na·ti/za·menzh·na

I'm single.
Jestem nieżonaty/niezamężna. m/f — nye·zho·na·ti/nye·za·menzh·na

age

How old is your ...?	*Ile lat ma pana/*	*ee·*le lat ma *pa·*na/
	pani ...? m/f pol	*pa·*nee ...
daughter	*córka*	*tsoor·*ka
son	*syn*	sin
How old are you?	*Ile pan/pani ma lat?* m/f pol	*ee·*le pan/*pa·*nee ma lat
	Ile masz lat? inf	*ee·*le mash lat
I'm ... years old.	*Mam ... lat.*	mam ... lat
He/She is ... years old.	*On/Ona ma ... lat.*	on/*o·*na ma ... lat

feelings

I'm (not) ...	*(Nie) Jestem ...*	(nye) *yes·*tem ...
Are you ...?	*Czy jest pan/pani ...?* m/f pol	chi yest pan/*pa·*nee ...
cold	*zmarznięty/a* m/f	zmar·*znyen·*ti/a
happy	*szczęśliwy/a* m/f	shchen·*shlee·*vi/a
hungry	*głodny/a* m/f	*gwod·*ni/a
sad	*smutny/a* m/f	*smoot·*ni/a
thirsty	*spragniony/a* m/f	sprag·*nyo·*ni/a

entertainment

going out

Where can I find ...?	*Gdzie mogę znaleźć ...?*	gjye *mo·*ge *zna·*lezhch ...
clubs	*kluby nocne*	*kloo·*bi *nots·*ne
gay venues	*kluby dla gejów*	*kloo·*bi dla *ge·*yoof
pubs	*puby*	*pa·*bi
I feel like going to a/the ...	*Mam ochotę pójść ...*	mam o·*kho·*te pooyshch ...
concert	*na koncert*	na *kon·*tsert
movies	*na film*	na feelm
party	*na imprezę*	na eem·*pre·*ze
restaurant	*do restauracji*	do res·tow·*ra·*tsyee
theatre	*na sztukę*	na *shtoo·*ke

interests

Do you like ...?	Czy lubisz ...? inf	chi loo·beesh ...
I like ...	Lubię ...	loo·bye ...
cooking	gotować	go·to·vach
movies	oglądać filmy	o·glon·dach feel·mi
reading	czytać	chi·tach
sport	sport	sport
travelling	podróżować	po·droo·zho·vach

Do you like art?	Czy lubisz sztukę? inf	chi loo·beesh shtoo·ke
I like art.	Lubię sztukę.	loo·bye shtoo·ke

Do you ...?	Czy ...? inf	chi ...
dance	tańczysz	tan'·chish
go to concerts	chodzisz na koncerty	kho·jeesh na kon·tser·ti
listen to music	słuchasz muzyki	swoo·khash moo·zi·kee

food & drink

finding a place to eat

Can you	Czy może pan/pani	chi mo·zhe pan/pa·nee
recommend a ...?	polecić ...? m/f	po·le·cheech ...
bar	bar	bar
café	kawiarnię	ka·vyar·nye
restaurant	restaurację	res·tow·rats·ye

I'd like ..., please.	Proszę ...	pro·she ...
a table for (five)	o stolik na (pięć) osób	o sto·leek na (pyench) o·soob
the (non)smoking section	dla (nie)palących	dla (nye·)pa·lon·tsikh

ordering food

breakfast	śniadanie n	shnya·da·nye
lunch	obiad m	o·byad
dinner	kolacja f	ko·la·tsya
snack	przekąska f	pshe·kons·ka

What would you recommend?

Co by pan polecił? m	tso bi pan po·*le*·cheew
Co by pani poleciła? f	tso bi *pa*·nee po·le·*chee*·wa

I'd like (the) ..., please. *Proszę ...* *pro·she ...*

bill	o rachunek	o ra·*khoo*·nek
drink list	o spis napojów	o spees na·*po*·yoof
menu	o jadłospis	o ya·*dwo*·spees
that dish	to danie	to *da*·nye

drinks

(cup of) coffee ...	(filiżanka) kawy ...	(fee·lee·*zhan*·ka) *ka*·vi ...
(cup of) tea ...	(filiżanka) herbaty ...	(fee·lee·*zhan*·ka) her·*ba*·ti ...
with milk	z mlekiem	z *mle*·kyem
without sugar	bez cukru	bez *tsoo*·kroo
(orange) juice	sok (pomarańczowy) m	sok (po·ma·ran'·*cho*·vi)
soft drink	napój m	*na*·pooy
... water	woda ...	*vo*·da ...
hot	gorąca	go·*ron*·tsa
mineral	mineralna	mee·ne·*ral*·na

in the bar

I'll have ...	Proszę ...	*pro*·she ...
I'll buy you a drink. inf	Kupię ci drinka. inf	*koo*·pye chee *dreen*·ka
What would you like? inf	Co zamówić dla ciebie? inf	tso za·*moo*·veech dla *chye*·bye
Cheers!	Na zdrowie!	na *zdro*·vye
brandy	brandy m	*bren*·di
champagne	szampan m	*sham*·pan
a shot of (vodka)	kieliszek (wódki)	kye·*lee*·shek (*vood*·kee)
a bottle/glass of beer	butelka/szklanka piwa	boo·*tel*·ka/*shklan*·ka *pee*·va
a bottle/glass	butelka/kieliszek	boo·*tel*·ka/kye·*lee*·shek
of ... wine	wina ...	*vee*·na...
red	czerwonego	cher·vo·*ne*·go
sparkling	musującego	moo·soo·*yon*·tse·go
white	białego	bya·*we*·go

self-catering

What's the local speciality?

*Co jest miejscową
specjalnością?*

tso yest myeys·*tso*·vom
spe·tsyal·*nosh*·chyom

What's that?

Co to jest?

tso to yest

How much (is a kilo of cheese)?

Ile kosztuje (kilogram sera)?

ee·le kosh·*too*·ye (kee·*lo*·gram *se*·ra)

I'd like ...	*Proszę ...*	*pro*·she ...
200 grams	*dwadzieścia deko*	dva·*jyesh*·chya *de*·ko
(two) kilos	*(dwa) kilo*	(dva) *kee*·lo
(three) pieces	*(trzy) kawałki*	(tshi) ka·*vow*·kee
(six) slices	*(sześć) plasterków*	(sheshch) plas·*ter*·koof

Less.	*Mniej.*	mney
Enough.	*Wystarczy.*	vis·*tar*·chi
More.	*Więcej.*	*vyen*·tsey

special diets & allergies

Is there a vegetarian restaurant near here?

*Czy jest tu gdzieś restauracja
wegetariańska?*

chi yest too gjyesh res·tow·*ra*·tsya
ve·ge·ta·*ryan'*·ska

Do you have vegetarian food?

Czy jest żywność wegetariańska?

chi yest *zhiv*·noshch ve·ge·tar·*yan'*·ska

Could you prepare	*Czy można przygotować*	chi *mo*·zhna pshi·go·to·vach
a meal without ...?	*jedzenie bez ...?*	ye·*dze*·nye bes ...
butter	*masła*	*mas*·wa
eggs	*jajek*	*yai*·ek
meat stock	*wywaru mięsnego*	vi·*va*·roo myens·*ne*·go

I'm allergic to ...	*Mam uczulenie na ...*	mam oo·choo·*le*·nye na ...
dairy produce	*produkty mleczne*	pro·*dook*·ti *mlech*·ne
gluten	*gluten*	*gloo*·ten
MSG	*glutaminian sodu*	gloo·ta·*mee*·nyan *so*·doo
nuts	*orzechy*	o·*zhe*·khi
seafood	*owoce morza*	o·*vo*·tse *mo*·zha

barszcz biały m	barshch *bya*·wi	thick sourish wheat & potato-starch soup with marjoram
barszcz czerwony m	barshch cher·*vo*·ni	beetroot soup with dumplings, hard-boiled egg slices or beans
bigos m	*bee*·gos	sauerkraut, cabbage & meat stew, simmered with mushrooms & prunes & flavoured with red wine
bliny m pl	*blee*·ni	small thick pancakes made from wheat or buckwheat flour & yeast
budyń m	*boo*·din'	milk-based cream dessert in a range of flavours (eg strawberry, vanilla or chocolate)
chłodnik m	*khwod*·neek	baby beetroot soup with yogurt & fresh vegetables, served cold
ćwikła f	*chfeek*·wa	boiled & grated beetroot with horseradish, served with roast or smoked meat & sausages
drożdżówka f	drozh·*joof*·ka	brioche (sweet yeast bun)
flaczki m pl	*flach*·kee	seasoned tripe & vegetables cooked in bouillon
galareta f	ga·la·*re*·ta	appetiser of meat or fish encased in aspic • sweet flavoured jelly
gofry m pl	*go*·fri	thick rectangular waffles served with toppings such as whipped cream, chocolate or jam
golonka f	go·*lon*·ka	boiled pigs' hocks served with sauerkraut or puréed yellow peas
gołąbki m pl	go·*womb*·kee	cabbage leaves stuffed with minced beef & rice
grahamka f	gra·*kham*·ka	small wholemeal roll
grochówka f	gro·*khoof*·ka	lentil soup

jabłecznik m	ya-*bwech*-neek	*apple strudel*
kapuśniak m	ka-*poosh*-nyak	*sauerkraut soup*
kisiel m	*kee*-shyel	*jelly-type dessert made with potato starch*
klopsiki m pl	klop-*shee*-kee	*meatballs made with ground beef, pork and/or veal*
knedle m pl	*kned*-le	*dumplings stuffed with plums, cherries or apples*
kopytka n pl	ko-*pit*-ka	*potato dumplings similar to gnocchi*
łosoś wędzony m	*wo*-sosh ven-*dzo*-ni	*smoked salmon*
makowiec m	ma-*ko*-vyets	*poppy-seed strudel*
melba f	*mel*-ba	*ice cream, fruit & whipped cream*
mizeria f	mee-*zer*-ya	*sliced cucumber in sour cream*
naleśniki m pl	na-lesh-*nee*-kee	*crèpes • pancakes*
nóżki w galarecie n pl	*noosh*-kee v ga-la-*re*-chye	*jellied pigs' knuckles*
pierogi m pl	pye-*ro*-gee	*ravioli-like dumplings made from noodle dough, usually stuffed with mincemeat, sauerkraut, mushroom, cheese & potato*
rosół z makaronem m	*ro*-soow z ma-ka-*ro*-nem	*bouillon with noodles*
sałatka jarzynowa f	sa-*wat*-ka ya-zhi-*no*-va	*salad made with potato, vegetables & mayonnaise*
sernik m	*ser*-neek	*cheesecake*
szaszłyk m	*shash*-wik	*shish kebab*
śledź w śmietanie m	shlej v shmye-*ta*-nye	*herring in sour cream*
tatar m	*ta*-tar	*minced sirloin served raw with onion, raw egg yolk & chopped dill cucumber*
zapiekanka f	za-pye-*kan*-ka	*half a bread roll filled with cheese & mushrooms, baked & served hot*

emergencies

basics

Help!	*Na pomoc!*	na *po*-mots
Stop!	*Stój!*	stooy
Go away!	*Odejdź!*	o-deyj
Thief!	*Złodziej!*	zwo-jyey
Fire!	*Pożar!*	po-zhar
Watch out!	*Uważaj!*	oo-va-zhai

Call ...!	*Zadzwoń po ...!*	zad-zvon' po ...
a doctor	*lekarza*	le-ka-zha
an ambulance	*karetkę*	ka-ret-ke
the police	*policję*	po-lee-tsye

It's an emergency.
To nagły wypadek. — to *nag*-wi vi-*pa*-dek

Could you help me, please?
Czy może pan/pani mi pomóc? m/f — chi *mo*-zhe pan/*pa*-nee mee *po*-moots

Can I use the telephone?
Czy mogę użyć telefon? — chi *mo*-ge oo-zhich te-*le*-fon

I'm lost.
Zgubiłem/Zgubiłam się. m/f — zgoo-*bee*-wem/zgoo-*bee*-wam shye

Where are the toilets?
Gdzie są toalety? — gjye som to-a-*le*-ti

police

Where's the police station?
Gdzie jest posterunek policji? — gje yest pos-te-*roo*-nek po-*lee*-tsyee

I want to report an offence.
Chciałem/Chciałam zgłosić przestępstwo. m/f — khchow-em/khchow-am *zgwo*-sheech pshe-*stemps*-tfo

I have insurance.
Mam ubezpieczenie. — mam oo-bes-pye-*che*-nye

I've been ...	Zostałem/Zostałam ... m/f	zo-*stow*-em/zo-*stow*-am ...
assaulted	napadnięty/a m/f	na-pad-*nyen*-ti/a
raped	zgwałcony/a m/f	zgvow-*tso*-ni/a
robbed	okradziony/a m/f	o-kra-*jyo*-ni/a

I've lost my ...	Zgubiłem/ Zgubiłam ... m/f	zgoo-*bee*-wem/ zgoo-*bee*-wam ...
backpack	plecak	*ple*-tsak
bag	torbę	*tor*-be
credit card	kartę kredytową	*kar*-te kre-di-*to*-vom
handbag	torebkę	to-*rep*-ke
jewellery	biżuterię	bee-zhoo-*ter*-ye
money	pieniądze	pye-*nyon*-dze
passport	paszport	*pash*-port
wallet	portfel	*port*-fel

I want to contact my ...	Chcę się skontaktować z ...	khtse shye skon-tak-*to*-vach z ...
consulate	moim konsulatem	*mo*-yeem kon-soo-*la*-tem
embassy	moją ambasadą	*mo*-yom am-ba-*sa*-dom

health

medical needs

Where's the nearest ...?	Gdzie jest najbliższy/a ...? m/f	gjye yest nai-*bleezh*-shi/a ...
dentist	dentysta m	den-*tis*-ta
doctor	lekarz m	*le*-kash
hospital	szpital m	*shpee*-tal
(night) pharmacist	apteka (nocna) f	ap-*te*-ka (*nots*-na)

I need a doctor (who speaks English).
Szukam lekarza (który mówi po angielsku).
shoo-kam le-*ka*-zha (*ktoo*-ri *moo*-vee po an-*gyel*-skoo)

Could I see a female doctor?
Czy mogę się widzieć z lekarzem kobietą?
chi *mo*-ge shye *vee*-jyech z le-*ka*-zhem ko-*bye*-tom

I've run out of my medication.
Skończyły mi się lekarstwa.
skon-*chi*-wi mee shye le-*kars*-tfa

symptoms, conditions & allergies

I'm sick.	Jestem chory/a. m/f	yes·tem kho·ri/a
It hurts here.	Tutaj boli.	too·tai bo·lee
I have (a) ...	Mam ...	mam ...

asthma	astma f	ast·ma
constipation	zatwardzenie n	zat·far·dze·nye
cough	kaszel m	ka·shel
diarrhoea	rozwolnienie n	roz·vol·nye·nye
fever	gorączka f	go·ronch·ka
headache	ból głowy m	bool gwo·vi
heart condition	stan serca m	stan ser·tsa
nausea	mdłości pl	mdwosh·chee
pain	ból m	bool
sore throat	ból gardła m	bool gar·dwa
toothache	ból zęba m	bool zem·ba

I'm allergic to ...	Mam alergię na ...	mam a·ler·gye na ...
antibiotics	antybiotyki	an·ti·byo·ti·kee
anti-inflammatories	leki przeciwzapalne	le·kee pshe·cheef·za·pal·ne
aspirin	aspirynę	as·pee·ri·ne
bees	pszczoły	pshcho·wi
codeine	kodeinę	ko·de·ee·ne
penicillin	penicylinę	pe·nee·tsi·lee·ne

antiseptic	środki odkażające pl	shrod·kee od·ka·zha·yon·tse
bandage	bandaż m	ban·dash
condoms	kondom pl	kon·dom
contraceptives	środki	shrod·kee
	antykoncepcyjne pl	an·ti·kon·tsep·tsiy·ne
diarrhoea medicine	rozwolnienie n	ros·vol·nye·nye
insect repellent	środek na owady m	shro·dek na o·va·di
laxatives	środek	shro·dek
	przeczyszczający m	pshe·chish·cha·yon·tsi
painkillers	środki	shrod·kee
	przeciwbólowe pl	pshe·cheef·boo·lo·ve
rehydration salts	sole fizjologiczne pl	so·le fee·zyo·lo·geech·ne
sleeping tablets	pigułki nasenne pl	pee·goow·kee na·se·ne

english–polish dictionary

Polish nouns in this dictionary have their gender indicated by ⓜ (masculine), ⓕ (feminine) or ⓝ (neuter).
If it's a plural noun, you'll also see pl. Adjectives are given in the masculine form only. Words are also marked
as a (adjective), v (verb), sg (singular), pl (plural), inf (informal) or pol (polite) where necessary.

A

accident *wypadek* ⓜ vi-*pa*-dek
accommodation *nocleg* ⓜ nots-leg
adaptor *zasilacz* ⓜ za-shee-lach
address *adres* ⓜ *a*-dres
after *po • za* po • za
air conditioning *klimatyzacja* ⓕ klee-ma-ti-*za*-tsya
airplane *samolot* ⓜ sa-*mo*-lot
airport *lotnisko* ⓝ lot-*nees*-ko
alcohol *alkohol* ⓜ al-ko-khol
all *wszystko* fshist-ko
allergy *alergia* ⓕ a-*ler*-gya
ambulance *karetka pogotowia* ⓕ
    ka-*ret*-ka po-go-*to*-vya
and *i* ee
ankle *kostka* ⓕ kost-ka
arm *ręka* ⓕ ren-ka
ashtray *popielniczka* ⓕ po-pyel-*neech*-ka
ATM *bankomat* ⓜ ban-ko-mat

B

baby *niemowlę* ⓝ nye-*mov*-le
back (body) *plecy* pl *ple*-tsi
backpack *plecak* ⓜ *ple*-tsak
bad *zły* zwi
bag *torba* ⓕ tor-ba
baggage claim *odbiór bagażu* ⓜ od-byoor ba-*ga*-zhoo
bank *bank* ⓜ bank
bar *bar* ⓜ bar
bathroom *łazienka* ⓕ wa-zhyen-ka
battery *bateria* ⓕ ba-*te*-rya
beautiful *piękny* pyen-kni
bed *łóżko* ⓝ woozh-ko
beer *piwo* ⓝ *pee*-vo
before *przed* pshet
behind *za* za
bicycle *rower* ⓜ *ro*-ver
big *duży* doo-zhi
bill *rachunek* ⓜ ra-khoo-nek
black *czarny* char-ni
blanket *koc* ⓜ kots

blood group *grupa krwi* ⓕ *groo*-pa krfee
blue *niebieski* nye-*byes*-kee
boat *łódź* ⓕ wooj
book (make a reservation) v *rezerwować*
    re-zer-*vo*-vach
bottle *butelka* ⓕ boo-*tel*-ka
bottle opener *otwieracz do butelek* ⓜ
    ot-*fye*-rach do boo-*te*-lek
boy *chłopiec* ⓜ khwo-pyets
brakes (car) *hamulce* ⓜ pl ha-*mool*-tse
breakfast *śniadanie* ⓝ shnya-*da*-nye
broken (faulty) *połamany* po-wa-*ma*-ni
bus *autobus* ⓜ ow-to-boos
business *firma* ⓕ feer-ma
buy *kupować* koo-po-vach

C

café *kawiarnia* ⓕ ka-*vyar*-nya
camera *aparat* ⓜ a-*pa*-rat
camp site *kamping* ⓜ kam-peeng
cancel *unieważnić* oo-nye-*vazh*-nyach
can opener *otwieracz do konserw* ⓜ
    ot-*fye*-rach do kon-serf
car *samochód* ⓜ sa-mo-khoot
cash *gotówka* ⓕ go-toof-ka
cash (a cheque) v *zrealizować czek*
    zre-a-lee-zo-vach chek
cell phone *telefon komórkowy* ⓜ
    te-*le*-fon ko-moor-*ko*-vi
centre *środek* ⓜ shro-dek
change (money) v *rozmieniać* roz-mye-nyach
cheap *tani* *ta*-nee
check (bill) *sprawdzenie* ⓝ sprav-*dze*-nye
check-in *zameldowanie* ⓝ za-mel-do-*va*-nye
chest *klatka piersiowa* ⓕ *klat*-ka pyer-*shyo*-va
child *dziecko* ⓝ *jye*-tsko
cigarette *papieros* ⓜ pa-*pye*-ros
city *miasto* ⓝ *myas*-to
clean a *czysty* chi-sti
closed *zamknięty* zam-knyen-ti
coffee *kawa* ⓕ *ka*-va
coins *monety* ⓕ pl mo-ne-ti
cold a *zimny* zheem-ni

collect call *rozmowa opłacona przez odbierającego* ①
roz-*mo*-va o-pwa-*tso*-na pshes od-bye-ra-*yon-tse*-go
come (by vehicle) *przyjść* pshiyshch
come (on foot) *przychodzić* pshi-*kho*-jeech
computer *komputer* ⑩ kom-*poo*-ter
condom *kondom* ⑩ kon-dom
contact lenses *soczewki kontaktowe* ① pl
so-*chef*-kee kon-tak-*to*-ve
cook ∨ *gotować* go-*to*-vach
cost *koszt* ⑩ kosht
credit card *karta kredytowa* ① *kar*-ta kre-di-*to*-va
cup *filiżanka* ① fee-lee-*zhan*-ka
currency exchange *kantor* ⑩ *kan*-tor
customs (immigration) *urząd celny* ⑩
oo-zhont *tsel*-ni

D

dangerous *niebezpieczny* nye-bes-*pyech*-ni
date (time) *data* ① *da*-ta
day *dzień* ⑩ jyen´
delay *opóźnienie* ① o-poozh-*nye*-nye
dentist *dentysta* ⑩ den-*tis*-ta
depart *odjeżdżać* od-*yezh*-jach
diaper *pieluszka* ① pye-*loosh*-ka
dictionary *słownik* ⑩ *swov*-neek
dinner *kolacja* ① ko-*la*-tsya
direct *bezpośredni* bes-po-*shred*-nee
dirty *brudny* *brood*-ni
disabled *niepełnosprawny* nye-pew-no-*sprav*-ni
discount *zniżka* ① *zneesh*-ka
doctor *lekarz* ⑩ *le*-kash
double bed *łóżko małżeńskie* ⑩
woozh-ko mow-*zhen´*-skye
double room *pokój dwuosobowy* ⑩
po-kooy dvoo-o-so-*bo*-vi
drink *napój* ⑩ *na*-pooy
drive ∨ *kierować* kye-*ro*-vach
drivers licence *prawo jazdy* ① *pra*-vo yaz-di
drugs (illicit) *narkotyki* ⑩ pl nar-ko-*ti*-kee
dummy (pacifier) *smoczek* ⑩ *smo*-chek

E

ear *ucho* ⑩ *oo*-kho
east *wschód* ⑩ vskhood
eat *jeść* yeshch
economy class *klasa oszczędnościowa* ①
kla-sa osh-chend-nosh-*chyo*-va
electricity *elektryczność* ① e-lek-*trich*-noshch
elevator *winda* ① *veen*-da
email *email* ⑩ *e*-mail

embassy *ambasada* ① am-ba-*sa*-da
emergency *nagły przypadek* ⑩ *nag*-wi pshi-*pa*-dek
English (language) *angielski* an-*gyel*-skee
entrance *wejście* ⑩ *veysh*-chye
evening *wieczór* ⑩ *vye*-choor
exchange rate *kurs wymiany* ⑩ koors vi-*mya*-ni
exit *wyjście* ⑩ *viysh*-chye
expensive *drogi* *dro*-gee
express mail *list ekspresowy* ⑩ leest eks-pre-*so*-vi
eye *oko* ⑩ *o*-ko

F

far *daleki* da-*le*-kee
fast *szybki* *shib*-kee
father *ojciec* ⑩ *oy*-chyets
film (camera) *film* ⑩ feelm
finger *palec* ⑩ *pa*-lets
first-aid kit *apteczka pierwszej pomocy* ①
ap-*tech*-ka pyerf-shey po-*mo*-tsi
first class *pierwsza klasa* ① pyerf-sha *kla*-sa
fish *ryba* ① *ri*-ba
food *żywność* ① *zhiv*-noshch
foot *stopa* ① *sto*-pa
fork *widelec* ⑩ vee-*de*-lets
free (of charge) *bezpłatny* bes-*pwat*-ni
friend *przyjaciel/przyjaciółka* ⑩/①
pshi-ya-chyel/pshi-ya-*choow*-ka
fruit *owoc* ⑩ *o*-vots
full *pełny* *pew*-ni
funny *zabawny* za-*bav*-ni

G

gift *prezent* ⑩ *pre*-zent
girl *dziewczyna* ① jyev-*chi*-na
glass (drinking) *szklanka* ① *shklan*-ka
glasses *okulary* pl o-koo-*la*-ri
go (by vehicle) *jechać* *ye*-khach
go (on foot) *iść* eeshch
good *dobry* *do*-bri
green *zielony* zhe-*lo*-ni
guide *przewodnik* ⑩ pshe-*vod*-neek

H

half *połówka* ① po-*woof*-ka
hand *ręka* ① *ren*-ka
handbag *torebka* ① to-*rep*-ka
happy *szczęśliwy* shchen-*shlee*-vi
have *mieć* myech
he *on* on

head *głowa* ① *gwo*-va
heart *serce* ① *ser*-tse
heat *upał* ⓜ *oo*-pow
heavy *ciężki* ⓜ *chyensh*-kee
help v *pomagać* po-*ma*-gach
here *tutaj* *too*-tai
high *wysoki* vi-*so*-kee
highway *szosa* ① *sho*-sa
hike v *wędrować* ven-*dro*-vach
holiday *święto* ① *shyven*-to
homosexual n *homoseksualista* ⓜ
ho-mo-sek-soo-a-*lees*-ta
hospital *szpital* ⓜ *shpee*-tal
hot *gorący* go-*ron*-tsi
hotel *hotel* ⓜ *ho*-tel
hungry *głodny* *gwo*-dni
husband *mąż* ⓜ monzh

I

I *ja* ya
identification (card) *dowód tożsamości* ⓜ
do-*vood* tozh-sa-*mosh*-chee
ill *chory* *kho*-ri
important *ważny* *vazh*-ni
included *wliczony* vlee-*cho*-ni
injury *rana* ① *ra*-na
insurance *ubezpieczenie* ① oo-bes-pye-*che*-nye
Internet *internet* ⓜ een-*ter*-net
interpreter *tłumacz/tłumaczka* ⓜ / ①
twoo-mach/twoo-*mach*-ka

J

jewellery *biżuteria* ① bee-zhoo-*ter*-ya
job *praca* ① *pra*-tsa

K

key *klucz* ⓜ klooch
kilogram *kilogram* ⓜ kee-*lo*-gram
kitchen *kuchnia* ① *kookh*-nya
knife *nóż* ⓜ noosh

L

laundry (place) *pralnia* ① *pral*-nya
lawyer *prawnik* ⓜ *prav*-neek
left (direction) *lewy* ⓜ *le*-vi
left-luggage office *przechowalnia bagażu* ①
pshe-kho-*val*-nya ba-*ga*-zhoo

leg *noga* ① *no*-ga
lesbian n *lesbijka* ① les-*beey*-ka
less *mniej* mnyey
letter (mail) *list* ⓜ leest
lift (elevator) *winda* ① *veen*-da
light *światło* ① *shvyat*-wo
like v *lubić* loo-beech
lock *zamek* ⓜ *za*-mek
long *długi* *dwoo*-gee
lost *zgubiony* zgoo-*byo*-ni
lost-property office *biuro rzeczy znalezionych* ⓝ
byoo-ro zhe-chi zna-le-*zhyo*-nikh
love v *kochać* ko-khach
luggage *bagaż* ① *ba*-gash
lunch *lunch* ⓜ lanch

M

mail (letters) *list* ⓜ leest
mail (postal system) *poczta* ① *poch*-ta
man *mężczyzna* ⓜ menzh-*chiz*-na
map (of country) *mapa* ① *ma*-pa
map (of town) *plan* ⓜ plan
market *rynek* ⓜ *ri*-nek
matches *zapałki* ① pl za-*pow*-kee
meat *mięso* ⓝ *myen*-so
medicine *lekarstwo* ⓝ le-*karst*-fo
menu *jadłospis* ⓜ ya-*dwo*-spees
message *wiadomość* ① *vya*-do-moshch
milk *mleko* ⓝ *mle*-ko
minute *minuta* ① mee-*noo*-ta
mobile phone *telefon komórkowy* ⓜ
te-*le*-fon ko-moor-*ko*-vi
money *pieniądze* ⓜ pl pye-*nyon*-dze
month *miesiąc* ⓜ *mye*-shonts
morning *rano* ⓝ *ra*-no
mother *matka* ① *mat*-ka
motorcycle *motor* ⓜ *mo*-tor
motorway *autostrada* ① ow-to-*stra*-da
mouth *usta* pl *oos*-ta
music *muzyka* ① moo-*zi*-ka

N

name *imię* ⓝ *ee*-mye
napkin *serwetka* ① ser-*vet*-ka
nappy *pieluszka* ① pye-*loosh*-ka
near *bliski* *blees*-kee
neck *szyja* ① *shi*-ya
new *nowy* *no*-vi
news *wiadomości* ① pl vya-do-*mosh*-chee
newspaper *gazeta* ① ga-*ze*-ta
night *noc* ① nots

no *nie* nye
noisy *hałaśliwy* ha-wa-*shlee*-vi
nonsmoking *niepalący* nye-pa-*lon*-tsi
north *północ* ⓕ *poow*-nots
nose *nos* ⓜ nos
now *teraz* *te*-ras
number *numer* ⓜ *noo*-mer

O

oil (engine) *olej* ⓜ o-ley
old *stary* *sta*-ri
one-way ticket *bilet w jedną stronę* ⓜ
  bee-let v *yed*-nom *stro*-ne
open a *otwarty* ot-*far*-ti
outside *na zewnątrz* na zev-nontsh

P

package *paczka* ⓕ *pach*-ka
paper *papier* ⓜ *pa*-pyer
park (car) v *parkować* par-ko-*vach*
passport *paszport* ⓜ *pash*-port
pay *płacić* pwa-*cheech*
pen *długopis* ⓜ dwoo-*go*-pees
petrol *benzyna* ⓕ ben-*zi*-na
pharmacy *apteka* ⓕ ap-*te*-ka
phonecard *karta telefoniczna* ⓕ *kar*-ta te-le-fo-*neech*-na
photo *zdjęcie* ⓝ *zdyen*-chye
plate *talerz* ⓜ *ta*-lesh
Poland *Polska* ⓕ *pol*-ska
police *policja* ⓕ po-*lee*-tsya
Polish (language) *polski* ⓜ *pol*-skee
postcard *pocztówka* ⓕ poch-*toof*-ka
post office *urząd pocztowy* ⓜ *oo*-zhond poch-*to*-vi
pregnant *w ciąży* v *chyon*-zhi
price *cena* ⓕ *tse*-na

Q

quiet *cichy* *chee*-khi

R

rain *deszcz* ⓜ deshch
razor *brzytwa* ⓕ *bzhit*-fa
receipt *rachunek* ⓜ ra-*khoo*-nek
red *czerwony* cher-*vo*-ni
refund *zwrot pieniędzy* ⓜ zvrot pye-*nyen*-dzi
registered mail *list polecony* ⓜ leest po-le-*tso*-ni
rent v *wynająć* vi-*na*-yonch

repair v *naprawić* na-*pra*-veech
reservation *rezerwacja* ⓕ re-zer-*va*-tsya
restaurant *restauracja* ⓕ res-tow-*ra*-tsya
return v *wracać* vra-*tsach*
return ticket *bilet powrotny* ⓜ *bee*-let po-*vro*-tni
right (direction) *prawoskrętny* pra-vo-*skrent*-ni
road *droga* ⓕ *dro*-ga
room *pokój* ⓜ *po*-kooy

S

safe a *bezpieczny* bes-*pyech*-ni
sanitary napkin *podpaski higieniczne* ⓕ pl
  pod-*pas*-kee hee-gye-*neech*-ne
seat *miejsce* ⓝ *myeys*-tse
send *wysyłać* vi-*si*-wach
service station *stacja obsługi* ⓕ *sta*-tsya ob-*swoo*-gee
sex *seks* ⓜ seks
shampoo *szampon* ⓜ *sham*-pon
share (a dorm) v *mieszkać z kimś* *myesh*-kach z keemsh
shaving cream *krem do golenia* ⓜ krem do go-*le*-nya
she *ona* *o*-na
sheet (bed) *prześcieradło* ⓝ pshesh-chye-*ra*-dwo
shirt *koszula* ⓕ ko-*shoo*-la
shoes *buty* ⓜ pl *boo*-ti
shop *sklep* ⓜ sklep
short *krótki* *kroot*-kee
shower *prysznic* ⓜ *prish*-neets
single room *pokój jednoosobowy* ⓜ
  po-kooy ye-dno-o-so-*bo*-vi
skin *skóra* ⓕ *skoo*-ra
skirt *spódnica* ⓕ spood-*nee*-tsa
sleep v *spać* spach
slowly *powoli* po-*vo*-lee
small *mały* *ma*-wi
smoke (cigarettes) v *palić* *pa*-leech
soap *mydło* ⓝ *mid*-wo
some *kilka* *keel*-ka
soon *wkrótce* *fkroot*-tse
south *południe* ⓝ po-*wood*-nye
souvenir shop *sklep z pamiątkami* ⓜ
  sklep z pa-*myont*-ka-mi
speak *mówić* *moo*-veech
spoon *łyżka* ⓕ *wish*-ka
stamp *znaczek* ⓜ *zna*-chek
stand-by ticket *bilet z listy rezerwowej* ⓜ
  bee-let z *lees*-ti re-zer-*vo*-vey
station (train) *stacja* ⓕ *sta*-tsya
stomach *żołądek* ⓜ zho-*won*-dek
stop v *przestać* *pshes*-tach
stop (bus) *przystanek* ⓜ pshis-*ta*-nek
street *ulica* ⓕ oo-*lee*-tsa
student *student* ⓜ *stoo*-dent

sun *słońce* ⓝ swon'-tse
sunscreen *krem przeciwsłoneczny* ⓜ
  krem pshe-cheef-swo-nech-ni
swim v *pływać* pwi-vach

T

tampon *tampon* ⓜ tam-pon
taxi *taksówka* ⓕ tak-soof-ka
teaspoon *łyżeczka* ⓕ wi-zhech-ka
teeth *zęby* ⓜ pl zem-bi
telephone *telefon* ⓜ te-le-fon
television *telewizja* ⓕ te-le-veez-ya
temperature (weather) *temperatura* ⓕ
  tem-pe-ra-too-ra
tent *namiot* ⓜ na-myot
that (one) *który* ktoo-ri
they *oni* o-nee
thirsty *spragniony* sprag-nyo-ni
this (one) *ten* ⓜ ten
throat *gardło* gard-wo
ticket *bilet* ⓜ bee-let
time *czas* ⓜ chas
tired *zmęczony* zmen-cho-ni
tissues *chusteczki* ⓕ pl khoos-tech-kee
today *dzisiaj* jee-shyai
toilet *toaleta* ⓕ to-a-le-ta
tomorrow *jutro* yoo-tro
tonight *dzisiaj wieczorem* jee-shyai vye-cho-rem
toothbrush *szczotka do zębów* ⓕ shchot-ka do zem-boof
toothpaste *pasta do zębów* ⓕ pas-ta do zem-boof
torch (flashlight) *latarka* ⓕ la-tar-ka
tour *wycieczka* ⓕ vi-chyech-ka
tourist office *biuro turystyczne* ⓝ byoo-ro too-ris-tich-ne
towel *ręcznik* ⓜ rench-neek
train *pociąg* ⓜ po-chyonk
translate *przetłumaczyć* pshe-twoo-ma-chich
travel agency *biuro podróży* ⓝ byoo-ro po-droo-zhi
travellers cheques *czeki podróżne* ⓜ pl
  che-kee po-droozh-ne
trousers *spodnie* pl spo-dnye
twin beds *dwa łóżka* ⓝ pl dva woosh-ka
tyre *opona* ⓕ o-po-na

U

underwear *bielizna* ⓕ bye-leez-na
urgent *pilny* peel-ni

V

vacant *wolny* vol-ni
vacation *wakacje* pl va-ka-tsye
vegetable *warzywo* ⓝ va-zhi-vo
vegetarian a *wegetariański* ve-ge-tar-yan'-skee
visa *wiza* ⓕ vee-za

W

waiter *kelner* ⓜ kel-ner
walk v *spacerować* spa-tse-ro-vach
wallet *portfel* ⓜ port-fel
warm a *ciepły* chyep-wi
Warsaw *Warszawa* ⓕ var-sha-va
wash (something) *prać* prach
watch *zegarek* ⓜ ze-ga-rek
water *woda* ⓕ vo-da
we *my* mi
weekend *weekend* ⓜ wee-kend
west *zachód* ⓜ za-khood
wheelchair *wózek inwalidzki* ⓜ
  voo-zek een-va-leets-kee
when *kiedy* kye-di
where *gdzie* gjye
white *biały* bya-wi
who *kto* kto
why *dlaczego* dla-che-go
wife *żona* ⓕ zho-na
window *okno* ⓝ ok-no
wine *wino* ⓝ vee-no
with *z* z
without *bez* bes
woman *kobieta* ⓕ ko-bye-ta
write *pisać* pee-sach

Y

yellow *żółty* zhoow-ti
yes *tak* tak
yesterday *wczoraj* fcho-rai
you sg inf *ty* ti
you sg pol *pan/pani* ⓜ/ⓕ pan/pa-nee
you pl inf *wy* vi
you pl pol *panowie/panie* ⓜ/ⓕ pa-no-vye/pa-nye
you pl pol *państwo* ⓜ&ⓕ pan'-stfo

Slovak

slovak alphabet

A a uh	*Á á* dl-hair a	*Ä ä* shi-ro-kair e	*B b* bair	*C c* tsair	*Č č* ch
D d dair	*Ď ď* dy	*Dz dz* dz	*Dž dž* j	*E e* e	*É é* dl-hair air
F f ef	*G g* gair	*H h* ha	*Ch ch* kh	*I i* i	*Í í* dl-hair ee
J j yair	*K k* ka	*L l* el	*Ĺ ĺ* dl-hair el	*Ľ ľ* ly	*M m* em
N n en	*Ň ň* ny	*O o* o	*Ó ó* dl-hair aw	*Ô ô* wo	*P p* pair
Q q quair	*R r* er	*Ŕ ŕ* dl-hair er	*S s* es	*Š š* sh	*T t* tair
Ť ť ty	*U u* u	*Ú ú* dl-hair oo	*V v* vair	*W w* dvo-yi-tair vair	*X x* iks
Y y ip-si-lon	*Ý ý* ee	*Z z* zet	*Ž ž* zh		

slovak

SLOVENČINA

introduction

The cosy position of the Slovak language (*slovenčina* slo·ven·chi·na) in Central Europe makes it a perfect base for learning or understanding the languages of other Slavic nations. It shares certain features with its close relatives in the West Slavic group – Czech and Polish. To a lesser extent, Slovak is similar to the South Slavic languages (particularly Slovene, from which it was distanced by the arrival of the Hungarians to their present day homeland in the 9th century). There are even similarities between Slovak and Ukranian, which represents the East Slavic branch.

Not surprisingly, however, the language that bears the closest resemblance to Slovak is Czech, since ties between the two now independent countries date back to the 9th century and the Great Moravian Empire. More recently, the 20th-century Czechoslovakian affair established even closer relations between Czech and Slovak, to the extent that the two languages are mutually intelligible (although less so in the colloquial form or among the younger generation). Hungarian influence on Slovak (mainly in the vocabulary) is a result of the centuries during which Slovaks formed first part of the Kingdom of Hungary, and later the Austro-Hungarian Empire.

The literary standard of Slovak emerged in the mid-19th century, during a national revival movement marked on the linguistic front by the work of Ľudovít Štúr. In earlier times, it was mostly a spoken language, subordinated in writing to Latin and Czech, although texts with elements of Slovak or written entirely in Slovak can be traced back to the 15th century. The Great Moravian Empire was originally the place of St Cyril and Methodius' mission, which used the Glagolitic script, the precursor of the Cyrillic alphabet, for Old Church Slavonic literature. However, the West Slavic languages, including Slovak, soon adopted the Roman alphabet due to the influence of the Catholic Church.

Since 1993, Slovak has stepped out of the shadow of its larger neighbour, Czech, with which it shared official status during the Czechoslovakian days. It is now the official language of about 5 million speakers in Slovakia and there are Slovak speaking minorities in Poland, Hungary, Romania, Ukraine, the northern Serbian province of Vojvodina, and of course, the Czech Republic.

Even if you don't speak Slovak, be sure to look up your name in the official Slovak calendar – in which each day corresponds to a personal name and entitles people to celebrate their 'name day' (*sviatok* svyuh·tok or *meniny* me·nyi·ni) with equal pomp as their birthday!

pronunciation

vowel sounds

Slovak is rich in vowels, including a number of vowel combinations (or 'diphthongs').

symbol	english equivalent	slovak example	transliteration
a	**father**	*pán*	pan
ai	**aisle**	*raňajky*	*ruh*·nyai·ki
air	**hair**	*volné*	*vol*·nair
aw	**law**	*pól*	pawl
e	**bet**	*sestra, mäso*	*ses*·truh, *me*·so
ee	**see**	*prosím, bývať*	pro·seem, bee·vuht'
ey	**hey**	*olej*	o·ley
i	**bit**	*izba, byt*	*iz*·buh, bit
o	**pot**	*meno*	*me*·no
oh	**oh**	*zmesou*	zme·soh
oo	**zoo**	*pavúk*	puh·vook
ow	**how**	*auto*	*ow*·to
oy	**toy**	*ahoj*	a·hoy
uh	**run**	*matka*	*muht*·kuh
wo	**quote**	*môžem*	mwo·zhem

word stress

In Slovak, stress always falls on the first syllable, but it's quite light.

consonant sounds

Slovak consonants are shown opposite. Most have equivalents in English.

symbol	english equivalent	slovak example	transliteration
b	bed	*obed*	o-bed
ch	cheat	*večer*	ve-cher
d	dog	*adresa*	uh-dre-suh
dy	during	*ďaleko, džem*	dyuh-le-ko, dyem
dz	adds	*prichádza*	pri-kha-dzuh
f	fat	*fotka*	fot-kuh
g	go	*margarin*	muhr-guh-reen
h	hat	*hlava*	hluh-vuh
k	kit	*oko*	o-ko
kh	loch	*chorý*	kho-ree
l	lot	*lampa*	luhm-puh
ly	million	*doľava*	do-lyuh-vuh
m	man	*matka*	muht-kuh
n	not	*noviny*	no-vi-ni
ny	canyon	*kuchyňa*	ku-khi-nyuh
p	pet	*pero*	pe-ro
r	run	*ráno*	ra-no
s	sun	*sukňa*	suk-nyuh
sh	shot	*štyri*	shti-ri
t	top	*tri*	tri
ts	hats	*anglicky*	uhng-lits-ki
ty	tutor	*ťava*	tyuh-vuh
v	very	*vízum, watt*	vee-zum, vuht
y	yes	*ja*	yuh
z	zero	*zub*	zub
zh	pleasure	*manžel*	muhn-zhel
'	a slight y sound	*meď*	meď

tools

language difficulties

Do you speak English?
Hovoríte po anglicky?   ho·vo·ree·tye po uhng·lits·ki

Do you understand?
Rozumiete?   ro·zu·mye·tye

I understand.
Rozumiem.   ro·zu·myem

I don't understand.
Nerozumiem.   nye·ro·zu·myem

What does (*jablko*) mean?
Čo znamená (jablko)?   cho znuh·me·na (yuh·bl·ko)

How do you ...?   *Ako sa ...?*   uh·ko suh ...
  pronounce this   *toto vyslovuje*   to·to vi·slo·vu·ye
  write (*cesta*)   *píše (cesta)*   pee·she (tses·tuh)

Could you please ...?   *Môžete prosím ...?*   mwo·zhe·tye pro·seem ...
  repeat that   *to zopakovať*   to zo·puh·ko·vuht'
  speak more slowly   *hovoriť pomalšie*   ho·vo·rit' po·muhl·shye
  write it down   *to napísať*   to nuh·pee·suht'

essentials

Yes.	*Áno.*	a·no
No.	*Nie.*	ni·ye
Please.	*Prosím.*	pro·seem
Thank you	*Ďakujem*	dyuh·ku·yem
(very much).	*(veľmi pekne).*	(veľ·mi pek·nye)
You're welcome.	*Prosím.*	pro·seem
Excuse me.	*Prepáčte.*	pre·pach·tye
Sorry.	*Prepáčte.*	pre·pach·tye

numbers

0	*nula*	nu·luh		15	*pätnásť*	pet·nast'
1	*jeden* m	ye·den		16	*šestnásť*	shes·nast'
	jedna f	yed·na		17	*sedemnásť*	se·dyem·nast'
	jedno n	yed·no		18	*osemnásť*	o·sem·nast'
2	*dva* m	dvuh		19	*devätnásť*	dye·vet·nast'
	dve n/f	dve		20	*dvadsať*	dvuh·tsuht'
3	*tri*	tri		21	*dvadsať-*	dvuh·tsuht'·
4	*štyri*	shti·ri			*jeden*	ye·den
5	*päť*	pet'		22	*dvadsaťdva*	dvuh·tsuht'·dvuh
6	*šesť*	shest'		30	*tridsať*	tri·tsuht'
7	*sedem*	se·dyem		40	*štyridsať*	shti·ri·tsuht'
8	*osem*	o·sem		50	*päťdesiat*	pe·dye·syuht
9	*deväť*	dye·vet'		60	*šesťdesiat*	shes·dye·syuht
10	*desať*	dye·suht'		70	*sedemdesiat*	se·dyem·dye·syuht
11	*jedenásť*	ye·de·nast'		80	*osemdesiat*	o·sem·dye·syuht
12	*dvanásť*	dvuh·nast'		90	*deväťdesiat*	dye·ve·dye·syuht
13	*trinásť*	tri·nast'		100	*sto*	sto
14	*štrnásť*	shtr·nast'		1000	*tisíc*	tyi·seets

time & dates

What time is it?	*Koľko je hodín?*	kol'·ko ye ho·dyeen
It's one o'clock.	*Je jedna hodina.*	ye yed·nuh ho·dyi·nuh
It's (two) o'clock.	*Sú (dve) hodiny.*	soo (dve) ho·dyi·ni
Quarter past (one).	*Štvrť na (dve).*	shtvrt' nuh (dve)
Half past (one).	*Pól (druhej).*	pol (dru·hey)
	(lit: half two)	
Quarter to (eight).	*Trištvrte na (osem).*	tri·shtvr·tye nuh (o·sem)
At what time ...?	*O koľkej ...?*	o kol'·key ...
At ...	*O ...*	o ...
am (before 10)	*ráno*	ra·no
pm (10 to 12)	*dobedu*	do·be·du
pm	*pobede*	po·be·dye

tools – SLOVAK

175

Monday	*pondelok*	pon·dye·lok
Tuesday	*utorok*	u·to·rok
Wednesday	*streda*	stre·duh
Thursday	*štvrtok*	shtvr·tok
Friday	*piatok*	pyuh·tok
Saturday	*sobota*	so·bo·tuh
Sunday	*nedeľa*	nye·dye·lyuh

January	*január*	yuh·nu·ar
February	*február*	feb·ru·ar
March	*marec*	muh·rets
April	*apríl*	uhp·reel
May	*máj*	mai
June	*jún*	yoon
July	*júl*	yool
August	*august*	ow·gust
September	*september*	sep·tem·ber
October	*október*	ok·taw·ber
November	*november*	no·vem·ber
December	*december*	de·tsem·ber

What date is it today?
  Koľkého je dnes? kol·kair·ho ye dnyes

It's (15 December).
  Je (pätnásteho decembra). ye (pet·nas·te·ho de·tsem·bruh)

since (May)	*od (mája)*	od (ma·yuh)
until (June)	*do (júna)*	do (yoo·nuh)
last night	*minulú noc*	mi·nu·loo nots

last/next ...	*minulý/budúci ...*	mi·nu·lee/bu·doo·tsi ...
week	*týždeň*	teezh·dyen'
month	*mesiac*	me·syuhts
year	*rok*	rok

yesterday/tomorrow ...	*včera/zajtra ...*	vche·ruh/zai·truh ...
morning	*ráno*	ra·no
afternoon	*popoludnie*	po·po·lud·ni·ye
evening	*večer*	ve·cher

weather

What's the weather like?	Aké je počasie?	uh·kair ye po·chuh·si·ye
It's ...		
cloudy	Je zamračené.	ye zuh·mruh·che·nair
cold	Je zima.	ye zi·muh
hot	Je horúco.	ye ho·roo·tso
raining	Prší.	pr·shee
snowing	Sneží.	sne·zhee
sunny	Je slnečno.	ye sl·nyech·no
warm	Je teplo.	ye tyep·lo
windy	Je veterno.	ye ve·tyer·no
spring	jar f	yuhr
summer	leto n	le·to
autumn	jeseň f	ye·sen'
winter	zima f	zi·muh

border crossing

I'm here ...	Som tu ...	som tu ...
on business	v obchodnej	v ob·khod·ney
	záležitosti	za·le·zhi·tos·tyi
on holiday	na dovolenke	nuh do·vo·len·ke

I'm here for ...	Som tu na ...	som tu nuh ...
(10) days	(desat) dni	(dye·suht') dnyee
(two) months	(dva) mesiace	(dvuh) me·syuh·tse
(three) weeks	(tri) týždne	(tri) teezhd·nye

I'm going to (Bratislava).
Idem do (Bratislavy).   i·dyem do (bruh·tyi·sluh·vi)

I'm staying at the (Hotel Grand).
Zostávam v (hoteli Grand).   zo·sta·vuhm v (ho·te·li gruhnd)

I have nothing to declare.
Nemám nič na preclenie.   nye·mam nyich nuh prets·le·ni·ye

I have something to declare.
Mám niečo na preclenie.   mam ni·ye·cho nuh prets·le·ni·ye

That's (not) mine.
To (nie) je moje.   to (ni·ye) ye mo·ye

transport

tickets & luggage

Where can I buy a ticket?
Kde si môžem kúpiť — kdye si *mwo*·zhem *koo*·pit'
cestovný lístok? — tses·tov·nee lees·tok

Do I need to book a seat?
Potrebujem si rezervovať — po·tre·bu·yem si re·zer·vo·vuht'
miestenku? — myes·tyen·ku

One ... ticket — *Jeden ... lístok* — ye·den ... lees·tok
(to Poprad), please. — *(do Popradu), prosím.* — (do pop·ruh·du) pro·seem
  one-way — *jednosmerný* — yed·no·smer·nee
  return — *spiatočný* — spyuh·toch·nee

I'd like to ... my — *Chcel/Chcela by som ...* — khtsel/*khtse*·luh bi som ...
ticket, please. — *môj lístok, prosím.* m/f — mwoy lees·tok pro·seem
  cancel — *zrušiť* — zru·shit'
  change — *zmeniť* — zme·nyit'
  collect — *vyzdvihnúť* — vizd·vih·noot'
  confirm — *potvrdiť* — po·tvr·dyit'

I'd like a ... seat, please. — *Prosím si ... miesto.* — pro·seem si ... mye·sto
  nonsmoking — *nefajčiarske* — nye·fai·chyuhr·ske
  smoking — *fajčiarske* — fai·chyuhr·ske

How much is it?
Kolko to stojí? — kol'·ko to sto·yee

Is there air conditioning?
Je tam klimatizácia? — ye tuhm *kli*·muh·ti·za·tsi·yuh

Is there a toilet?
Je tam toaleta? — ye tuhm to·uh·le·tuh

How long does the trip take?
Kolko trvá cesta? — kol'·ko *tr*·va tses·tuh

Is it a direct route?
Je to priamy smer? — ye to *pryuh*·mi smer

I'd like a luggage locker.
Chcel/Chcela by som skrinku — khtsel/*khtse*·luh bi som skrin·ku
na batožinu. m/f — nuh *buh*·to·zhi·nu

My luggage has been ...	*Moja batožina ...*	mo-yuh *buh*-to-zhi-nuh ...
damaged	*bola poškodená*	bo-luh *posh*-ko-dye-na
lost	*sa stratila*	suh *struh*-tyi-luh
stolen	*bola ukradnutá*	bo-luh *u*-kruhd-nu-ta

getting around

Where does flight (number 333) arrive?
Kam prilieta let   kuhm *pri*-li-ye-tuh let
(číslo 333)?   (*chees*-lo *tri*-sto-tri-tsat'-tri)

Where does flight (number 333) depart?
Odkiaľ odlieta let   *od*-kyuhl *od*-li-ye-tuh let
(číslo 333)?   (*chees*-lo *tri*-sto-tri-tsat'-tri)

Where's (the) ...?	*Kde je ...?*	kdye ye ...
arrivals hall	*príletová hala*	pree-le-to-va huh-luh
departures hall	*odletová hala*	od-le-to-va huh-luh
duty-free shop	*duty-free obchod*	dyu-ti-free ob-khod
gate (12)	*vchod (dvanásť)*	vkhod (dvuh-nast')

Is this the ...	*Je toto ...*	ye to-to ...
to (Komárno)?	*do (Komárna)?*	do (ko-mar-nuh)
boat	*loď*	lod'
bus	*autobus*	ow-to-bus
plane	*lietadlo*	li-ye-tuhd-lo
train	*vlak*	vluhk

What time's the ... bus?	*Kedy príde ... autobus?*	ke-di pree-dye ... ow-to-bus
first	*prvý*	pr-vee
last	*posledný*	po-sled-nee
next	*nasledujúci*	nuh-sle-du-yoo-tsi

At what time does it arrive/leave?
O koľkej prichádza/odchádza?   o kol'-key pri-kha-dzuh/od-kha-dzuh

How long will it be delayed?
Koľko je spozdenie?   kol'-ko ye spoz-dye-ni-ye

What station/stop is this?
Ktorá stanica/zastávka je toto?   kto-ra stuh-nyi-tsuh/zuhs-tav-kuh ye to-to

What's the next station/stop?
Ktorá je nasledujúca   kto-ra ye nuh-sle-du-yoo-tsuh
stanica/zastávka?   stuh-nyi-tsuh/zuhs-tav-kuh

Does it stop at (Štúrovo námestie)?
Stojí to na (Štúrovom námestí)?   *sto*·yee to nuh (*shtoo*·ro·vom *na*·mes·tyee)

Please tell me when we get to (Hlavné námestie).
Môžete ma prosím upozorniť   *mwo*·zhe·tye muh *pro*·seem u·po·zor·nyit'
keď budeme na ...   ked' *bu*·dye·me nuh ...

How long do we stop here?
Ako dlho tu budeme stát'?   *uh*·ko *dl*·ho tu *bu*·dye·me stat'

Is this seat available?
Je toto miesto voľné?   ye *to*·to *mye*·sto *vol*·nair

That's my seat.
Toto je moje miesto.   *to*·to ye *mo*·ye *mye*·sto

I'd like a taxi ...   *Chcel/Chcela by*   khtsel/*khtse*·luh bi
   som taxík na ... m/f   som *tuhk*·seek nuh ...
   at (9am)   *(deviatu ráno)*   (*dye*·vyuh·tu *ra*·no)
   now   *teraz*   te·ruhz
   tomorrow   *zajtra*   *zai*·truh

Is this taxi available?
Je tento taxík voľný?   ye *ten*·to *tuhk*·seek *vol*'·nee

How much is it to ...?
Koľko to bude stát' do ...?   *kol*'·ko to *bu*·dye stat' do ...

Please put the meter on.
Zapnite taxameter, prosím.   *zuhp*·nyi·tye *tuhk*·suh·me·ter *pro*·seem

Please take me to (this address).
Zavezte ma (na túto adresu),   zuh·*vez*·tye muh (nuh *too*·to *uh*·dre·su)
prosím.   *pro*·seem

Please ...   *..., prosím.*   ... *pro*·seem
   slow down   *Spomaľte*   spo·*muhl*'·tye
   stop here   *Zastavte tu*   *zuhs*·tuhv·tye tu
   wait here   *Počkajte tu*   *poch*·kai·tye tu

car, motorbike & bicycle hire

I'd like to hire a ...   *Chcel/Chcela by som si*   khtsel/*khtse*·luh bi som si
   prenajať ... m/f   *pre*·nuh·yuht' ...
   bicycle   *bicykel*   *bi*·tsi·kel
   car   *auto*   *ow*·to
   motorbike   *motorku*   *mo*·tor·ku

with ...	s ...	s ...
a driver	šoférom	sho·fair·rom
air conditioning	klimatizáciou	kli·muh·ti·za·tsi·oh
antifreeze	protimrazovou	pro·tyi·mruh·zo·voh
	zmesou	zme·soh
snow chains	snehovými	snye·ho·vee·mi
	reťazami	re·tyuh·zuh·mi

How much for	Koľko stojí	koľ·ko sto·yee
... hire?	prenájom na ...?	pre·na·yom nuh ...
hourly	hodinu	ho·dyi·nu
daily	deň	dyen'
weekly	týždeň	teezh·dyen'

air	stlačený vzduch m	stluh·che·nee vzdukh
oil	olej m	o·ley
petrol	benzín m	ben·zeen
tyres	pneumatiky f pl	pne·u·muh·ti·ki

I need a mechanic.
Potrebujem automechanika. — po·tre·bu·yem ow·to·me·khuh·ni·kuh

I've run out of petrol.
Minul sa mi benzín. — mi·nul suh mi ben·zeen

I have a flat tyre.
Dostal/Dostala som defekt. m/f — dos·tuhl/dos·tuh·luh som de·fekt

directions

Where's the ...?	Kde je ...?	kdye ye ...
bank	banka	buhn·kuh
city centre	mestské centrum	mes·kair tsen·trum
hotel	hotel	ho·tel
market	trh	trh
police station	policajná stanica	po·li·tsai·na stuh·nyi·tsuh
post office	pošta	posh·tuh
public toilet	verejný záchod	ve·rey·nee za·khod
tourist office	turistická	tu·ris·tits·ka
	kancelária	kuhn·tse·la·ri·yuh

Is this the road to ...?	Je toto cesta na ...?	ye to·to tses·tuh nuh ...

SLOVENČINA – transport

Can you show me (on the map)?
  Môžete mi ukázať (na mape)? — mwo·zhe·tye mi u·ka·zuhť (nuh *muh*·pe)

What's the address?
  Aká je adresa? — uh·ka ye uh·dre·suh

How far is it?
  Ako je to ďaleko? — uh·ko ye to dyuh·le·ko

How do I get there?
  Ako sa tam dostanem? — uh·ko suh tuhm dos·tuh·nyem

Turn ...	*Zabočte ...*	zuh·boch·tye ...
at the corner	*na rohu*	nuh ro·hu
at the traffic lights	*na svetelnej križovatke*	nuh sve·tyel·ney kri·zho·vuht·ke
left	*doľava*	do·lyuh·vuh
right	*doprava*	do·pruh·vuh

It's ...	*Je to ...*	ye to ...
behind ...	*za ...*	zuh ...
far away	*ďaleko*	dyuh·le·ko
here	*tu*	tu
in front of ...	*pred ...*	pred ...
left	*vľavo*	vlyuh·vo
near (to ...)	*blízko (k ...)*	bleez·ko (k ...)
next to ...	*vedľa ...*	ved·lyuh ...
on the corner	*na rohu*	nuh ro·hu
opposite ...	*oproti ...*	o·pro·tyi ...
right	*vpravo*	vpruh·vo
straight ahead	*rovno*	rov·no
there	*tam*	tuhm

by bus	*autobusom*	ow·to·bu·som
by taxi	*taxíkom*	tuhk·see·kom
by train	*vlakom*	vluh·kom
on foot	*peši*	pe·shi

north	*sever*	se·ver
south	*juh*	yooh
east	*východ*	vee·khod
west	*západ*	za·puhd

182

Vchod/Východ	vkhod/*vee*·khod	**Entrance/Exit**
Otvorené/Zatvorené	ot·vo·re·nair/zuht·vo·re·nair	**Open/Closed**
Ubytovanie	u·bi·to·vuh·ni·ye	**Rooms Available**
Plne obsadené	pl·nye ob·suh·dye·nair	**No Vacancies**
Informácie	in·for·ma·tsi·ye	**Information**
Policajná stanica	po·li·tsai·na *stuh*·nyi·tsuh	**Police Station**
Zakázané	zuh·ka·zuh·nair	**Prohibited**
Záchody/WC/Toalety	za·kho·di/*vair*·tsair/*to*·uh·le·ti	**Toilets**
Páni	pa·nyi	**Men**
Dámy	da·mi	**Women**
Horúca/Studená	ho·roo·tsuh/*stu*·dye·na	**Hot/Cold**

accommodation

finding accommodation

Where's a ...?	Kde je ...?	kdye ye ...
camping ground	táborisko	*ta*·bo·ris·ko
guesthouse	penzión	*pen*·zi·awn
hotel	hotel	*ho*·tel
youth hostel	nocľaháreň	*nots*·lyuh·ha·ren'
	pre mládež	pre mla·dyezh

Can you recommend somewhere ...?	Môžete odporučiť niečo ...?	*mwo*·zhe·tye od·po·ru·chit' ni·ye·cho ...
cheap	lacné	*luhts*·nair
good	dobré	dob·rair
nearby	nablízku	nuh·bleez·ku

I have a reservation.	Mám rezerváciu.	mam re·zer·va·tsi·yu
My name's ...	Volám sa ...	*vo*·lam suh ...
Do you have a twin room?	Máte dve oddelené postele?	ma·tye dve od·dye·le·nair pos·tye·le
Do you have a single room?	Máte jednoposteľovú izbu?	ma·tye yed·no·pos·tye·lyo·voo iz·bu
Do you have a double room?	Máte izbu s manželskou posteľou?	ma·tye iz·bu s muhn·zhels·koh pos·tye·lyoh

How much is it per ...?	Koľko to stojí na ...?	kolʼ·ko to sto·yee nuh ...
night	noc	nots
person	osobu	o·so·bu

Can I pay by ...?	Môžem platiť ...?	mwo·zhem pluh·tyitʼ ...
credit card	kreditnou kartou	kre·dit·noh kuhr·toh
travellers cheque	cestovnými šekmi	tses·tov·nee·mi shek·mi

I'd like to stay for (two) nights.
Chcel/Chcela by som   khtsel/khtse·luh bi som
zostať (dve) noci. m/f   zos·tuhtʼ (dve) no·tsi

From (2 July) to (6 July).
Od (druhého júla)   od (dru·hair·ho yoo·luh)
do (šiesteho júla).   do (shyes·te·ho yoo·luh)

Can I see it?
Môžem to vidieť?   mwo·zhem to vi·di·yetʼ

Am I allowed to camp here?
Môžem tu stanovať?   mwo·zhem tu stuh·no·vuhtʼ

Is there a camp site nearby?
Je tu nablízku táborisko?   ye tu nuh·blees·ku ta·bo·ris·ko

requests & queries

When/Where is breakfast served?
Kedy/Kde sa podávajú   ke·di/kdye suh po·da·vuh·yoo
raňajky?   ruh·nyai·ki

Please wake me at (seven).
Zobuďte ma o (siedmej), prosím.   zo·budʼ·tye muh o (syed·mey) pro·seem

Could I have my key, please?
Prosím si môj kľúč.   pro·seem si mwoy klyooch

Can I get another (blanket)?
Môžem dostať inú (prikrývku)?   mwo·zhem dos·tuhtʼ i·noo (pri·kreev·ku)

Is there a/an ...?	Je tam ...?	ye tuhm ...
elevator	výťah	vee·tyah
safe	bezpečnostný trezor	bez·pech·nos·nee tre·zor

The room is too ...	Izba je príliš ...	iz·buh ye pree·lish ...
expensive	drahá	druh·ha
noisy	hlučná	hluch·na
small	malá	muh·la

The ... doesn't work.	... nefunguje.	... nye·fun·gu·ye
air conditioning	Klimatizácia	kli·muh·ti·za·tsi·yuh
fan	Ventilátor	ven·ti·la·tor
toilet	Toaleta	to·uh·le·tuh

This ... isn't clean.	Tento ... nie je čistý.	ten·to ... ni·ye ye chis·tee
pillow	vankúš	vuhn·koosh
towel	uterák	u·tye·rak

This sheet isn't clean.
Táto plachta nie je chistaa.　　ta·to pluhkh·tuh ni·ye ye chis·ta

checking out

What time is checkout?
O koľkej sa odhlasuje?　　o kol'·key suh od·hluh·su·ye

Can I leave my luggage here?
Môžem si tu nechať batožinu?　　mwo·zhem si tu nye·khuht' buh·to·zhi·nu

Could I have my ...?	Poprosím vás o ...	po·pro·seem vas o ...
deposit	moju zálohu	mo·yu za·lo·hu
passport	môj cestovný pas	mwoy tses·tov·nee puhs
valuables	moje cennosti	mo·ye tsen·nos·tyi

communications & banking

the internet

Where's the local Internet café?
Kde je miestne internet café?　　kdye ye myes·ne in·ter·net kuh·fair

How much is it per hour?
Koľko stojí na hodinu?　　kol'·ko sto·yee nuh ho·dyi·nu

I'd like to ...	Chcel/Chcela	khtsel/khtse·luh
	by som ... m/f	bi som ...
check my email	si skontrolovať email	si skon·tro·lo·vuht' ee·meyl
get Internet access	sa pripojiť na	suh pri·po·yit' nuh
	internet	in·ter·net
use a printer	použiť tlačiareň	po·u·zhit' tluh·chyuh·ren'
use a scanner	použiť scanner	po·u·zhit' ske·ner

mobile/cell phone

I'd like a ...	Chcel/Chcela	khtsel/khtse·luh
	by som ... m/f	bi som ...
mobile/cell phone	si prenajať	si pre·nuh·yuht'
for hire	mobilný telefón	mo·bil·nee te·le·fawn
SIM card for your	SIM kartu pre vašu	sim kuhr·tu pre vuh·shu
network	sieť	syet'

| What are the rates? | Aké sú poplatky? | uh·kair soo pop·luht·ki |

telephone

What's your phone number?
Aké je vaše telefónne číslo?   uh·kair ye vuh·she te·le·faw·ne chees·lo

The number is ...
Číslo je ...   chees·lo ye ...

Where's the nearest public phone?
Kde je najbližší verejný telefón?   kdye ye nai·blizh·shee ve·rey·nee te·le·fawn

I'd like to buy a phonecard.
Chcel/Chcela by som si kúpiť   khtsel/khtse·luh bi som si koo·pit'
telefónnu kartu. m/f   te·le·faw·nu kuhr·tu

I want to ...	Chcem ...	khtsem ...
call (Singapore)	volať	vo·luht'
	(do Singapúru)	(do sin·guh·poo·ru)
make a local call	volať miestne číslo	vo·luht' myes·ne chees·lo
reverse the	hovor na účet	ho·vor nuh oo·chet
charges	volaného	vo·luh·nair·ho

How much does ... cost?	Koľko ...?	koľ·ko ...
a (three)-minute	stoja (tri) minúty	sto·yuh (tri) mi·noo·ti
call	volania	vo·luh·ni·yuh
each extra	stojí každá	sto·yee kuhzh·da
minute	ďalšia minúta	dyuhl·shyuh mi·noo·tuh

(One) euro per minute.
(Jedno) euro za minútu.   (yed·no) e·u·ro zuh mi·noo·tu

(Forty) Slovak crowns per minute.
(Štyridsať) korún za minútu.   (shti·ri·tsat') ko·roon zuh mi·noo·tu

post office

I want to send a ...	Chcel/Chcela by som poslať ... m/f	khtsel/khtse·luh bi som pos·luht' ...
fax	fax	fuhks
letter	list	list
parcel	balík	buh·leek
postcard	pohľadnicu	po·hlyuhd·nyi·tsu

I want to buy a/an ...	Chcel/Chcela by som si kúpiť ... m/f	khtsel/khtse·luh bi som si koo·pit' ...
envelope	obálku	o·bal·ku
stamp	známku	znam·ku

Please send it (to Australia) by ...	Prosím pošlite to (do Austrálie) ...	pro·seem posh·li·tye to (do ows·tra·li·ye) ...
airmail	leteckou poštou	le·tyets·koh posh·toh
express mail	expresne	eks·pres·nye
registered mail	doporučene	do·po·ru·che·nye
surface mail	obyčajnou poštou	o·bi·chai·noh posh·toh

Is there any mail for me?
Je tam nejaká pošta pre mňa?   ye tuhm nye·yuh·ka posh·tuh pre mnyuh

bank

Where's a/an ...?	Kde je ...?	kdye ye ...
ATM	nejaký bankomat	nye·yuh·kee buhn·ko·muht
foreign exchange office	nejaká zmenáreň	nye·yuh·ka zme·na·ren'

| I'd like to ... | Chcel/Chcela by som ... m/f | khtsel/khtse·luh bi som ... |

Where can I ...?	Kde môžem ...?	kdye mwo·zhem ...
arrange a transfer	zariadiť prevod	zuh·ryuh·dyit' pre·vod
cash a cheque	preplatiť šek	pre·pluh·tyit' shek
change a travellers cheque	zameniť cestovný šek	zuh·me·nyit' tses·tov·nee shek
change money	zameniť peniaze	zuh·me·nyit' pe·ni·yuh·ze
get a cash advance	dostať vopred hotovosť	dos·tuht' vo·pred ho·to·vost'
withdraw money	vybrať peniaze	vib·ruht' pe·ni·yuh·ze

What's the ...?	Aký je ...?	uh·kee ye ...
charge for that	za to poplatok	zuh to pop·luh·tok
exchange rate	výmenný kurz	vee·men·nee kurz

It's ...	Je to ...	ye to ...
(12) euros	(dvanásť) euro	(dvuh·nast') e·u·ro
(100) Slovak crowns	(sto) korún	(sto) ko·roon
free	zadarmo	zuh·duhr·mo

What's the commission?
Aká je provízia? uh·ka ye pro·vee·zi·yuh

What time does the bank open?
O koľkej otvára banka? o koľ·key ot·va·ruh buhn·kuh

Has my money arrived yet?
Prišli už moje peniaze? prish·li uzh mo·ye pe·ni·yuh·ze

sightseeing

getting in

What time does it open/close?
*O koľkej otvárajú/
zatvárajú?* o koľ·key ot·va·ruh·yoo/
zuht·va·ruh·yoo

What's the admission charge?
Koľko je vstupné? koľ·ko ye vstup·nair

Is there a discount for students/children?
*Je nejaká zľava pre
študentov/deti?* ye nye·yuh·ka zlyuh·vuh pre
shtu·den·tov/dye·tyi

| I'd like a ... | Chcel/Chcela
by som ... m/f | khtsel/khtse·luh
bi som ... |
|---|---|---|
| catalogue | katalóg | kuh·tuh·lawg |
| guide | sprievodcu | sprye·vod·tsu |
| local map | miestnu mapu | myest·nu muh·pu |

| I'd like to see ... | Rád/Rada by som
videl/videla ... m/f | rad/ruh·duh bi som
vi·dyel/vi·dye·luh ... |
|---|---|---|
| What's that? | Čo je to? | cho ye to |
| Can I take a photo? | Môžem
fotografovať? | mwo·zhem
fo·to·gruh·fo·vuhť |

tours

When's the next ...?	Kedy je ďalší ...?	ke·di ye dyuhl·shee ...
day trip	celodenný výlet	tse·lo·den·nee vee·let
tour	zájazd	za·yuhzd

Is ... included?	Je zahrnuté ...?	ye zuh·hr·nu·tair ...
accommodation	ubytovanie	u·bi·to·vuh·ni·ye
the admission charge	vstupné	vstup·nair
food	jedlo	yed·lo

Is transport included?
Je zahrnutá doprava?　　　　ye zuh·hr·nu·ta do·pruh·vuh

How long is the tour?
Koľko trvá zájazd?　　　　koľ·ko tr·va za·yuhzd

What time should we be back?
O koľkej by sme mali byť späť?　　o koľ·key bi sme muh·li biť speť

sightseeing

castle	zámok m	za·mok
cathedral	katedrála f	kuh·ted·ra·luh
church	kostol m	kos·tol
main square	hlavné námestie n	hluhv·nair na·mes·ti·ye
monastery	kláštor m	klash·tor
monument	pamätník m	puh·met·nyeek
museum	múzeum n	moo·ze·um
old city	staré mesto n	stuh·rair mes·to
palace	palác m	puh·lats
ruins	zrúcaniny pl	zroo·tsuh·nyi·ni
stadium	štadión m	shtuh·di·awn
statue	socha f	so·khuh

shopping

enquiries

Where's a ...?	*Kde je ...?*	kdye ye ...
bank	*banka*	*buhn*·kuh
bookshop	*kníhkupectvo*	*knyeeh*·ku·pets·tvo
camera shop	*fotografický obchod*	*fo*·to·gruh·fits·kee *ob*·khod
department store	*obchodný dom*	*ob*·khod·nee dom
grocery store	*potraviny*	*po*·truh·vi·ni
market	*trh*	trh
newsagency	*predajňa novín*	pre·dai·nyuh *no*·veen
supermarket	*samoobsluha*	suh·mo·ob·slu·huh

Where can I buy (a padlock)?
Kde si môžem kúpiť   kdye si *mwo*·zhem koo·pit'
(visiaci zámok)?   (*vi*·syuh·tsi *za*·mok)

I'm looking for ...
Hľadám ...   hlyuh·dam ...

Can I look at it?
Môžem sa na to pozrieť?   mwo·zhem suh nuh to *poz*·ryet'

Do you have any others?
Máte nejaké iné?   ma·tye nye·yuh·kair *i*·nair

Does it have a guarantee?
Je na to záruka?   ye nuh to *za*·ru·kuh

Can I have it sent abroad?
Môžem si to dať poslať do   mwo·zhem si to duht' *pos*·luht' do
zahraničia?   zuh·hruh·nyi·chyuh

Can I have my ... repaired?
Môžem si dať opraviť môj ...?   mwo·zhem si duht' *o*·pruh·vit' mwoy ...

It's faulty.
Je to pokazené.   ye to *po*·kuh·ze·nair

I'd like ..., please.	*Poprosil/Poprosila*	*po*·pro·sil/*po*·pro·si·luh
	by som ... m/f	bi som ...
a bag	*tašku*	*tuhsh*·ku
a refund	*vrátenie peňazi*	*vra*·tye·ni·ye pe·nyuh·zee
to return this	*toto vrátiť*	*to*·to *vra*·tyit'

paying

How much is it?
Koľko to stojí?   *kol'*·ko to sto·yee

Can you write down the price?
Môžete napísať cenu?   *mwo*·zhe·tye *nuh*·pee·suht' *tse*·nu

That's too expensive.
To je príliš drahé.   to ye *pree*·lish *druh*·hair

What's your lowest price?
Aká je vaša najnižšia cena?   *uh*·ka ye *vuh*·shuh *nai*·nizh·shyuh *tse*·nuh

I'll give you (five) euros.
Dám vám (päť) euro.   dam vam (pet') *e*·u·ro

I'll give you (100) Slovak crowns.
Dám vám (sto) korún.   dam vam (sto) *ko*·roon

There's a mistake in the bill.
V účte je chyba.   v *ooch*·tye ye *khi*·buh

Do you accept ...?	*Príjmate ...?*	*pree*·muh·tye ...
credit cards	*kreditné karty*	*kre*·dit·nair *kuhr*·ti
debit cards	*debetné karty*	*de*·bet·nair *kuhr*·ti
travellers cheques	*cestovné šeky*	*tses*·tov·nair *she*·ki

I'd like ..., please.	*Prosím si ...*	*pro*·seem si ...
a receipt	*potvrdenie*	*pot*·vr·dye·ni·ye
my change	*môj výdavok*	mwoy *vee*·duh·vok

clothes & shoes

Can I try it on?	*Môžem si to vyskúšať?*	*mwo*·zhem si to *vis*·koo·shuht'
My size is (42).	*Moja velkosť je*	*mo*·yuh *vel'*·kost' ye
	(štyridsaťdva).	(*shti*·rid·suht'·dvuh)
It doesn't fit.	*Nesedí mi to.*	*nye*·se·dyee mi to

small	*malý*	*muh*·lee
medium	*stredný*	*stred*·nee
large	*veľký*	*vel'*·kee

books & music

I'd like a ...
newspaper
  (in English)
pen

Môžem dostať ...
noviny
(v angličtine)
pero

mwo·zhem dos·tuhť ...
no·vi·ni
(v uhn·glich·tyi·nye)
pe·ro

Is there an English-language bookshop?
Je tu anglické kníhkupectvo?   ye tu uhn·glits·kair kneeh·ku·pets·tvo

I'm looking for something by (Milan Lasica/Boris Filan).
Hľadám niečo od (Milana Lasicu/   hlyuh·dam ni·ye·cho od (mi·luh·nuh luh·si·tsu/
Borisa Filana).   bo·ri·suh fi·luh·nuh)

Can I listen to this?
Môžem si to vypočuť?   mwo·zhem si to vi·po·chuť

photography

Can you ...?
  burn a CD from
    my memory card

  develop this film
  load my film

Mohli by ste ...?
napáliť CD z
mojej pamäťovej
karty
vyvolať tento film
zaviesť môj film

mo·hli bi stye ...
nuh·pa·liť tsair·dair z
mo·yey puh·me·tyo·vey
kuhr·ti
vi·vo·luhť ten·to film
zuh·vyesť mwoy film

I need a/an ... film
for this camera.
  APS
  B&W
  colour
  slide
  (200) speed

Potrebujem ... film
do tohto fotoaparátu.
APS
čiernobiely
farebný
navíjací
(dvestovku) citlivosť

po·tre·bu·yem ... film
do to·hto fo·to·uh·puh·ra·tu
a pair es
chyer·no·bye·li
fuh·reb·nee
nuh·vee·yuh·tsee
(dve·stov·ku) tsit·li·vosť

When will it be ready?   *Kedy to bude hotové?*   ke·di to bu·dye ho·to·vair

meeting people

greetings, goodbyes & introductions

Hello/Hi.	*Dobrý deň/Ahoj.*	do·bree dyen'/*uh*·hoy
Good night.	*Dobrú noc.*	do·broo nots
Goodbye/Bye.	*Do videnia/Ahoj.*	do vi·dye·ni·yuh/*uh*·ho
Mr/Mrs	*pán/pani*	pan/*puh*·nyi
Miss	*slečna*	slech·nuh
How are you?	*Ako sa máte/máš?* pol/inf	uh·ko suh *ma*·tye/mash
Fine, thanks.	*Dobre, ďakujem.*	do·bre dyuh·ku·yem
And you?	*A vy/ty?* pol/inf	uh vi/ti
What's your name?	*Ako sa voláte/*	uh·ko suh vo·la·tye/
	voláš? pol/inf	vo·lash
My name is ...	*Volám sa ...*	vo·lam suh ...
I'm pleased to meet you.	*Teší ma.*	tye·shee muh
This is my ...	*Toto je môj/moja ...* m/f	to·to ye mwoy/*mo*·yuh ...
boyfriend	*priateľ*	pryuh·tyel'
brother	*brat*	bruht
daughter	*dcéra*	tsair·ruh
father	*otec*	o·tyets
friend	*kamarát* m	kuh·muh·rat
	kamarátka f	kuh·muh·rat·kuh
girlfriend	*priateľka*	pryuh·tyel'·kuh
husband	*manžel*	muhn·zhel
mother	*matka*	muht·kuh
partner (intimate)	*partner/partnerka* m/f	part·ner/part·ner·kuh
sister	*sestra*	ses·truh
son	*syn*	sin
wife	*manželka*	muhn·zhel·kuh
What's your ...?	*Aká je vaša ...?*	uh·ka ye vuh·shuh ...
address	*adresa*	uhd·re·suh
email address	*emailová adresa*	ee·mey·lo·va uhd·re·suh
Here's my ...	*Tu je môj ...*	tu ye mwoy ...
What's your ...?	*Aké je vaše ...?*	uh·kair ye vuh·she ...
fax number	*faxové číslo*	fuhk·so·vair chees·lo
phone number	*telefónne číslo*	te·le·fuhwn·ne chees·lo

occupations

What's your occupation?
Aké je vaše povolanie?   uh·kair ye *vuh*·she po·vo·luh·ni·ye

I'm a/an ...	Som ...	som ...
artist	*umelec/umelkyňa* m/f	u·me·lets/u·mel·ki·nyuh
businessperson	*podnikateľ* m	pod·nyi·kuh·tyel'
	podnikateľka f	pod·nyi·kuh·tyel'·kuh
farmer	*pestovateľ* m	pes·to·vuh·tyel'
	pestovateľka f	pes·to·vuh·tyel'·ka
manual worker	*robotník* m	ro·bot·nyeek
	robotníčka f	ro·bot·nyeech·kuh
office worker	*úradník* m	oo·ruhd·nyeek
	úradníčka f	oo·ruhd·nyeech·kuh
scientist	*vedecký*	ve·dyets·kee
	pracovník m	pruh·tsov·nyeek
	vedecká	ve·dets·ka
	pracovníčka f	pruh·tsov·nyeech·kuh
student	*študent/študentka* m/f	shtu·dent/shtu·dent·kuh
tradesperson	*živnostník* m	zhiv·nos·nyeek
	živnostníčka f	zhiv·nos·nyeech·kuh

background

Where are you from?	*Odkiaľ ste?*	od·kyuhl' stye
I'm from ...	*Som z ...*	som z ...
Australia	*Austrálie*	ows·tra·li·ye
Canada	*Kanady*	kuh·nuh·di
England	*Anglicka*	uhng·lits·kuh
New Zealand	*Nového Zélandu*	no·vair·ho zair·luhn·du
the USA	*USA*	oo·es·a

Are you married?	*Ste ženatý/vydatá?* m/f	stye zhe·nuh·tee/vi·duh·ta
I'm ...	*Som ...*	som ...
married	*ženatý/vydatá* m/f	zhe·nuh·tee/vi·duh·ta
single	*slobodný* m	slo·bod·nee
	slobodná f	slo·bod·na

age

How old ...?	Koľko ... rokov?	koľ·ko ... ro·kov
are you	máte/máš pol/inf	ma·tye/mash
is your daughter	má vaša dcéra	ma vuh·shuh tsair·ruh
is your son	má váš syn	ma vash sin

| I'm ... years old. | Ja mám ... rokov. | yuh mam ... ro·kov |
| He/She is ... years old. | On/Ona má ... rokov. | on/onuh ma ... ro·kov |

feelings

I'm (not) ...	(Nie) Je mi ...	(ni·ye) ye mi ...
Are you ...?	Je vám ...?	ye vam ...
cold	zima	zi·muh
hot	teplo	tye·plo

I'm (not) ...	(Nie) Som ...	(ni·ye) som ...
Are you ...?	Ste ...?	stye ...
happy	šťastný/šťastná m/f	shtyuhs·nee/shtyuhs·na
hungry	hladný/hladná m/f	hluhd·nee/hluhd·na
sad	smutný/smutná m/f	smut·nee/smut·na
thirsty	smädný/smädná m/f	smed·nee/smed·na

entertainment

going out

Where can I find ...?	Kde nájdem ...?	kdye nai·dyem ...
clubs	kluby	klu·bi
gay venues	podniky pre	pod·nyi·ki pre
	homosexuálov	ho·mo·sek·su·a·lov
pubs	krčmy	krch·mi

I feel like going to a/the ...	Mám chuť ísť ...	mam khuť eesť ...
concert	na koncert	nuh kon·tsert
movies	do kina	do ki·nuh
restaurant	do reštaurácie	do resh·tow·ra·tsi·ye
theatre	do divadla	do dyi·vuhd·luh

interests

Do you like …?	*Máte radi …?*	*ma·tye ruh·di …*
I like …	*Mám rád/rada …* m/f	mam rad/*ruh·duh …*
I don't like …	*Nemám rád/ rada …* m/f	*nye·*mam rad/ *ruh·duh …*
art	*umenie*	*u·*me·ni·ye
cooking	*varenie*	*vuh·*re·ni·ye
movies	*filmy*	*fil·*mi
nightclubs	*nočné kluby*	*noch·*nair *klu·*bi
reading	*čítanie*	*chee·*tuh·ni·ye
shopping	*nakupovanie*	*nuh·*ku·po·vuh·ni·ye
sport	*šport*	shport
travelling	*cestovanie*	*tses·*to·vuh·ni·ye
Do you like to …?	*Radi …?*	*ruh·*dyi …
dance	*tancujete*	*tuhn·*tsu·ye·tye
go to concerts	*chodíte na koncerty*	*kho·*dyee·tye nuh *kon·*tser·ti
listen to music	*počúvate hudbu*	*po·*choo·vuh·tye *hud·*bu

food & drink

finding a place to eat

Can you recommend a …?	*Môžete mi odporučiť …?*	*mwo·*zhe·tye mi *od·*po·ru·chit' …
bar	*bar*	buhr
café	*kaviareň*	*kuh·*vyuh·ren'
restaurant	*reštauráciu*	*resh·*tow·ra·tsi·yu
I'd like …, please.	*Chcel/Chcela by som …, prosím.* m/f	khtsel/*khtse·*luh bi som … *pro·*seem
a table for (four)	*stôl pre (štyroch)*	stwol pre (*shti·*rokh)
the nonsmoking section	*nefajčiarsku časť*	*nye·*fai·chyuhr·sku chuhst'
the smoking section	*fajčiarsku časť*	*fai·*chyuhr·sku chuhst'

ordering food

breakfast	*raňajky* pl	ruh-nyai-ki
lunch	*obed* m	o-bed
dinner	*večera* f	ve-che-ruh
snack	*občerstvenie* n	ob-cherst-ve-ni-ye

| What would you recommend? | *Čo by ste mi odporučili?* | cho bi stye mi od-po-ru-chi-li |

I'd like (the) ..., please. *Prosím si ...* pro-seem si ...

bill	*účet*	oo-chet
drink list	*nápojový lístok*	na-po-yo-vee lees-tok
menu	*jedálny lístok*	ye-dal-ni lees-tok
that dish	*toto jedlo*	to-to yed-lo

drinks

(cup of) coffee/tea ...	*(šálka) kávy/čaju ...*	(shal-kuh) ka-vi/chuh-yu ...
with milk	*s mliekom*	s mlye-kom
without sugar	*bez cukru*	bez tsuk-ru

(orange) juice	*(pomarančový) džús* m	(po-muh-ruhn-cho-vee) dyoos
soft drink	*nealkoholický nápoj* m	nye-uhl-ko-ho-lits-kee na-poy
(boiled/mineral) water	*(prevarená/minerálna) voda* f	(pre-vuh-re-na/mi-ne-ral-nuh) vo-duh

in the bar

I'll have ...	*Dám si ...*	dam si ...
I'll buy you a drink.	*Kúpim ti/vám drink.* inf/pol	koo-pim tyi/vam drink
What would you like?	*Čo si dáš/dáte?* inf/pol	cho si dash/da-tye
Cheers!	*Nazdravie!*	nuhz-druh-vi-ye

| a shot of (whisky) | *štamperlík (whisky)* | shtuhm-per-leek (vis-ki) |
| a bottle/glass of beer | *fľaša/pohár piva* | flyuh-shuh/po-har pi-vuh |

a bottle/glass of ...wine	*fľaša/pohár ... vína*	flyuh-shuh/po-har ... vee-nuh
red	*červeného*	cher-ve-nair-ho
sparkling	*šumivého*	shu-mi-vair-ho
white	*bieleho*	bye-le-ho

self-catering

What's the local speciality?
Čo je miestna špecialita? — cho ye *myes*-nuh *shpe*-tsyuh-li-tuh

What's that?
Čo je to? — cho ye to

How much is (a kilo of cheese)?
Koľko stojí (kilo syra)? — *koľ*-ko *sto*-yee (*ki*-lo *si*-ruh)

I'd like ...	*Môžem dostať ...*	mwo-zhem *dos*-tuht' ...
(100) grams	*(sto) gramov*	(sto) *gruh*-mov
(two) kilos	*(dve) kilá*	(dve) *ki*-la
(three) pieces	*(tri) kusy*	(tri) *ku*-si
(six) slices	*(šesť) plátkov*	(shesť) *plat*-kov

Less.	*Menej.*	*me*-nyey
Enough.	*Stačí.*	*stuh*-chee
More.	*Viac.*	vyuhts

special diets & allergies

Is there a vegetarian restaurant near here?
Je tu nablízku vegetariánska — ye tu nuh-*bleez*-ku ve-ge-tuh-ri-yan-skuh
reštaurácia? — resh-tow-ra-tsi-yuh

Do you have vegetarian food?
Máte vegetariánske jedlá? — ma-tye ve-ge-tuh-ri-yan-ske *yed*-la

Could you prepare	*Mohli by ste pripraviť*	mo-hli bi stye *pri*-pruh-vit'
a meal without ...?	*jedlo bez ...?*	*yed*-lo bez ...
butter	*masla*	*muhs*-luh
eggs	*vajec*	*vuh*-yets
meat stock	*mäsového vývaru*	me-so-vair-ho *vee*-vuh-ru

I'm allergic to ...	*Som alergický/*	som uh-*ler*-gits-kee/
	alergická na ... m/f	uh-*ler*-gits-ka nuh ...
dairy produce	*mliečne produkty*	*mlyech*-ne pro-duk-ti
gluten	*lepok*	*le*-pok
MSG	*zvýrazňovač*	zvee-ruhz-nyo-vuhch
	chute	*khu*-tye
nuts	*orechy*	*o*-re-khi
seafood	*dary mora*	*duh*-ri mo-ruh

menu reader

balkánský šalát m	*buhl*-kan-ski *shuh*-lat	*lettuce, tomato, onion & cheese salad*
bravčové pečené s rascou n	*bruhv*-cho-vair *pe*-che-nair s *ruhs*-tsoh	*roast pork with caraway seeds*
držková polievka f	*drzh*-ko-va *po*-lyev-kuh	*sliced tripe soup*
dusené hovädzie na prírodno n	*du*-se-nair *ho*-ve-dzye nuh *pree*-rod-no	*braised beef slices in sauce*
guláš m	*gu*-lash	*thick, spicy beef & potato soup*
hovädzí guláš m	*ho*-ve-dzee *gu*-lash	*beef chunks in brown sauce*
hovädzí vývar m	*ho*-ve-dzee *vee*-vuhr	*beef in broth*
hrachová polievka f	*hruh*-kho-va *po*-lyev-kuh	*thick pea soup with bacon*
jablkový závin m	*yuh*-bl-ko-vee *za*-vin	*apple strudel*
kapor na víne m	*kuh*-por nuh *vee*-nye	*carp braised in wine*
koložvárska kapusta f	*ko*-lozh-var-skuh *kuh*-pus-tuh	*goulash with beef, pork, lamb & sauerkraut in a cream sauce*
krokety m pl	*kro*-ke-ti	*deep-fried mashed potato*
kuracia polievka f	*ku*-ruh-tsyuh *po*-lyev-kuh	*chicken soup*
kurací paprikáš m	*ku*-ruh-tsee *puhp*-ri-kash	*chicken braised in red (paprika) sauce*
kyslá uhorka f	*kis*-la *u*-hor-kuh	*dill pickle (gherkin)*
opékané zemiaky f pl	*o*-pe-kuh-nair *ze*-myuh-ki	*fried potatoes*
ovocné knedle f pl	*o*-vots-nair *kned*-le	*fruit dumplings*
palacinky f pl	*puh*-luh-tsin-ki	*pancakes*
paradajková polievka s cibuľkou f	*puh*-ruh-dai-ko-va *po*-lyev-kuh s *tsi*-buľ-koh	*tomato & onion soup*

pečené zemiaky f pl	pe-che-nair ze-myuh-ki	roast potatoes
plnená paprika v paradajkovej omáčke f	pl-nye-na puhp-ri-kuh v puh-ruh-dai-ko-vey o-mach-ke	capsicum stuffed with minced meat & rice, served with tomato sauce
polievka z bažanta f	po-lyev-kuh z buh-zhuhn-tuh	pheasant soup
praženica f	pruh-zhe-nyi-tsuh	scrambled eggs
prírodný rezeň m	pree-rod-nee re-zen'	unbreaded pork or veal schnitzel
rizoto n	ri-zo-to	mixture of pork, onion, peas & rice
ruské vajcia n pl	rus-kair vai-tsyuh	hard-boiled egg, potato & salami, with mayonnaise
rybacia polievka f	ri-buh-tsyuh po-lyev-kuh	fish soup
ryžový nákyp m	ri-zho-vee na-kip	rice soufflé
salámový tanier s oblohou m	suh-la-mo-vee tuh-nyer s ob-lo-hoh	salami platter with fresh or pickled vegetables
sviečková na smotane f	svyech-ko-va nuh smo-tuh-nye	roast beef with sour cream sauce & spices
špenát m	shpe-nat	finely chopped spinach, cooked with onion, garlic & cream
šunka pečená s vajcom f	shun-kuh pe-che-na s vai-tsom	fried ham with egg
tatárska omáčka f	tuh-tar-skuh o-mach-kuh	creamy tartar sauce
tatársky biftek m	tuh-tar-ski bif-tek	raw steak
teľacie pečené n	tye-lyuh-tsye pe-che-nair	roast veal
tlačenka s octom a cibuľou f	tluh-chen-kuh s ots-tom uh tsi-bu-loh	jellied meat loaf with vinegar & onion
vyprážané rybacie filé n	vi-pra-zhuh-nair ri-buh-tsye fi-lair	fillet of fish fried in breadcrumbs

emergencies

basics

Help!	Pomoc!	*po*-mots
Stop!	Stoj!	stoy
Go away!	Choďte preč!	*khoď*-tye prech
Thief!	Zlodej!	*zlo*-dyey
Fire!	Oheň!	*o*-hen'
Watch out!	Pozor!	*po*-zor
Call a doctor!	Zavolajte lekára!	zuh-vo-lai-tye *le*-ka-ruh
Call an ambulance!	Zavolajte záchranku!	zuh-vo-lai-tye *zakh*-ruhn-ku
Call the police!	Zavolajte políciu!	zuh-vo-lai-tye *po*-lee-tsi-yu

It's an emergency!
Je to pohotovostný prípad!   ye to *po*-ho-to-vos-nee *pree*-puhd

Could you help me, please?
Môžete mi prosím pomóct?   *mwo*-zhe-tye mi *pro*-seem *po*-mwotst'

I have to use the telephone.
Potrebujem telefón.   po-tre-bu-yem *te*-le-fawn

I'm lost.
Stratil/Stratila som sa. m/f   *struh*-tyil/*struh*-tyi-luh som suh

Where are the toilets?
Kde sú tu záchody?   kdye soo tu *za*-kho-di

police

Where's the police station?
Kde je policajná stanica?   kdye ye *po*-li-tsai-na *stuh*-nyi-tsuh

I want to report an offence. (serious/minor)
Chcem nahlásiť zločin/priestupok.   khtsem *nuh*-hla-sit' *zlo*-chin/*prye*-stu-pok

I've been ...	Bol/Bola som ... m/f	bol/*bo*-luh som ...
assaulted	prepadnutý m	pre-*puhd*-nu-tee
	prepadnutá f	pre-*puhd*-nu-ta
raped	znásilnený m	zna-sil-*nye*-nee
	znásilnená f	zna-sil-*nye*-na
robbed	okradnutý m	o-*kruhd*-nu-tee
	okradnutá f	o-*kruhd*-nu-ta

I've lost my ...	Stratil/Stratila som ... m/f	struh·tyil/struh·tyi·luh som ...
My ... was/were stolen.	Ukradli mi ...	u·kruhd·li mi ...
backpack	plecniak	plets·ni·yuhk
bags	batožinu	buh·to·zhi·nu
credit card	kreditnú kartu	kre·dit·noo kuhr·tu
handbag	kabelku	kuh·bel·ku
jewellery	šperky	shper·ki
money	peniaze	pe·nyuh·ze
passport	cestovný pas	tses·tov·nee puhs
travellers cheques	cestovné šeky	tses·tov·nair she·ki
wallet	peňaženku	pe·nyuh·zhen·ku
I want to contact my ...	Chcem sa spojiť s ...	khtsem suh spo·yit' s ...
consulate	mojím konzulátom	mo·yeem kon·zu·la·tom
embassy	mojou ambasádou	mo·yoh uhm·buh·sa·doh

health

medical needs

Where's the nearest ...?	Kde je najbližší/ najbližšia ...? m/f	kdye ye nai·blizh·shee/ nai·blizh·shyuh ...
dentist	zubár m	zu·bar
doctor	doktor m	dok·tor
hospital	nemocnica f	ne·mots·nyi·tsuh
(night) pharmacist	(pohotovostná) lekáreň f	(po·ho·to·vost·na) le·ka·ren'

I need a doctor (who speaks English).
Potrebujem lekára, (ktorý hovorí po anglicky).
po·tre·bu·yem le·ka·ruh (kto·ree ho·vo·ree po uhng·lits·ki)

Could I see a female doctor?
Mohla by som navštíviť ženského lekára?
mo·hluh bi som nuhv·shtyee·vit' zhen·skair·ho le·ka·ruh

I've run out of my medication.
Minuli sa mi lieky.
mi·nu·li suh mi li·ye·ki

symptoms, conditions & allergies

| I'm sick. | Som chorý/chorá. m/f | som kho·ree/kho·ra |
| It hurts here. | Tu ma to bolí. | tu muh to bo·lee |

I have (a) ...		
asthma	Mám astmu.	mam uhst·mu
bronchitis	Mám zápal priedušiek.	mam za·puhl prye·du·shyek
constipation	Mám zápchu.	mam zap·khu
cough	Mám kašeľ.	mam kuh·shel
diarrhoea	Mám hnačku.	mam hnuhch·ku
fever	Mám horúčku.	mam ho·rooch·ku
headache	Bolí ma hlava.	bo·lee muh hluh·vuh
heart condition	Mám srdcovú príhodu.	mam srd·tso·voo pree·ho·du
nausea	Je mi nazvracanie.	ye mi nuhz·vruh·tsuh·ni·ye
pain	Mám bolesti.	mam bo·les·tyi
sore throat	Bolí ma hrdlo.	bo·lee muh hrd·lo
toothache	Bolí ma zub.	bo·lee muh zub

I'm allergic to ...	Som alergický/	som uh·ler·gits·kee/
	alergická na... m/f	uh·ler·gits·ka nuh ...
antibiotics	antibiotiká	uhn·ti·bi·o·ti·ka
anti-inflammatories	protizápalové lieky	pro·ti·za·puh·lo·vair lye·ki
aspirin	aspirín	uhs·pi·reen
bees	včely	fche·li
codeine	kodeín	ko·de·een
penicillin	penicilín	pe·ni·tsi·leen

antiseptic	antiseptikum n	uhn·ti·sep·ti·kum
bandage	obväz m	ob·vez
condoms	kondómy m pl	kon·daw·mi
contraceptives	antikoncepcia f	uhn·ti·kon·tsep·tsi·yuh
diarrhoea medicine	lieky proti hnačke m	li·ye·ki pro·tyi hnuhch·ke
insect repellent	repelent proti hmyzu m	re·pe·lent pro·tyi hmi·zu
laxatives	preháňadlá n pl	pre·ha·nyuhd·la
painkillers	analgetiká n pl	uh·nuhl·ge·ti·ka
rehydration salts	rehydratujúce soli f pl	re·hid·ruh·tu·yoo·tse so·li
sleeping tablets	tabletky na spanie f pl	tuhb·let·ki nuh spuh·ni·ye

english–slovak dictionary

Slovak nouns in this dictionary have their gender indicated by ⓜ (masculine), ⓕ (feminine) or ⓝ (neuter). If it's a plural noun, you'll also see pl. Adjectives are given in the masculine form only. Words are also marked as a (adjective), v (verb), sg (singular), pl (plural), inf (informal) or pol (polite) where necessary.

A

accident *nehoda* ⓕ *nye*-ho-duh
accommodation *ubytovanie* ⓝ *u*-bi-to-vuh-ni-ye
adaptor *rozvodka* ⓕ *roz*-vod-kuh
address *adresa* ⓕ *uh*-dre-suh
after *po* po
air-conditioned *klimatizovaný* *kli*-muh-ti-zo-vuh-nee
airplane *lietadlo* ⓝ *li*-ye-tuhd-lo
airport *letisko* ⓝ *le*-tis-ko
alcohol *alkohol* ⓜ *uhl*-ko-hol
all (everything) *všetko* *fshet*-ko
allergy *alergia* ⓕ *uh*-ler-gi-yuh
ambulance *ambulancia* ⓕ *uhm*-bu-luhn-tsi-yuh
and *a* uh
ankle *členok* ⓜ *chle*-nok
arm *rameno* ⓝ *ruh*-me-no
ashtray *popolník* ⓜ *po*-pol-nyeek
ATM *bankomat* ⓜ *buhn*-ko-muht

B

baby *dieťatko* ⓝ *di*-ye-tyuht-ko
back (body) *chrbát* ⓜ *khr*-baat
backpack *ruksak* ⓜ *ruk*-suhk
bad *zlý* zlee
bag *taška* ⓕ *tuhsh*-kuh
baggage claim *úložňa batožiny* ⓕ
  oo-lozh-nyuh buh-to-zhi-ni
bank *banka* ⓕ *buhn*-kuh
bar *bar* ⓜ buhr
bathroom *kúpeľňa* ⓕ *koo*-pel'-nyuh
battery *batéria* ⓕ *buh*-tair-ri-yuh
beautiful *krásny* *kras*-ni
bed *posteľ* ⓕ *pos*-tyel'
beer *pivo* ⓝ *pi*-vo
before *pred* pred
behind *za* zuh
bicycle *bicykel* ⓜ *bi*-tsi-kel
big *veľký* *vel'*-kee
bill *účet* ⓜ *oo*-chet
black *čierny* *chyer*-ni
blanket *prikrývka* ⓕ *pri*-kreev-kuh

blood group *krvná skupina* ⓕ *krv*-na *sku*-pi-nuh
blue *modrý* *mod*-ree
boat *loď* ⓕ lod'
book (make a reservation) v *rezervovať*
  re-zer-vo-vuht'
bottle *fľaša* ⓕ *flyuh*-shuh
bottle opener *otvárač na fľašu* ⓜ
  ot-va-ruhch nuh *flyuh*-shu
boy *chlapec* ⓜ *khluh*-pets
brakes (car) *brzdy* ⓕ pl *brz*-di
breakfast *raňajky* pl *ruh*-nyai-ki
broken (faulty) *pokazený* po-kuh-ze-nee
bus *autobus* ⓜ *ow*-to-bus
business *obchod* ⓜ *ob*-khod
buy *kúpiť* *koo*-pit'

C

café *kaviareň* ⓕ *kuh*-vyuh-ren'
camera *fotoaparát* ⓜ *fo*-to-uh-puh-rat
camp site *táborisko* ⓝ *ta*-bo-ris-ko
cancel *zrušiť* *zru*-shit'
can opener *otvárač na konzervu* ⓜ
  ot-va-ruhch nuh kon-zer-vu
car *auto* ⓝ *ow*-to
cash *hotovosť* ⓕ *ho*-to-vost'
cash (a cheque) v *preplatiť (šek)* *prep*-luh-tyit' (shek)
cell phone *mobil* ⓜ *mo*-bil
centre *centrum* ⓝ *tsen*-trum
change (money) v *zameniť (peniaze)*
  zuh-me-nyit' (pe-ni-yuh-ze)
cheap *lacný* *luhts*-nee
check (bill) *účet* ⓜ *oo*-chet
check-in *registrácia* ⓕ *re*-gis-tra-tsi-yuh
chest *hruď* ⓕ hrud'
child *dieťa* ⓝ *di*-ye-tyuh
cigarette *cigareta* ⓕ *tsi*-guh-re-tuh
city *mesto* ⓝ *mes*-to
clean a *čistý* *chis*-tee
closed *zatvorený* *zuht*-vo-re-nee
coffee *káva* ⓕ *ka*-vuh
coins *mince* ⓕ pl *min*-tse
cold a *studený* *stu*-dye-nee

collect call *hovor na účet volaného* m
  ho-vor nuh oo-chet vo-luh-nair-ho
come *prísť* preest'
computer *počítač* m *po-chee-tuhch*
condom *kondóm* m *kon-duhwm*
contact lenses *kontaktné šošovky* f pl
  kon-tuhkt-nair sho-shov-ki
cook v *variť vuh-rit'*
cost *cena* f *tse-nuh*
credit card *kreditná karta* f *kre-dit-na kuhr-tuh*
cup *šálka* f *shaal-ka*
currency exchange *výmena peňazí* f
  vee-me-nuh pe-nyuh-zee
customs (immigration) *colnica* f *tsol-nyi-tsuh*

D

dangerous *nebezpečný* *ne-bez-pech-nee*
date (time) *dátum* m *da-tum*
day *deň* m *dyen'*
delay *meškanie* f *mesh-kuh-ni-ye*
dentist *zubár* m *zu-bar*
depart *odchádzať* *od-kha-dzat'*
diaper *plienka* f *pli-yen-kuh*
dictionary *slovník* m *slov-nyeek*
dinner *večera* f *ve-che-ruh*
direct a *priamy pryuh-mi*
dirty *špinavý shpi-nuh-vee*
disabled *postihnutý pos-tyih-nu-tee*
discount *zľava* f *zlyuh-vuh*
doctor *lekár* m *le-kar*
double bed *dvojitá posteľ* f *dvo-yi-ta pos-tyel'*
double room *dvojposteľová izba* f
  dvoy-pos-tye-lyo-va iz-buh
drink *nápoj* m *na-poy*
drive v *riadiť ryuh-dyit'*
drivers licence *vodičský preukaz* m
  vo-dyich-skee pre-u-kuhz
drug (illicit) *droga* f *dro-guh*
dummy (pacifier) *cumeľ* m *tsu-meľ*

E

ear *ucho* n *u-kho*
east *východ* *vee-khod*
eat *jesť* yest'
economy class *ekonomická trieda* f
  e-ko-no-mits-ka trye-duh
electricity *elektrika* f *e-lek-tri-kuh*
elevator *výťah* m *vee-tyah*
email *email* m *ee-meyl*
embassy *veľvyslanectvo* n *veľ-vis-luh-nyets-tvo*
emergency *pohotovosť* f *po-ho-to-vost'*

English (language) *angličtina* f *uhng-lich-tyi-nuh*
entrance *vchod* m *vkhod*
evening *večer* m *ve-cher*
exchange rate *výmenný kurz* m *vee-men-nee kurz*
exit *východ* m *vee-khod*
expensive *drahý druh-hee*
express mail *expresná pošta* f *eks-pres-na posh-tuh*
eye *oko* n *o-ko*

F

far *ďaleko* *dyuh-le-ko*
fast *rýchly reekh-li*
father *otec* m *o-tyets*
film (camera) *film* m film
finger *prst* m *prst*
first-aid kit *lekárnička* f *le-kar-nyich-kuh*
first class *prvá trieda* f *pr-va trye-duh*
fish *ryba* f *ri-buh*
food *jedlo* n *yed-lo*
foot *noha* f *no-huh*
fork *vidlička* f *vid-lich-kuh*
free (of charge) *zadarmo* *zuh-duhr-mo*
friend *priateľ/priateľka* m/f *pryuh-teľ /prya-tyeľ-ka*
fruit *ovocie* n *o-vo-tsye*
full *plný* *pl-nee*
funny *smiešny smyesh-ni*

G

gift *dar* m *duhr*
girl *dievča* n *di-yev-chuh*
glass (drinking) *pohár* m *po-har*
glasses *okuliare* pl *o-ku-lyuh-re*
go *ísť* eest'
good *dobrý dob-ree*
green *zelený ze-le-nee*
guide *sprievodca* m *sprye-vod-tsuh*

H

half *polovica* f *po-lo-vi-tsuh*
hand *ruka* f *ru-kuh*
handbag *kabelka* f *kuh-bel-kuh*
happy *šťastný shtyuhs-nee*
have *mať muhť*
he *on* on
head *hlava* f *hluh-vuh*
heart *srdce* n *srd-tse*
heat *teplo* n *tyep-lo*
heavy *ťažký tyuhzh-kee*
help v *pomôcť pom-wotst'*

here *tu* tu
high *vysoký* vi-so-kee
highway *diaľnica* ① di-yuhl-nyi-tsuh
hike v *ísť na turistiku* eest' nuh tu-ris-ti-ku
holiday *dovolenka* ① do-vo-len-kuh
homosexual *homosexuál* ⑩ ho-mo-sek-su-al
hospital *nemocnica* ① ne-mots-nyi-tsuh
hot *horúci* ho-roo-tsi
hotel *hotel* ⑩ ho-tel
hungry *hladný* hluhd-nee
husband *manžel* ⑩ muhn-zhel

I

I *ja* yuh
identification (card) *občiansky preukaz* ⑩ ob-chyuhns-ki pre-u-kuhz
ill *chorý* kho-ree
important *dôležitý* dwo-le-zhi-tee
included *zahrnutý* zuh-hr-nu-tee
injury *poranenie* ⑩ po-ruh-nye-ni-ye
insurance *poistenie* ⑩ po-is-tye-ni-ye
Internet *internet* ⑩ in-ter-net
interpreter *tlmočník* ⑩ tl-moch-nyeek

J

jewellery *šperky* ⑩ pl shper-ki
job *zamestnanie* ⑩ zuh-mest-nuh-ni-ye

K

key *kľúč* ⑩ kl'ooch
kilogram *kilogram* ⑩ ki-log-ruhm
kitchen *kuchyňa* ① ku-khi-nyuh
knife *nôž* ⑩ nwozh

L

laundry (place) *práčovňa* ① pra-chov-nyuh
lawyer *právnik* ⑩ prav-nyik
left (direction) *vľavo* vluh-vo
left-luggage office *úschovňa batožiny* ① oos-khov-nyuh buh-to-zhi-ni
leg *noha* ① no-huh
lesbian *lesbia* ① les-bi-yuh
less *menej* me-nyey
letter (mail) *list* ⑩ list
lift (elevator) *výťah* ⑩ vee-tyah
light *svetlo* ⑩ svet-lo
like v *mať rád* muht' rad

lock *zámok* ⑩ za-mok
long *dlhý* dl-hee
lost *stratený* struh-tye-nee
lost-property office *straty a nálezy* ① struh-ti uh na-le-zi
love v *ľúbiť* lyoo-bit'
luggage *batožina* ① buh-to-zhi-nuh
lunch *obed* ⑩ o-bed

M

mail *pošta* ① posh-tuh
man *muž* ⑩ muzh
map *mapa* ① muh-puh
market *trh* ⑩ trh
matches *zápalky* ① pl za-puhl-ki
meat *mäso* ⑩ me-so
medicine *liek* ⑩ li-yek
menu *jedálny lístok* ⑩ ye-dal-ni lees-tok
message *správa* ① spra-vuh
milk *mlieko* ⑩ mli-ye-ko
minute *minúta* ① mi-noo-tuh
mobile phone *mobil* ⑩ mo-bil
money *peniaze* ① pl pe-ni-yuh-ze
month *mesiac* ⑩ me-syuhts
morning *ráno* ⑩ ra-no
mother *matka* ① muht-kuh
motorcycle *motorka* ① mo-tor-kuh
motorway *hlavná cesta* ① hluhv-na tses-tuh
mouth *ústa* pl oos-tuh
music *hudba* ① hud-buh

N

name *meno* ⑩ me-no
napkin *obrúsok* ⑩ ob-roo-sok
nappy *plienka* ① plyen-kuh
near *blízko* bleez-ko
neck *krk* ⑩ krk
new *nový* no-vee
news *správy* ① pl spra-vi
newspaper *noviny* pl no-vi-ni
night *noc* ① nots
no *nie* ni-ye
noisy *hlučný* hluch-nee
nonsmoking *nefajčiarsky* ne-fai-chyuhr-ski
north *sever* se-ver
nose *nos* ⑩ nos
now *teraz* te-ruhz
number *číslo* ⑩ chees-lo

O

oil (engine) *olej* (m) o-ley
old *starý* stuh-ree
one-way ticket *jednosmerný lístok* (m)
　yed-no-smer-nee lees-tok
open a *otvorený* ot-vo-re-nee
outside *vonku* von-ku

P

package *balík* (m) buh-leek
paper *papier* (m) puh-pyer
park (car) v *zaparkovať* zuh-puhr-ko-vuht'
passport *cestovný pas* (m) tses-tov-nee puhs
pay *platiť* pluh-tyit'
pen *pero* (n) pe-ro
petrol *benzín* (m) ben-zeen
pharmacy *lekáreň* (f) le-ka-ren'
phonecard *telefónna karta* (f)
　te-le-fuhwn-nuh kuhr-tuh
photo *fotografia* (f) fo-to-gruh-fi-yuh
plate *tanier* (m) tuh-ni-yer
police *polícia* (f) po-lee-tsi-yuh
postcard *pohľadnica* (f) poh-lyuhd-nyi-tsuh
post office *pošta* (f) posh-tuh
pregnant *tehotná* tye-hot-na
price *cena* (f) tse-nuh

Q

quiet *tichý* tyi-khee

R

rain *dážď* (m) dazhd'
razor *žiletka* (f) zhi-let-kuh
receipt *potvrdenie* (n) pot-vr-dye-ni-ye
red *červený* cher-ve-nee
refund *vrátenie peňazí* (n)
　vra-tye-ni-ye pe-nyuh-zee
registered mail *doporučená pošta* (f)
　do-po-ru-che-na posh-tuh
rent v *prenajať* pre-nuh-yuht'
repair v *opraviť* o-pruh-vit'
reservation *rezervácia* (f) re-zer-va-tsi-yuh
restaurant *reštaurácia* (f) resh-tow-ra-tsi-yuh
return v *vrátiť* vra-tyit'
return ticket *spiatočný lístok* (m)
　spyuh-toch-nee lees-tok
right (direction) *vpravo* vpruh-vo

S

road *cesta* (f) tses-tuh
room *izba* (f) iz-buh

S

safe a *bezpečný* bez-pech-nee
sanitary napkin *dámska vložka* (f) dams-kuh
　vlozh-kuh
seat *sedadlo* (n) se-duhd-lo
send *poslať* pos-luht'
service station *benzínová stanica* (f)
　ben-zee-no-va stuh-nyi-tsuh
sex *sex* (m) seks
shampoo *šampón* (m) shuhm-puhwn
share (a dorm) *deliť sa (o izbu)*
　dye-lit' suh (o iz-bu)
shaving cream *krém na holenie* (m)
　krairm nuh ho-le-ni-ye
she *ona* o-nuh
sheet (bed) *plachta* (f) pluhkh-tuh
shirt *košeľa* (f) ko-she-lyuh
shoes *topánky* (f) pl to-pan-ki
shop *obchod* (m) ob-khod
short *krátky* krat-ki
shower *sprcha* (f) spr-khuh
single room *jednoposteľová izba* (f)
　yed-no-pos-tye-lyo-va iz-buh
skin *koža* (f) ko-zhuh
skirt *sukňa* (f) suk-nyuh
sleep v *spať* spuht'
Slovakia *Slovensko* (n) slo-vens-ko
Slovak (language) *slovenčina* (f) slo-ven-chi-na
Slovak a *slovenský* slo-vens-kee
slowly *pomaly* po-muh-li
small *malý* muh-lee
smoke (cigarettes) v *fajčiť* fai-chit'
soap *mydlo* (n) mid-lo
some *nejaký* nye-yuh-kee
soon *skoro* sko-ro
south *juh* yooh
souvenir shop *obchod so suvenírmi* (m)
　ob-khod zo su-ve-neer-mi
speak *hovoriť* ho-vo-rit'
spoon *lyžica* (f) li-zhi-tsuh
stamp *známka* (f) znam-kuh
stand-by ticket *lístok na čakacom zozname* (m)
　lees-tok nuh chuh-kuh-tsom zoz-nuh-me
station (train) *železničná stanica* (f)
　zhe-lez-nich-na stuh-ni-tsuh
stomach *žalúdok* (m) zhuh-loo-dok
stop v *stáť* stat'

stop (bus) *autobusová zastávka* ⓕ
ow-to-bu-so-va zuhs-tav-kuh

street *ulica* ⓕ u-li-tsuh

student *študent/študentka* ⓜ/ⓕ
shtu-dent/shtu-dent-ka

sun *slnko* ⓝ sln-ko

sunscreen *ochranný faktor* ⓜ o-khruhn-nee fuhk-tor

swim v *plávať* pla-vuhť

T

tampons *tampóny* ⓜ pl tuhm-puhw-ni

taxi *taxík* ⓜ tuhk-seek

teaspoon *lyžička* ⓕ li-zhich-ku

teeth *zuby* ⓜ pl zu-bi

telephone *telefón* ⓜ te-le-fuhwn

television *televízia* ⓕ te-le-vee-zi-yuh

temperature (weather) *teplota* ⓕ tep-lo-tuh

tent *stan* ⓜ stuhn

that (one) *to* to

they *oni* o-nyi

thirsty *smädný* smed-nee

this (one) *toto* to-to

throat *hrdlo* ⓝ hrd-lo

ticket *lístok* ⓜ lees-tok

time *čas* ⓜ chuhs

tired *unavený* u-nuh-ve-nee

tissues *servítky* ⓕ pl ser-veet-ki

today *dnes* dnyes

toilet *záchod* ⓜ za-khod

tomorrow *zajtra* zai-truh

tonight *dnes večer* dnyes ve-cher

toothbrush *zubná kefka* ⓕ zub-na kef-kuh

toothpaste *zubná pasta* ⓕ zub-na puhs-tuh

torch (flashlight) *baterka* ⓕ buh-ter-kuh

tour *zájazd* ⓜ za-yuhzd

tourist office *turistická kancelária* ⓕ
tu-ris-tits-ka kuhn-tse-la-ri-yuh

towel *uterák* ⓜ u-tye-rak

train *vlak* ⓜ vluhk

translate *prekladať* pre-kluh-duhť

travel agency *cestovná kancelária* ⓕ
tses-tov-na kuhn-tse-la-ri-yuh

travellers cheque *cestovný šek* ⓜ tses-tov-nee shek

trousers *nohavice* pl no-huh-vi-tse

twin beds *dve oddelené postele* ⓕ pl
dve od-dye-le-nair pos-tye-le

tyre *pneumatika* ⓕ pne-u-muh-ti-kuh

U

underwear *spodné prádlo* ⓝ spod-nair prad-lo

urgent *súrny* soor-ni

V

vacant *voľný* voly-nee

vacation *dovolenka* ⓕ do-vo-len-kuh

vegetable *zelenina* ⓕ ze-le-nyi-nuh

vegetarian a *vegetariánsky* ve-ge-tuh-ri-yans-ki

visa *vízum* ⓝ vee-zum

W

waiter *čašník* ⓜ chuhsh-nyeek

walk v *kráčať* kra-chuhť

wallet *peňaženka* ⓕ pe-nyuh-zhen-kuh

warm a *teplý* tep-lee

wash (something) *umývať* u-mee-vuhť

watch *hodinky* pl ho-dyin-ki

water *voda* ⓕ vo-duh

we *my* mi

weekend *víkend* ⓜ vee-kend

west *západ* za-puhd

wheelchair *invalidný vozík* ⓜ in-vuh-lid-nee vo-zeek

when *kedy* ke-di

where *kde* kdye

white *biely* bye-li

who *kto* kto

why *prečo* pre-cho

wife *manželka* ⓕ muhn-zhel-kuh

window *okno* ⓝ ok-no

wine *víno* ⓝ vee-no

with *s* s

without *bez* bez

woman *žena* ⓕ zhe-nuh

write *písať* pee-suhť

Y

yellow *žltý* zhl-tee

yes *áno* a-no

yesterday *včera* vche-ruh

you sg inf *ty* ti

you sg pol & pl *vy* vi

Slovene

slovene alphabet

A a	B b	C c	Č č	D d
a	buh	tsuh	chuh	duh
E e	F f	G g	H h	I i
e	fuh	guh	huh	ee
J j	K k	L l	M m	N n
yuh	kuh	luh	muh	nuh
O o	P p	R r	S s	Š š
o	puh	ruh	suh	shuh
T t	U u	V v	Z z	Ž ž
tuh	oo	vuh	zuh	zhuh

SLOVENŠČINA

■ slovene

introduction

The language spoken by about 2 million people 'on the sunny side of the Alps', Slovene (*slovenščina* slo·vensh·chee·na) is sandwiched between German, Italian and Hungarian, against the backdrop of its wider South Slavic family. Its distinctive geographical position parallels its unique evolution, beginning with Slav settlement in this corner of Europe back in the 6th century, then becoming the official language of Slovenia – first as a part of Yugoslavia and since 1991 an independent republic.

Although Croatian and Serbian are its closest relatives within the South Slavic group, Slovene is nevertheless much closer to Croatia's northwestern and coastal dialects. It also shares some features with the more distant West Slavic languages (through contact with a dialect of Slovak, from which it was later separated by the arrival of the Hungarians to Central Europe in the 9th century). Unlike any other modern Slavic language, it has preserved the archaic Indo-European dual grammatical form, which means, for example, that instead of *pivo* pee·vo (a beer) or *piva* pee·va (beers), you and a friend could simply order *pivi* pee·vee (two beers).

German, Italian and Hungarian words entered Slovene during the centuries of foreign rule (in the Austro-Hungarian Empire or under the control of Venice), as these were the languages of the elite when all three countries coexisted, while the common people spoke one of the Slovene dialects. Croatian and Serbian influence on Slovene was particularly significant during the 20th century within the Yugoslav state.

For a language with a relatively small number of speakers, Slovene abounds in regional variations – eight major dialect groups have been identified, which are further divided into fifty or so regional dialects. Some of these cover the neighbouring areas of Austria, Italy and Hungary. The modern literary language is based largely on the central dialects and was shaped through a gradual process that lasted from the 16th to the 19th century.

Slovenia has been called 'a nation of poets', and what better way to get immersed in that spirit than to plunge into this beautiful language first? While you're soaking up the atmosphere of the capital, Ljubljana (whose central square is graced with a monument in honour of the nation's greatest poet, France Prešeren), remember that its name almost equals 'beloved' (*ljubljena* lyoob·lye·na) in Slovene!

pronunciation

vowel sounds

The vowels in Slovene can be pronounced differently, depending on whether they're stressed or unstressed, long or short. Don't worry about these distinctions though, as you shouldn't have too much trouble being understood if you follow our coloured pronunciation guide. Note that we've used the symbols oh and ow to help you pronounce vowels followed by the letters *l* and *v* in written Slovene – when they appear at the end of a syllable, these combinations sometimes produce a sound similar to the 'w' in English.

symbol	english equivalent	slovene example	transliteration
a	father	*dan*	dan
ai	aisle	*srajca*	*srai*-tsa
e	bet	*center*	*tsen*-ter
ee	see	*riba*	*ree*-ba
o	pot	*oče*	*o*-che
oh	oh	*pol, nov*	poh, noh
oo	zoo	*jug*	yoog
ow	how	*ostal, prav*	os-*tow*, prow
uh	ago	*pes*	puhs

word stress

Slovene has free stress, which means there's no general rule regarding which syllable the stress falls on – it simply has to be learned. You'll be fine if you just follow our coloured pronunciation guides, in which the stressed syllable is always in italics.

consonant sounds

Most Slovene consonant sounds are pronounced more or less as they are in English. Don't be intimidated by the vowel-less words such as *trg* tuhrg (square) or *vrt* vuhrt (garden) – we've put a slight 'uh' sound before the *r*, which serves as a semi-vowel between the two other consonants.

symbol	english equivalent	slovene example	transliteration
b	**b**ed	*brat*	brat
ch	**ch**eat	*hči*	hchee
d	**d**og	*datum*	da·toom
f	**f**at	*telefon*	te·le·fon
g	**g**o	*grad*	grad
h	**h**at	*hvala*	hva·la
k	**k**it	*karta*	kar·ta
l	**l**ot	*ulica*	oo·lee·tsa
m	**m**an	*mož*	mozh
n	**n**ot	*naslov*	nas·loh
p	**p**et	*pošta*	po·shta
r	**r**un (rolled)	*brez*	brez
s	**s**un	*sin*	seen
sh	**sh**ot	*tuš*	toosh
t	**t**op	*sto*	sto
ts	ha**ts**	*cesta*	tse·sta
v	**v**ery	*vlak*	vlak
y	**y**es	*jesen*	ye·sen
z	**z**ero	*zima*	zee·ma
zh	plea**s**ure	*žena*	zhe·na
'	a slight y sound	*kašelj, manj*	ka·shel', man'

tools

language difficulties

Do you speak English?
Ali govorite angleško?
a·lee go·vo·ree·te ang·lesh·ko

Do you understand?
Ali razumete?
a·lee ra·zoo·me·te

I (don't) understand.
(Ne) Razumem.
(ne) ra·zoo·mem

What does (danes) mean?
Kaj pomeni (danes)?
kai po·me·nee (da·nes)

Could you repeat that?
Lahko ponovite?
lah·ko po·no·vee·te

How do you ...?
Kako se ...?
ka·ko se ...

  pronounce this word
izgovori to besedo
eez·go·vo·ree to be·se·do

  write (hvala)
napiše (hvala)
na·pee·she (hva·la)

Could you please ...?
Prosim ...
pro·seem ...

  speak more slowly
govorite počasneje
go·vo·ree·te po·cha·sne·ye

  write it down
napišite
na·pee·shee·te

essentials

Yes.	*Da.*	da
No.	*Ne.*	ne
Please.	*Prosim.*	pro·seem
Thank you (very much).	*Hvala (lepa).*	hva·la (le·pa)
You're welcome.	*Ni za kaj.*	nee za kai
Excuse me.	*Dovolite.*	do·vo·lee·te
Sorry.	*Oprostite.*	op·ros·tee·te

numbers

0	*nula*	noo-la	16	*šestnajst*	shest-naist
1	*en/ena* m/f	en/e-na	17	*sedemnajst*	se-dem-naist
2	*dva/dve* m/f	dva/dve	18	*osemnajst*	o-sem-naist
3	*trije/tri* m/f	tree-ye/tree	19	*devetnajst*	de-vet-naist
4	*štirje* m	shtee-rye	20	*dvajset*	dvai-set
	štiri f	shtee-ree	21	*enaindvajset*	e-na-een-dvai-set
5	*pet*	pet	22	*dvaindvajset*	dva-een-dvai-set
6	*šest*	shest			
7	*sedem*	se-dem	30	*trideset*	tree-de-set
8	*osem*	o-sem	40	*štirideset*	shtee-ree-de-set
9	*devet*	de-vet	50	*petdeset*	pet-de-set
10	*deset*	de-set	60	*šestdeset*	shest-de-set
11	*enajst*	e-naist	70	*sedemdeset*	se-dem-de-set
12	*dvanajst*	dva-naist	80	*osemdeset*	o-sem-de-set
13	*trinajst*	tree-naist	90	*devetdeset*	de-vet-de-set
14	*štirinajst*	shtee-ree-naist	100	*sto*	sto
15	*petnajst*	pet-naist	1000	*tisoč*	tee-soch

time & dates

What time is it?	*Koliko je ura?*	ko-lee-ko ye oo-ra
It's one o'clock.	*Ura je ena.*	oo-ra ye e-na
It's (10) o'clock.	*Ura je (deset).*	oo-ra ye (de-set)
Quarter past (one).	*Četrt čez (ena).*	che-tuhrt chez (e-na)
Half past (one).	*Pol (dveh).* (lit: half two)	pol (dveh)
Quarter to (one).	*Petnajst do (enih).*	pet-naist do (e-neeh)
At what time ...?	*Ob kateri uri ...?*	ob ka-te-ree oo-ree ...
At ...	*Ob ...*	ob ...
am	*dopoldne*	do-poh-dne
pm	*popoldne*	po-poh-dne
Monday	*ponedeljek*	po-ne-del-yek
Tuesday	*torek*	to-rek
Wednesday	*sreda*	sre-da
Thursday	*četrtek*	che-tuhr-tek
Friday	*petek*	pe-tek
Saturday	*sobota*	so-bo-ta
Sunday	*nedelja*	ne-del-ya

January	*januar*	ya·noo·ar
February	*februar*	feb·roo·ar
March	*marec*	ma·rets
April	*april*	ap·*reel*
May	*maj*	mai
June	*junij*	yoo·neey
July	*julij*	yoo·leey
August	*avgust*	av·*goost*
September	*september*	sep·*tem*·ber
October	*oktober*	ok·*to*·ber
November	*november*	no·*vem*·ber
December	*december*	de·*tsem*·ber

What date is it today?
   Katerega smo danes?   ka·*te*·re·ga smo *da*·nes

It's (18 October).
   Smo (osemnajstega oktobra).   smo (o·sem·*nai*·ste·ga) ok·*tob*·ra

| since (May) | *od (maja)* | od (*ma*·ya) |
| until (June) | *do (junija)* | do (*yoo*·nee·ya) |

last ...
night	*prejšnji večer*	*preysh*·nyee ve·*cher*
week	*prejšnji teden*	*preysh*·nyee *te*·den
month	*prejšnji mesec*	*preysh*·nyee me·*sets*
year	*prejšnje leto*	*preysh*·nye *le*·to

next ...
week	*naslednji teden*	nas·*led*·nyee *te*·den
month	*naslednji mesec*	nas·*led*·nyee me·*sets*
year	*naslednje leto*	nas·*led*·nye *le*·to

yesterday/tomorrow ...	*včeraj/jutri ...*	vche·rai/yoot·ree ...
morning	*zjutraj*	zyoot·rai
afternoon	*popoldne*	po·*poh*·dne
evening	*zvečer*	zve·*cher*

weather

| What's the weather like? | Kakšno je vreme? | kak-shno ye vre-me |
| It's raining/snowing. | Dežuje/Sneži. | de-zhoo-ye/sne-zhee |

It's	... je.	... ye
cloudy	Oblačno	ob-lach-no
cold	Mrzlo	muhr-zlo
hot	Vroče	vro-che
sunny	Sončno	sonch-no
warm	Toplo	top-lo
windy	Vetrovno	vet-roh-no

spring	pomlad f	pom-lad
summer	poletje n	po-let-ye
autumn	jesen f	ye-sen
winter	zima f	zee-ma

border crossing

I'm here ...	Tu sem ...	too sem ...
on business	poslovno	pos-lov-no
on holiday	na počitnicah	na po-cheet-nee-tsah

I'm here for ...	Ostanem ...	os-ta-nem ...
(10) days	(deset) dni	(de-set) dnee
(two) months	(dva) meseca	(dva) me-se-tsa
(three) weeks	(tri) tedne	(tree) ted-ne

I'm going to ...
Namenjen/Namenjena sem v ... m/f   na-men-yen/na-men-ye-na sem v ...

I'm staying at the (Slon).
Stanujem v (Slonu).   sta-noo-yem v (slo-noo)

I have nothing to declare.
Ničesar nimam za prijaviti.   nee-che-sar nee-mam za pree-ya-vee-tee

I have something to declare.
Nekaj imam za prijaviti.   ne-kai ee-mam za pree-ya-vee-tee

That's mine.
To je moje.   to ye mo-ye

That's not mine.
To ni moje.   to nee mo-ye

transport

tickets & luggage

Where can I buy a ticket?
Kje lahko kupim vozovnico?　　kye lah·*ko koo*·peem vo·*zov*·nee·tso

Do I need to book a seat?
Ali moram rezervirati sedež?　　a·lee *mo*·ram re·zer·*vee*·ra·tee *se*·dezh

One ... ticket to	*... vozovnico do*	*...* vo·*zov*·nee·tso do
(Koper), please.	*(Kopra), prosim.*	(*ko*·pra) *pro*·seem
one-way	*Enosmerno*	e·no·*smer*·no
return	*Povratno*	pov·*rat*·no
I'd like to ... my	*Želim ... vozovnico,*	zhe·*leem ...* vo·*zov*·nee·tso
ticket, please.	*prosim.*	*pro*·seem
cancel	*preklicati*	prek·*lee*·tsa·tee
change	*zamenjati*	za·*men*·ya·tee
collect	*dvigniti*	*dveeg*·nee·tee
confirm	*potrditi*	po·tuhr·*dee*·tee
I'd like a ... seat,	*Želim ... sedež,*	zhe·*leem ...* se·dezh
please.	*prosim.*	*pro*·seem
nonsmoking	*nekadilski*	ne·ka·*deel*·skee
smoking	*kadilski*	ka·*deel*·skee

How much is it?
Koliko stane?　　*ko*·lee·ko *sta*·ne

Is there air conditioning?
Ali ima klimo?　　a·lee ee·*ma klee*·mo

Is there a toilet?
Ali ima stranišče?　　a·lee ee·*ma* stra·*neesh*·che

How long does the trip take?
Kako dolgo traja potovanje?　　ka·*ko dol*·go *tra*·ya po·to·*van*·ye

Is it a direct route?
Je to direktna proga?　　ye to dee·*rekt*·na *pro*·ga

I'd like a luggage locker.
Želim garderobno omarico.　　zhe·*leem* gar·de·*rob*·no o·*ma*·ree·tso

My luggage has been ...   *Moja prtljaga je ...*   *mo*-ya puhrt-*lya*-ga ye ...

damaged	*poškodovana*	posh-ko-do-*va*-na
lost	*izgubljena*	eez-goob-*lye*-na
stolen	*ukradena*	oo-*kra*-de-na

getting around

Where does flight (AF 46) arrive/depart?
Kje pristane/odleti let   kye pree-*sta*-ne/od-le-*tee* let
številka (AF 46)?   shte-*veel*-ka (a fuh *shtee*-ree shest)

Where's (the) ...?   *Kje je/so ...?* sg/pl   kye ye/so ...

arrivals hall	*prihodi* pl	pree-*ho*-dee
departures hall	*odhodi* pl	od-*ho*-dee
duty-free shop	*brezcarinska*	brez-tsa-*reen*-ska
	trgovina sg	tuhr-go-*vee*-na
gate (12)	*izhod (dvanajst)* sg	eez-*hod* (*dva*-naist)

Is this the ... to (Venice)?   *Je to ... za (Benetke)?*   ye to ... za (be-*net*-ke)

boat	*ladja*	*lad*-ya
bus	*avtobus*	*av*-to-boos
plane	*letalo*	le-*ta*-lo
train	*vlak*	vlak

What time's the ... bus?   *Kdaj odpelje ... avtobus?*   kdai od-*pel*-ye ... *av*-to-boos

first	*prvi*	*puhr*-vee
last	*zadnji*	*zad*-nyee
next	*naslednji*	nas-*led*-nyee

At what time does it arrive/leave?
Kdaj prispe/odpelje?   kdai prees-*pe*/od-*pel*-ye

How long will it be delayed?
Koliko je zamujen?   *ko*-lee-ko ye za-moo-*yen*

What station is this?
Katera postaja je to?   ka-*te*-ra pos-*ta*-ya ye to

What stop is this?
Katero postajališče je to?   ka-*te*-ro pos-ta-ya-*leesh*-che ye to

What's the next station?
Katera je naslednja postaja?   ka-*te*-ra ye nas-*led*-nya pos-*ta*-ya

What's the next stop?
Katero je naslednje postajališče?   ka-*te*-ro ye nas-*led*-nye pos-ta-ya-*leesh*-che

Does it stop at (Postojna)?
Ali ustavi v (Postojni)? — a-lee oos-*ta*-vee v (pos-*toy*-nee)

Please tell me when we get to (Kranj).
Prosim povejte mi, — pro-*seem* po-*vey*-te mee
ko prispemo v (Kranj). — ko prees-*pe*-mo v (kran)

How long do we stop here?
Kako dolgo stojimo tu? — ka-*ko dol*-go sto-*yee*-mo too

Is this seat available?
Je ta sedež prost? — ye ta se-dezh prost

That's my seat.
To je moj sedež. — to ye moy se-dezh

I'd like a taxi ...	*Želim taksi ...*	zhe-*leem* tak-see ...
at (9am)	*ob (devetih*	ob (de-ve-teeh
	dopoldne)	do-*poh*-dne)
now	*zdaj*	zdai
tomorrow	*jutri*	*yoot*-ree

Is this taxi available?
Je ta taksi prost? — ye ta tak-see prost

How much is it to ...?
Koliko stane do ...? — ko-lee-ko sta-ne do ...

Please put the meter on.
Prosim, vključite taksimeter. — pro-seem vklyoo-chee-te tak-see-me-ter

Please take me to (this address).
Prosim, peljite me na (ta naslov). — pro-seem pel-yee-te me na (ta nas-loh)

Please ...	*Prosim ...*	pro-seem ...
slow down	*vozite počasneje*	vo-zee-te po-chas-ne-ye
stop here	*ustavite tukaj*	oos-*ta*-vee-te *too*-kai
wait here	*počakajte tukaj*	po-*cha*-kai-te *too*-kai

car, motorbike & bicycle hire

I'd like to hire a ...	*Želim najeti ...*	zhe-*leem* na-*ye*-tee ...
bicycle	*kolo*	ko-*lo*
car	*avto*	*av*-to
motorbike	*motor*	mo-*tor*

with ...	s ...	s ...
a driver	*šoferjem*	sho-*fer*-yem
air conditioning	*klimo*	*klee*-mo
antifreeze	*sredstvom proti*	*sreds*-tvom *pro*-tee
	zmrzovanju	zmuhr-zo-*van*-yoo
snow chains	*snežnimi*	*snezh*-nee-mee
	verigami	ve-*ree*-ga-mee
How much for	*Koliko stane najem*	ko-*lee*-ko *sta*-ne na-*yem*
... hire?	*na ...?*	na ...
hourly	*uro*	*oo*-ro
daily	*dan*	dan
weekly	*teden*	*te*-den
air	*zrak* m	zrak
oil	*olje* n	*ol*-ye
petrol	*bencin* m	ben-*tseen*
tyres	*gume* f	*goo*-me

I need a mechanic.
Potrebujem mehanika.   pot-re-*boo*-yem me-*ha*-nee-ka

I've run out of petrol.
Zmanjkalo mi je bencina.   zman'-ka-lo mee ye ben-*tsee*-na

I have a flat tyre.
Počila mi je guma.   po-chee-la mee ye *goo*-ma

directions

Where's the ...?	*Kje je ...?*	kye ye ...
bank	*banka*	*ban*-ka
city centre	*center mesta*	*tsen*-ter *mes*-ta
hotel	*hotel*	ho-*tel*
market	*tržnica*	*tuhrzh*-nee-tsa
police station	*policijska*	po-lee-*tseey*-ska
	postaja	pos-*ta*-ya
post office	*pošta*	*posh*-ta
public toilet	*javno stranišče*	*yav*-no stra-*neesh*-che
tourist office	*turistični*	too-*rees*-teech-nee
	urad	*oo*-rad

Is this the road to (Ptuj)?
Pelje ta cesta do (Ptuja)?   pel·ye ta tses·ta do (ptoo·ya)

Can you show me (on the map)?
Mi lahko pokažete   mee lah·ko po·ka·zhe·te
(na zemljevidu)?   (na zem·lye·vee·doo)

What's the address?
Na katerem naslovu je?   na ka·te·rem nas·lo·voo ye

How far is it?
Kako daleč je?   ka·ko da·lech ye

How do I get there?
Kako pridem tja?   ka·ko pree·dem tya

Turn ...	*Zavijte ...*	za·veey·te ...
at the corner	*na vogalu*	na vo·ga·loo
at the traffic lights	*pri semaforju*	pree se·ma·for·yoo
left/right	*levo/desno*	le·vo/des·no

It's ...		
behind ...	*Za ...*	za ...
far away	*Daleč.*	da·lech
here	*Tukaj.*	too·kai
in front of ...	*Pred ...*	pred ...
left	*Levo.*	le·vo
near (to ...)	*Blizu ...*	blee·zoo ...
next to ...	*Poleg ...*	po·leg ...
on the corner	*Na vogalu.*	na vo·ga·loo
opposite ...	*Nasproti ...*	nas·pro·tee ...
right	*Desno.*	des·no
straight ahead	*Naravnost naprej.*	na·rav·nost na·prey
there	*Tam.*	tam

by bus	*z avtobusom*	z av·to·boo·som
by taxi	*s taksijem*	s tak·see·yem
by train	*z vlakom*	z vla·kom
on foot	*peš*	pesh

north	*sever*	se·ver
south	*jug*	yoog
east	*vzhod*	vzhod
west	*zahod*	za·hod

222

Vhod/Izhod	vhod/eez-hod	**Entrance/Exit**
Odprto/Zaprto	od-puhr-to/za-puhr-to	**Open/Closed**
Proste sobe	pros-te so-be	**Rooms Available**
Ni prostih mest	nee pros-teeh mest	**No Vacancies**
Informacije	een-for-ma-tsee-ye	**Information**
Policijska postaja	po-lee-tseey-ska pos-ta-ya	**Police Station**
Prepovedano	pre-po-ve-da-no	**Prohibited**
Stranišče	stra-neesh-che	**Toilets**
Moški	mosh-kee	**Men**
Ženske	zhen-ske	**Women**
Vroče/Mrzlo	vro-che/muhr-zlo	**Hot/Cold**

accommodation

finding accommodation

Where's a ...?	Kje je ... ?	kye ye ...
camping ground	kamp	kamp
guesthouse	gostišče	gos-teesh-che
hotel	hotel	ho-tel
youth hostel	mladinski hotel	mla-deen-skee ho-tel
Can you recommend a ... hotel?	Mi lahko priporočite ... hotel?	mee lah-ko pree-po-ro-chee-te ... ho-tel
cheap	poceni	po-tse-nee
good	dober	do-ber

Can you recommend a hotel nearby?
Mi lahko priporočite hotel v bližini?
mee lah-ko pree-po-ro-chee-te ho-tel oo blee-zhee-nee

I'd like to book a room, please.
Želim rezervirati sobo, prosim.
zhe-leem re-zer-vee-ra-tee so-bo pro-seem

I have a reservation.
Imam rezervacijo.
ee-mam re-zer-va-tsee-yo

My name's ...
Ime mi je ...
ee-me mee ye ...

Do you have a twin room?
Imate sobo z ločenima posteljama?   ee·*ma*·te *so*·bo z *lo*·che·nee·ma *pos*·tel·ya·ma

Do you have a ... room?	*Ali imate ... sobo?*	a·lee ee·*ma*·te ... *so*·bo
single	*enoposteljno*	e·no·*pos*·tel'·no
double	*dvoposteljno*	dvo·*pos*·tel'·no

How much is it per ...?	*Koliko stane na ...?*	ko·*lee*·ko *sta*·ne na ...
night	*noč*	noch
person	*osebo*	o·*se*·bo

Can I pay by ...?	*Lahko plačam s ...?*	lah·ko pla·cham s ...
credit card	*kreditno kartico*	kre·*deet*·no *kar*·tee·tso
travellers cheque	*potovalnim čekom*	po·to·*val*·neem *che*·kom

I'd like to stay for (three) nights.
Rad bi ostal (tri) noči. m   rada bee os·*tow* (tree) no·*chee*
Rada bi ostala (tri) noči. f   *ra*·da bee os·*ta*·la (tree) no·*chee*

From (2 July) to (6 July).
Od (drugega julija)   od (*droo*·ge·ga *yoo*·lee·ya)
do (šestega julija).   do (*shes*·te·ga *yoo*·lee·ya)

Can I see the room?
Lahko vidim sobo?   lah·ko vee·deem *so*·bo

Am I allowed to camp here?
Smem tu kampirati?   smem too kam·*pee*·ra·tee

Is there a camp site nearby?
Je v bližini kakšen kamp?   ye v blee·*zhee*·nee *kak*·shen kamp

requests & queries

When/Where is breakfast served?
Kdaj/Kje strežete zajtrk?   kdai/kye *stre*·zhe·te *zai*·tuhrk

Please wake me at (seven).
Prosim, zbudite me ob (sedmih).   pro·seem zboo·*dee*·te me ob (*sed*·meeh)

Could I have my key, please?
Lahko prosim dobim ključ?   lah·ko pro·sim do·*beem* klyooch

Can I get another (blanket)?
Lahko dobim drugo (odejo)?   lah·ko do·*beem droo*·go (o·*de*·yo)

Is there an elevator/a safe?
Imate dvigalo/sef?   ee·*ma*·te dvee·*ga*·lo/sef

The room is too...	Soba je ...	so-ba ye ...
expensive	predraga	pre-dra-ga
noisy	prehrupna	pre-hroop-na
small	premajhna	pre-mai-hna

This ... isn't clean.	Ta ... ni čista.	ta ... nee chees-ta
pillow	blazina	bla-zee-na
sheet	rjuha	ryoo-ha
towel	brisača	bree-sa-cha

The fan doesn't work.
Ventilator je pokvarjen.   ven-tee-la-tor ye pok-var-yen

The air conditioning doesn't work.
Klima je pokvarjena.   klee-ma ye pok-var-ye-na

The toilet doesn't work.
Stranišče je pokvarjeno.   stra-neesh-che ye pok-var-ye-no

checking out

What time is checkout?
Kdaj se moram odjaviti?   kdai se mo-ram od-ya-vee-tee

Can I leave my luggage here?
Lahko pustim prtljago tu?   lah-ko poos-teem puhrt-lya-go too

Could I have my ..., please?	Lahko prosim dobim ...?	lah-ko pro-seem do-beem ...
deposit	moj polog	moy po-log
passport	moj potni list	moy pot-nee leest
valuables	moje dragocenosti	mo-ye dra-go-tse-nos-tee

communications & banking

the internet

Where's the local Internet café?
Kje je najbližja internetna kavarna?   kye ye nai-bleezh-ya een-ter-net-na ka-var-na

How much is it per hour?
Koliko stane ena ura?   ko-lee-ko sta-ne e-na oo-ra

I'd like to ...	Želim ...	zhe·leem ...
check my email	preveriti elektronsko pošto	pre·ve·ree·tee e·lek·tron·sko posh·to
get Internet access	dostop do interneta	dos·top do een·ter·ne·ta
use a printer	uporabiti tiskalnik	oo·po·ra·bee·tee tees·kal·neek
use a scanner	uporabiti optični čitalnik	oo·po·ra·bee·tee op·teech·nee chee·tal·neek

mobile/cell phone

I'd like a ...	Želim ...	zhe·leem ...
mobile/cell phone for hire	najeti mobilni telefon	na·ye·tee mo·beel·nee te·le·fon
SIM card for your network	SIM kartico za vaše omrežje	seem kar·tee·tso za va·she om·rezh·ye

What are the rates? — *Kakšne so cene?* — kak·shne so tse·ne

telephone

What's your phone number?
Lahko izvem vašo telefonsko številko? — lah·ko eez·vem va·sho te·le·fon·sko shte·veel·ko

The number is ...
Številka je ... — shte·veel·ka ye ...

Where's the nearest public phone?
Kje je najbližja govorilnica? — kye ye nai·bleezh·ya go·vo·reel·nee·tsa

I'd like to buy a phonecard.
Želim kupiti telefonsko kartico. — zhe·leem koo·pee·tee te·le·fon·sko kar·tee·tso

I want to ...	Želim ...	zhe·leem ...
call (Singapore)	poklicati (Singapur)	pok·lee·tsa·tee (seen·ga·poor)
make a local call	klicati lokalno	klee·tsa·tee lo·kal·no
reverse the charges	klicati na stroške klicanega	klee·tsa·tee na strosh·ke klee·tsa·ne·ga

How much does ... cost?	Koliko stane ...?	ko·lee·ko sta·ne ...
a (three)-minute call	(tri)minutni klic	(tree·)mee·noot·nee kleets
each extra minute	vsaka dodatna minuta	vsa·ka do·dat·na mee·noo·ta

post office

I want to send a ...	Želim poslati ...	zhe-*leem* pos-*la*-tee ...
letter	pismo	*pees*-mo
parcel	paket	pa-*ket*
postcard	razglednico	raz-*gled*-nee-tso

I want to buy a/an ...	Želim kupiti ...	zhe-*leem* koo-*pee*-tee ...
envelope	kuverto	koo-*ver*-to
stamp	znamko	*znam*-ko

Please send it by ...	Prosim, pošljite ...	*pro*-seem posh-*lyee*-te ...
airmail	z letalsko pošto	z le-*tal*-sko *posh*-to
express mail	s hitro pošto	s *heet*-ro *posh*-to
registered mail	s priporočeno pošto	s pree-po-ro-*che*-no *posh*-to
surface mail	z navadno pošto	z na-*vad*-no *posh*-to

bank

Where's a/an ...?	Kje je ...?	kye ye ...
ATM	bankomat	ban-ko-*mat*
foreign exchange office	menjalnica	men-*yal*-nee-tsa

I'd like to ...	Želim ...	zhe-*leem* ...
Where can I ...?	Kje je mogoče ...?	kye ye mo-*go*-che ...
cash a cheque	unovčiti ček	oo-*nov*-chee-tee chek
change a travellers cheque	zamenjati potovalni ček	za-*men*-ya-tee po-to-*val*-nee chek
change money	zamenjati denar	za-*men*-ya-tee de-*nar*
withdraw money	dvigniti denar	dveeg-nee-tee de-*nar*

What's the ...?	Kakšen/Kakšna je ...? m/f	kak-shen/kak-shna ye ...
commission	provizija f	pro-*vee*-zee-ya
exchange rate	menjalni tečaj m	men-*yal*-nee te-*chai*

Can I arrange a transfer of money?
Lahko uredim prenos denarja?   lah-ko oo-re-*deem* pre-*nos* de-*nar*-ya

What time does the bank open?
Kdaj se banka odpre?   kdai se *ban*-ka od-*pre*

Has my money arrived yet?
Je moj denar že prispel?   ye moy de-*nar* zhe prees-*pe*-oo

sightseeing

getting in

What time does it open/close?
Kdaj se odpre/zapre?   kdai se od·*pre*/za·*pre*

What's the admission charge?
Koliko stane vstopnica?   ko·lee·ko *sta*·ne *vstop*·nee·tsa

Is there a discount for students/children?
Imate popust za   ee·*ma*·te po·*poost* za
študente/otroke?   shtoo·*den*·te/ot·ro·ke

I'd like a ...	*Želim ...*	zhe·*leem* ...
catalogue	*katalog*	ka·ta·*log*
guide	*vodnik*	vod·*neek*
local map	*zemljevid kraja*	zem·lye·*veed* kra·ya

I'd like to see ...   *Želim videti ...*   zhe·*leem* vee·de·tee ...
What's that?   *Kaj je to?*   kai ye to
Can I take a photo?   *Ali lahko fotografiram?*   a·lee lah·ko fo·to·gra·*fee*·ram

tours

When's the next ...?	*Kdaj je naslednji ...?*	kdai ye nas·*led*·nyee ...
boat trip	*izlet s čolnom*	eez·*let* s *choh*·nom
day trip	*dnevni izlet*	dnev·nee eez·*let*
tour	*izlet*	eez·*let*

Is ... included?	*Je ... vključena?*	ye ... vklyoo·che·na
accommodation	*nastanitev*	nas·ta·*nee*·tev
the admission charge	*vstopnina*	vstop·*nee*·na
food	*hrana*	*hra*·na

Is transport included?
Je prevoz vključen?   ye pre·*voz* vklyoo·chen

How long is the tour?
Koliko časa traja izlet?   ko·lee·ko *cha*·sa *tra*·ya eez·*let*

What time should we be back?
Kdaj naj se vrnemo?   kdai nai se *vuhr*·ne·mo

castle	grad m	grad
cathedral	stolnica f	stol·nee·tsa
church	cerkev f	tser·kev
main square	glavni trg m	glav·nee tuhrg
monastery	samostan m	sa·mos·tan
monument	spomenik m	spo·me·neek
museum	muzej m	moo·zey
old city	staro mesto n	sta·ro mes·to
palace	palača f	pa·la·cha
ruins	ruševine f	roo·she·vee·ne
stadium	stadion m	sta·dee·on
statue	kip m	keep

shopping

enquiries

Where's a ...?	Kje je ...?	kye ye ...
bank	banka	ban·ka
bookshop	knjigarna	knyee·gar·na
camera shop	trgovina s	tuhr·go·vee·na s
	fotografsko opremo	fo·to·graf·sko op·re·mo
department store	blagovnica	bla·gov·nee·tsa
grocery store	trgovina s	tuhr·go·vee·na s
	špecerijo	shpe·tse·ree·yo
market	tržnica	tuhrzh·nee·tsa
newsagency	kiosk	kee·osk
supermarket	trgovina	tuhr·go·vee·na

Where can I buy (a padlock)?
  Kje lahko kupim (ključavnico)?   kye lah·ko koo·peem (klyoo·chav·nee·tso)

I'm looking for ...
  Iščem ...   eesh·chem ...

Can I look at it?
  Lahko pogledam?   lah·ko pog·le·dam

Do you have any others?
Imate še kakšnega/kakšno? m/f — ee·*ma*·te she *kak*·shne·ga/*kak*·shno

Does it have a guarantee?
Ali ima garancijo? — *a*·lee ee·*ma* ga·ran·*tsee*·yo

Can I have it sent abroad?
Mi lahko pošljete v tujino? — mee lah·*ko* posh·lye·te v too·*yee*·no

Can I have my ... repaired?
Mi lahko popravite ...? — mee lah·*ko* po·*pra*·vee·te ...

It's faulty.
Ne deluje. — ne de·*loo*·ye

I'd like ..., please. — *Želim ..., prosim.* — zhe·*leem* ... *pro*·seem
  a bag — *vrečko* — *vrech*·ko
  a refund — *vračilo denarja* — vra·*chee*·lo de·*nar*·ya
  to return this — *vrniti tole* — vr·*nee*·tee *to*·le

paying

How much is this?
Koliko stane? — ko·lee·ko *sta*·ne

Can you write down the price?
Lahko napišete ceno? — lah·*ko* na·*pee*·she·te *tse*·no

That's too expensive.
To je predrago. — to ye pre·dra·*go*

What's your lowest price?
Povejte vašo najnižjo ceno. — po·*vey*·te *va*·sho nai·*neezh*·yo *tse*·no

I'll give you (five) euros.
Dam vam (pet) evrov. — dam vam (pet) *ev*·roh

There's a mistake in the bill.
Na računu je napaka. — na ra·*choo*·noo ye na·*pa*·ka

Do you accept ...? — *Ali sprejemate ...?* — *a*·lee spre·ye·ma·te ...
  credit cards — *kreditne kartice* — kre·*deet*·ne *kar*·tee·tse
  debit cards — *debetne kartice* — de·*bet*·ne *kar*·tee·tse
  travellers cheques — *potovalne čeke* — po·to·*val*·ne *che*·ke

I'd like ..., please. — *Želim ..., prosim.* — zhe·*leem* ... *pro*·seem
  a receipt — *račun* — ra·*choon*
  my change — *drobiž* — dro·*beezh*

clothes & shoes

Can I try it on?	Lahko pomerim?	lah·ko po·me·reem
My size is (42).	Nosim številko	no·seem shte·veel·ko
	(dvainštirideset).	(dva-een-shtee·ree·de·set)
It doesn't fit.	Ni mi prav.	nee mee prow
... size	... številka	... shte·veel·ka
small	majhna	mai·hna
medium	srednja	sred·nya
large	velika	ve·lee·ka

books & music

I'd like a ...	Želim ...	zhe·leem ...
newspaper	časopis	cha·so·pees
(in English)	(v angleščini)	(v ang·lesh·chee·nee)
pen	pisalo	pee·sa·lo

I'm looking for an English-language bookshop.

| Iščem angleško knjigarno. | eesh·chem ang·lesh·ko knye·gar·no |

I'm looking for a book/music by (Miha Mazzini/Zoran Predin).

| Iščem knjigo/glasbo | eesh·chem knye·go/glaz·bo |
| (Mihe Mazzinija/Zorana Predina). | (mee·he ma·tsee·nee·ya/zo·ra·na pre·dee·na) |

Can I listen to this?

| Lahko tole poslušam? | lah·ko to·le pos·loo·sham |

photography

Can you ...?	Lahko ...?	lah·ko ...
burn a CD from	zapečete CD z moje	za·pe·che·te tse·de z mo·ye
my memory card	spominske kartice	spo·meen·ske kar·tee·tse
develop this film	razvijete ta film	raz·vee·ye·te ta feelm
load this film	vstavite ta film	vsta·vee·te ta feelm
I need a/an ... film	Potrebujem ... film	pot·re·boo·yem ... feelm
for this camera.	za ta fotoaparat.	za ta fo·to·a·pa·rat
APS	APS	a pe es
B&W	črno-bel	chuhr·no·be·oo
colour	barvni	barv·nee
(200) speed	(dvesto) ASA	(dve·sto) a·sa

I need a slide film for this camera.
Potrebujem film za diapozitive za ta fotoaparat.
pot·re·*boo*·yem feelm za dee·a·po·zee·*tee*·ve za ta fo·to·a·pa·*rat*

When will it be ready?
Kdaj bo gotovo?
kdai bo go·*to*·vo

meeting people

greetings, goodbyes & introductions

Hello/Hi.	*Zdravo.*	*zdra*·vo
Good night.	*Lahko noč.*	*lah*·ko noch
Goodbye/Bye.	*Na svidenje/Adijo.*	na *svee*·den·ye/a·*dee*·yo
See you later.	*Se vidiva.*	se *vee*·dee·va
Mr/Mrs	*gospod/gospa*	gos·*pod*/gos·*pa*
Miss	*gospodična*	gos·po·*deech*·na
How are you?	*Kako ste/si?* pol/inf	ka·*ko* ste/see
Fine, thanks.	*Dobro, hvala.*	*dob*·ro hva·la
And you?	*Pa vi/ti?* pol/inf	pa vee/tee
What's your name?	*Kako vam/ti je ime?* pol/inf	ka·*ko* vam/tee ye ee·*me*
My name is …	*Ime mi je …*	ee·*me* mee ye …
I'm pleased to	*Veseli me, da sem vas*	ve·se·*lee* me da sem vas
meet you.	*spoznal/spoznala.* m/f	spoz·*now*/spoz·*na*·la
This is my …	*To je moj/moja …* m/f	to ye moy/*mo*·ya …
boyfriend	*fant*	fant
brother	*brat*	brat
daughter	*hči*	hchee
father	*oče*	*o*·che
friend	*prijatelj* m	pree·*ya*·tel'
	prijateljica f	pree·*ya*·tel·yee·tsa
girlfriend	*punca*	*poon*·tsa
husband	*mož*	mozh
mother	*mama*	*ma*·ma
partner (intimate)	*partner/partnerka* m/f	*part*·ner/*part*·ner·ka
sister	*sestra*	*ses*·tra
son	*sin*	seen
wife	*žena*	*zhe*·na

Here's my phone number.
Tu je moja telefonska številka.   too ye *mo*·ya te·le·*fon*·ska shte·*veel*·ka

What's your phone number?
Mi poveste vašo telefonsko številko?   mee po·*ves*·te *va*·sho te·le·*fon*·sko shte·*veel*·ko

Here's my ...	*Tu je moj/moja ...* m/f	too ye moy/*mo*·ya ...
What's your ...?	*Kakšen je vaš ...?* m	*kak*·shen ye vash ...
	Kakšna je vaša ...? f	*kak*·shna ye *va*·sha ...
(email) address	*(elektronski) naslov* m	(e·lek·*tron*·skee) nas·*loh*
fax number	*številka faksa* f	shte·*veel*·ka *fak*·sa

occupations

What's your occupation?	*Kaj ste po poklicu?*	kai ste po pok·*lee*·tsoo
I'm a/an ...	*... sem.*	... sem
artist	*Umetnik* m	oo·*met*·neek
	Umetnica f	oo·*met*·nee·tsa
farmer	*Kmet/Kmetica* m/f	kmet/kme·*tee*·tsa
office worker	*Uradnik* m	oo·*rad*·neek
	Uradnica f	oo·*rad*·nee·tsa
scientist	*Znanstvenik* m	znans·tve·neek
	Znanstvenica f	znans·tve·nee·tsa
student	*Študent/Študentka* m/f	shtoo·*dent*/ shtoo·*dent*·ka
tradesperson	*Trgovec/Trgovka* m/f	tuhr·*go*·vets/ tuhr·*gov*·ka

background

Where are you from?	*Od kod ste?*	od kod ste
I'm from ...	*Iz ... sem.*	eez ... sem
Australia	*Avstralije*	av·*stra*·lee·ye
Canada	*Kanade*	*ka*·na·de
England	*Anglije*	*an*·glee·ye
New Zealand	*Nove Zelandije*	*no*·ve ze·*lan*·dee·ye
the USA	*Združenih držav*	zdroo·zhe·neeh dr·zhav
Are you married?	*Ste poročeni?*	ste po·ro·*che*·nee
I'm married.	*Poročen/Poročena*	po·ro·*chen*/po·ro·*che*·na
	sem. m/f	sem
I'm single.	*Samski/Samska sem.* m/f	*sam*·skee/*sam*·ska sem

age

How old ...?	Koliko ...?	ko-lee-ko ...
are you	si star/stara m/f inf	see star/sta-ra
are you	ste stari m&f pol	ste sta-ree
is your daughter	je stara vaša hči	ye sta-ra va-sha hchee
is your son	je star vaš sin	ye star vash seen
I'm ... years old.	Imam ... let.	ee-mam ... let
He/She is ... years old.	... let ima.	... let ee-ma

feelings

I'm ...	... sem.	... sem
hungry	Lačen/Lačna m/f	la-chen/lach-na
thirsty	Žejen/Žejna m/f	zhe-yen/zhey-na
tired	Utrujen m	oot-roo-yen
	Utrujena f	oot-roo-ye-na
I'm not ...	Nisem ...	nee-sem ...
hungry	lačen/lačna m/f	la-chen/lach-na
thirsty	žejen/žejna m/f	zhe-yen/zhey-na
tired	utrujen/utrujena m/f	oot-roo-yen/oot-roo-ye-na
Are you ... ?	Ste ... ?	ste ...
hungry	lačni	lach-nee
thirsty	žejni	zhey-nee
tired	utrujeni	oot-roo-ye-nee
I'm ...	... mi je.	... mee ye
hot	Vroče	vro-che
well	Dobro	dob-ro
I'm not ...	Ni mi ...	nee mee ...
Are you ...?	Vam je ...?	vam ye ...
hot	vroče	vro-che
well	dobro	dob-ro
I'm (not) cold.	(Ne) Zebe me.	ne ze-be me
Are you cold?	Vas zebe?	vas ze-be

entertainment

going out

Where can I find ...?	*Kje je kakšen ...?*	kye ye *kak*·shen ...
clubs	*klub*	kloob
gay venues	*homoseksualski bar*	ho·mo·sek·soo·*al*·skee bar
pubs	*bar*	bar
I feel like going to a/the ...	*Želim iti ....*	zhe·*leem* ee·tee ...
concert	*na koncert*	na kon·*tsert*
movies	*v kino*	oo *kee*·no
party	*na zabavo*	na za·*ba*·vo
restaurant	*v restavracijo*	oo res·tav·*ra*·tsee·yo
theatre	*v gledališče*	oo gle·da·*leesh*·che

interests

Do you like ...?	*Vam je všeč ...?*	vam ye vshech ...
I like ...	*Všeč mi je ...*	vshech mee ye ...
I don't like ...	*Ni mi všeč ...*	nee mee vshech ...
art	*umetnost*	oo·*met*·nost
cooking	*kuhanje*	*koo*·han·ye
reading	*branje*	*bran*·ye
shopping	*nakupovanje*	na·koo·po·*van*·ye
sport	*šport*	shport
Do you like ...?	*So vam všeč ...?*	so vam vshech ...
I like ...	*Všeč so mi ...*	vshech so mee ...
I don't like ...	*Niso mi všeč ...*	*nee*·so mee vshech ...
movies	*filmi*	*feel*·mee
nightclubs	*nočni bari*	*noch*·nee ba·ree
travelling	*potovanja*	po·to·*van*·ya
Do you like to ...?	*Ali radi ...?*	*a*·lee ra·dee ...
dance	*plešete*	*ple*·she·te
go to concerts	*hodite na koncerte*	ho·dee·te na kon·*tser*·te
listen to music	*poslušate glasbo*	pos·*loo*·sha·te *glas*·bo

food & drink

finding a place to eat

Can you recommend a ...?	Mi lahko priporočite ...?	mee lah-ko pree-po-ro-chee-te ...
bar	bar	bar
café	kavarno	ka-var-no
restaurant	restavracijo	res-tav-ra-tsee-yo
I'd like ..., please.	Želim ..., prosim.	zhe-leem ... pro-seem
a table for (five)	mizo za (pet)	mee-zo za (pet)
the (non)smoking section	prostor za (ne)kadilce	pros-tor za (ne-)ka-deel-tse

ordering food

breakfast	zajtrk m	zai-tuhrk
lunch	kosilo n	ko-see-lo
dinner	večerja f	ve-cher-ya
snack	malica f	ma-lee-tsa
today's special	danes nudimo	da-nes noo-dee-mo
What would you recommend?	Kaj priporočate?	kai pree-po-ro-cha-te
I'd like (the) ..., please.	Želim ..., prosim.	zhe-leem ... pro-seem
bill	račun	ra-choon
drink list	meni pijač	me-nee pee-yach
menu	jedilni list	ye-deel-nee leest
that dish	to jed	to yed

drinks

cup of coffee ...	skodelica kave ...	sko-de-lee-tsa ka-ve ...
cup of tea ...	skodelica čaja ...	sko-de-lee-tsa cha-ya ...
with milk	z mlekom	z mle-kom
without sugar	brez sladkorja	brez slad-kor-ya

(orange) juice	(pomarančni) sok m	(po·ma·*ranch*·nee) sok
soft drink	brezalkoholna	brez·al·ko·*hol*·na
	pijača f	pee·*ya*·cha
... water	... voda	... *vo*·da
boiled	prekuhana	pre·*koo*·ha·na
(sparkling)	mineralna	mee·ne·*ral*·na
mineral	(gazirana)	(ga·*zee*·ra·na)

in the bar

I'll have ...
Jaz bom ... yaz bom ...

I'll buy you a drink.
Povabim te na pijačo. inf po·*va*·beem te na pee·*ya*·cho

What would you like?
Kaj boš? inf kai bosh

Cheers!
Na zdravje! na *zdrav*·ye

brandy	vinjak m	*veen*·yak
champagne	šampanjec m	sham·*pan*·yets
cocktail	koktajl m	kok·*tail*
cognac	konjak m	*kon*·yak
a shot of (whisky)	kozarček (viskija)	ko·*zar*·chek (*vees*·kee·ya)

a ... of beer	... piva	... *pee*·va
glass	kozarec	ko·*za*·rets
jug	vrč	vuhrch
pint	vrček	*vuhr*·chek

a bottle/glass	steklenica/kozarec	stek·le·*nee*·tsa/ko·*za*·rets
of ... wine	... vina	... *vee*·na
red	rdečega	rde·*che*·ga
sparkling	penečega	pe·*ne*·che·ga
white	belega	*be*·le·ga

self-catering

What's the local speciality?
Kaj je lokalna specialiteta?   kai ye lo-*kal*-na spe-tsee-a-lee-*te*-ta

What's that?
Kaj je to?   kai ye to

How much is (a kilo of cheese)?
Koliko stane (kila sira)?   ko-lee-ko *sta*-ne (*kee*-la *see*-ra)

I'd like ...	Želim ...	zhe-*leem* ...
(200) grams	(dvesto) gramov	(*dve*-sto) *gra*-mov
(two) kilos	(dva) kilograma	(dva) kee-lo-*gra*-ma
(three) pieces	(tri) kose	(tree) *ko*-se
(six) slices	(šest) rezin	(shest) re-*zeen*

Less.	Manj.	man'
Enough.	Dovolj.	do-*vol*
More.	Več.	vech

special diets & allergies

Is there a vegetarian restaurant near here?
Je tu blizu vegetarijanska   ye too *blee*-zoo ve-ge-ta-ree-*yan*-ska
restavracija?   res-tav-*ra*-tsee-ya

Do you have vegetarian food?
Ali imate vegetarijansko hrano?   *a*-lee ee-*ma*-te ve-ge-ta-ree-*yan*-sko *hra*-no

Could you prepare	Lahko pripravite	lah-ko pree-*pra*-vee-te
a meal without ...?	obed brez ...?	o-bed brez ...
butter	masla	*mas*-la
eggs	jajc	yaits
meat stock	mesne osnove	*mes*-ne os-*no*-ve

I'm allergic to ...	Alergičen/Alergična	a-*ler*-gee-chen/a-*ler*-geech-na
	sem na ... m/f	sem na ...
dairy produce	mlečne izdelke	*mlech*-ne eez-*del*-ke
gluten	gluten	gloo-ten
MSG	MSG	em es ge
nuts	oreške	o-*resh*-ke
seafood	morsko hrano	*mor*-sko *hra*-no

menu reader

bograč m	*bog-rach*	beef goulash
brancin na maslu m	*bran-tseen na mas-loo*	sea bass in butter
čebulna bržola f	*che-bool-na br-zho-la*	braised beef with onions
čevapčiči m	*che-vap-chee-chee*	spicy beef or pork meatballs
drobnjakovi štruklji m	*drob-nya-ko-vee shtrook-lyee*	dumplings of cottage cheese & chives
dunajski zrezek m	*doo-nai-skee zre-zek*	breaded veal or pork cutlet
francoska solata f	*fran-tsos-ka so-la-ta*	diced potatoes & vegetables with mayonnaise
gobova kremna juha f	*go-bo-va krem-na yoo-ha*	creamed mushroom soup
goveja juha z rezanci f	*go-ve-ya yoo-ha z re-zan-tsee*	beef broth with little egg noodles
jota f	*yo-ta*	beans, sauerkraut & potatoes or barley cooked with pork
kisle kumarice f	*kees-le koo-ma-ree-tse*	pickled cucumbers
kmečka pojedina f	*kmech-ka po-ye-dee-na*	smoked meats with sauerkraut
kranjska klobasa z gorčico f	*kran'-ska klo-ba-sa z gor-chee-tso*	sausage with mustard
kraški pršut z olivami m	*krash-kee puhr-shoot z o-lee-va-mee*	air-dried ham with black olives
krofi m	*kro-fee*	jam-filled doughnuts
kuhana govedina s hrenom f	*koo-ha-na go-ve-dee-na s hre-nom*	boiled beef with horseradish
kuhana postrv f	*koo-ha-na pos-tuhrv*	boiled trout
kumarična solata f	*koo-ma-reech-na so-la-ta*	cucumber salad
ljubljanski zrezek m	*lyoob-lyan-skee zre-zek*	breaded cutlet with cheese

mešano meso na žaru n	*me*-sha-no me-*so* na *zha*-roo	*mixed grill*
ocvrt oslič m	ots-*vuhrt* os-*leech*	*fried cod*
ocvrt piščanec m	ots-*vuhrt* peesh-*cha*-nets	*fried chicken*
orada na žaru f	o-*ra*-da na *zha*-roo	*grilled sea bream*
palačinke f	pa-la-*cheen*-ke	*thin pancakes with marmalade, nuts or chocolate*
pečena postrv f	pe-*che*-na pos-*tuhrv*	*grilled trout*
pečene sardele f	pe-*che*-ne sar-*de*-le	*grilled sardines*
pleskavica f	*ples*-ka-vee-tsa	*spicy meat patties*
pariški zrezek m	pa-*reesh*-kee *zre*-zek	*cutlet fried in egg batter*
puranov zrezek s šampinjoni m	poo-*ra*-nov *zre*-zek s sham-peen-*yo*-nee	*turkey steak with white mushrooms*
ražnjiči m	*razh*-nyee-chee	*shish kebab*
riba v marinadi f	*ree*-ba v ma-ree-*na*-dee	*marinated fish*
ričet m	*ree*-chet	*barley stew with smoked pork ribs*
rižota z gobami f	ree-*zho*-ta z *go*-ba-mee	*risotto with mushrooms*
sadna kupa f	*sad*-na *koo*-pa	*fruit salad with whipped cream*
srbska solata f	*suhrb*-ska so-*la*-ta	*salad of tomatoes & green peppers with onions & cheese*
svinjska pečenka f	sveen'-ska pe-*chen*-ka	*roast pork*
škampi na žaru m	*shkam*-pee na *zha*-roo	*grilled prawns*
školjke f	*shkol'*-ke	*clams*
zelena solata f	ze-*le*-na so-*la*-ta	*lettuce salad*
zelenjavna juha f	ze-len-*yav*-na *yoo*-ha	*vegetable soup*

emergencies

basics

Help!	Na pomoč!	na po-moch
Stop!	Ustavite (se)!	oos-ta-vee-te (se)
Go away!	Pojdite stran!	poy-dee-te stran
Thief!	Tat!	tat
Fire!	Požar!	po-zhar
Watch out!	Pazite!	pa-zee-te

Call ...!	Pokličite ...!	pok-lee-chee-te ...
a doctor	zdravnika	zdrav-nee-ka
an ambulance	rešilca	re-sheel-tsa
the police	policijo	po-lee-tsee-yo

It's an emergency.
Nujno je. — nooy-no ye

Could you help me, please?
Pomagajte mi, prosim. — po-ma-gai-te mee pro-seem

I have to use the telephone.
Poklicati moram. — pok-lee-tsa-tee mo-ram

I'm lost.
Izgubil/Izgubila sem se. m/f — eez-goo-beew/eez-goo-bee-la sem se

Where are the toilets?
Kje je stranišče? — kye ye stra-neesh-che

police

Where's the police station?
Kje je policijska postaja? — kye ye po-lee-tseey-ska pos-ta-ya

I want to report an offence.
Želim prijaviti prestopek. — zhe-leem pree-ya-vee-tee pres-to-pek

I have insurance.
Zavarovan/Zavarovana sem. m/f — za-va-ro-van/za-va-ro-va-na sem

I've been ...	... so me.	... so me
assaulted	Napadli	na-pad-lee
raped	Posilili	po-see-lee-lee
robbed	Oropali	o-ro-pa-lee

I've lost my ...	Izgubil/Izgubila sem ... m/f	eez-*goo*-beew/eez-goo-*bee*-la sem ...
My ... was/were stolen.	Ukradli so mi ...	ook-*rad*-lee so mee ...
backpack	nahrbtnik	na-*huhrbt*-neek
bags	torbe	*tor*-be
credit card	kreditno kartico	kre-*deet*-no *kar*-tee-tso
handbag	ročno torbico	*roch*-no tor-*bee*-tso
jewellery	nakit	na-*keet*
money	denar	de-*nar*
passport	potni list	*pot*-nee leest
travellers cheques	potovalne čeke	po-to-*val*-ne *che*-ke
wallet	denarnico	de-*nar*-nee-tso
I want to contact my ...	Želim poklicati ... svoj/svojo ... m/f	zhe-*leem* pok-*lee*-tsa-tee ... svoy/*svo*-yo ...
consulate	konzulat m	kon-zoo-*lat*
embassy	ambasado f	am-ba-*sa*-do

health

medical needs

Where's the nearest ...?	Kje je najbližji/ najbližja ... ? m/f	kye ye nai-*bleezh*-yee/ nai-*bleezh*-ya ...
dentist	zobozdravnik m	zo-bo-zdrav-*neek*
doctor	zdravnik m	zdrav-*neek*
hospital	bolnišnica f	bol-*neesh*-nee-tsa
(night) pharmacist	(nočna) lekarna f	(*noch*-na) le-*kar*-na

I need a doctor (who speaks English).
Potrebujem zdravnika
(ki govori angleško).
pot-re-*boo*-yem zdrav-*nee*-ka
(kee go-vo-*ree* ang-*lesh*-ko)

Could I see a female doctor?
Bi me lahko pregledala
zdravnica?
bee me lah-*ko* preg-*le*-da-la
zdrav-*nee*-tsa

I've run out of my medication.
Zmanjkalo mi je zdravil.
zman'-ka-lo mee ye zdra-*veel*

symptoms, conditions & allergies

I'm sick.	Bolan/Bolna sem. m/f	bo-*lan*/*boh*-na sem
It hurts here.	Tu me boli.	too me bo-*lee*
I have (a) ...	Imam ...	ee-*mam* ...
asthma	astmo	*ast*-mo
bronchitis	bronhitis	bron-*hee*-tees
constipation	zapeko	za-*pe*-ko
diarrhoea	drisko	drees-ko
fever	vročino	vro-*chee*-no
headache	glavobol	gla-vo-*bol*
heart condition	srčno bolezen	*suhr*-chno bo-*le*-zen
toothache	zobobol	zo-bo-*bol*
pain	bolečine	bo-le-*chee*-ne
I'm nauseous.	Slabo mi je.	sla-*bo* mee ye
I'm coughing.	Kašljam.	*kash*-lyam
I have a sore throat.	Boli me grlo.	bo-*lee* me *guhr*-lo
I'm allergic to ...	Alergičen/Alergična	a-*ler*-gee-chen/a-*ler*-geech-na
	sem na ... m/f	sem na ...
antibiotics	antibiotike	an-tee-bee-*o*-tee-ke
anti-inflammatories	protivnetna	pro-teev-*net*-na
	zdravila	zdra-*vee*-la
aspirin	aspirin	as-pee-*reen*
bees	čebelji pik	che-*bel*-yee peek
codeine	kodein	ko-de-*een*
penicillin	penicilin	pe-nee-tsee-*leen*
antiseptic	razkužilo n	raz-koo-*zhee*-lo
bandage	obveza f	ob-*ve*-za
condoms	kondomi m pl	kon-*do*-mee
contraceptives	kontracepcija f	kon-tra-*tsep*-tsee-ya
diarrhoea medicine	zdravilo za drisko n	zdra-*vee*-lo za drees-ko
insect repellent	sredstvo proti	sreds-tvo *pro*-tee
	mrčesu n	muhr-*che*-soo
laxatives	odvajala n pl	od-va-*ya*-la
painkillers	analgetiki m pl	a-nal-*ge*-tee-kee
rehydration salts	sol za rehidracijo f	sol za re-heed-*ra*-tsee-yo
sleeping tablets	uspavalne tablete f pl	oos-pa-*val*-ne tab-*le*-te

english–slovene dictionary

Slovene nouns in this dictionary have their gender indicated by ⓜ (masculine), ⓕ (feminine) or ⓝ (neuter). If it's a plural noun, you'll also see pl. Adjectives are given in the masculine form only. Words are also marked as a (adjective), v (verb), sg (singular), pl (plural), inf (informal) or pol (polite) where necessary.

A

accident *nesreča* ⓕ nes-re-cha
accommodation *nastanitev* ⓕ na-sta-*nee*-tev
adaptor *adapter* ⓜ a-*dap*-ter
address *naslov* ⓜ nas-*loh*
after *po* po
air-conditioned *klimatiziran* klee-ma-tee-*zee*-ran
airplane *letalo* ⓝ le-*ta*-lo
airport *letališče* ⓝ le-ta-*leesh*-che
alcohol *alkohol* ⓜ al-ko-*hol*
all *vse* vse
allergy *alergija* ⓕ a-ler-*gee*-ya
ambulance *rešilni avto* ⓜ re-*sheel*-nee *av*-to
and *in* een
ankle *gleženj* ⓜ *gle*-zhen'
arm *roka* ⓕ ro-ka
ashtray *pepelnik* ⓜ pe-*pel*-neek
ATM *bankomat* ⓜ ban-ko-*mat*

B

baby *dojenček* ⓜ do-yen-chek
back (body) *hrbet* ⓜ *huhr*-bet
backpack *nahrbtnik* ⓜ na-*huhrbt*-neek
bad *slab* slab
bag *torba* ⓕ tor-ba
baggage *prtljaga* ⓕ puhrt-*lya*-ga
baggage claim *prevzem prtljage* ⓕ prev-zem puhrt-*lya*-ge
bank *banka* ⓕ *ban*-ka
bar *bar* ⓜ bar
bathroom *kopalnica* ⓕ ko-*pal*-nee-tsa
battery *baterija* ⓕ ba-te-*ree*-ya
beautiful *lep* lep
bed *postelja* ⓕ *pos*-tel-ya
beer *pivo* ⓝ *pee*-vo
before *prej* prey
behind *zadaj* za-dai
bicycle *bicikel* ⓜ bee-*tsee*-kel
big *velik* ve-leek
bill *račun* ⓜ ra-*choon*
black *črn* chuhrn

blanket *odeja* ⓕ o-*de*-ya
blood group *krvna skupina* ⓕ *kuhrv*-na skoo-*pee*-na
blue *moder* mo-der
boat (ship) *ladja* ⓕ *lad*-ya
boat (small) *čoln* ⓝ chohn
book (make a reservation) v *rezervirati* re-zer-vee-ra-tee
bottle *steklenica* ⓕ stek-le-*nee*-tsa
bottle opener *odpirač* ⓜ od-pee-*rach*
boy *fant* ⓜ fant
brakes (car) *zavore* ⓕ pl za-*vo*-re
breakfast *zajtrk* ⓜ *zai*-tuhrk
broken (faulty) *pokvarjen* pok-*var*-yen
bus *avtobus* ⓜ av-to-*boos*
business *posel* ⓜ po-se-oo
buy *kupiti* koo-*pee*-tee

C

café *kavarna* ⓕ ka-*var*-na
camera *fotoaparat* ⓜ fo-to-a-pa-*rat*
camera shop *trgovina s fotografsko opremo* ⓕ tr-go-*vee*-na s fo-to-*graf*-sko o-*pre*-mo
campsite *kamp* ⓜ kamp
can opener *odpirač za pločevinke* ⓜ od-pee-*rach* za plo-che-*veen*-ke
cancel *preklicati* prek-lee-tsa-tee
car *avtomobil* ⓜ av-to-mo-*beel*
cash *gotovina* ⓕ go-to-*vee*-na
cash (a cheque) v *unovčiti (ček)* oo-nov-*chee*-tee (chek)
cell phone *mobilni telefon* ⓜ mo-*beel*-nee te-le-*fon*
centre *center* ⓜ *tsen*-ter
change (money) v *menjati (denar)* men-ya-tee (de-*nar*)
cheap *poceni* po-*tse*-nee
check (bill) *račun* ⓜ ra-*choon*
check-in *prijava za let* ⓕ pree-*ya*-va za let
chest *prsni koš* ⓜ *puhr*-snee kosh
child *otrok* ⓜ ot-*rok*
cigarette *cigareta* ⓕ tsee-ga-*re*-ta
city *mesto* ⓝ *mes*-to
clean a *čist* cheest
closed *zaprt* za-*puhrt*
coffee *kava* ⓕ ka-va
coins *kovanci* ⓜ pl ko-*van*-tsee

cold a *hladen* hla-den

collect call *klic na stroške klicanega* m
 kleets na strosh-ke klee-tsa-ne-ga

come *priti* pree-tee

computer *računalnik* m ra-choo-nal-neek

condom *kondom* m kon-dom

contact lenses *kontaktne leče* f pl kon-takt-ne le-che

cook v *kuhati* koo-ha-tee

cost *strošek* m stro-shek

credit card *kreditna kartica* f kre-deet-na kar-tee-tsa

cup *skodelica* f sko-de-lee-tsa

currency exchange *menjava* m men-ya-va

customs (immigration) *carina* f tsa-ree-na

D

dangerous *nevaren* ne-va-ren

date (time) *datum* m da-toom

day *dan* m dan

delay *zamuda* f za-moo-da

dentist *zobozdravnik* m zo-boz-drav-neek

depart *oditi* o-dee-tee

diaper *plenica* f ple-nee-tsa

dictionary *slovar* m slo-var

dinner *večerja* f ve-cher-ya

direct *direkten* dee-rek-ten

dirty *umazan* oo-ma-zan

disabled (person) *invaliden* een-va-lee-den

discount *popust* m po-poost

doctor *zdravnik* m zdrav-neek

double bed *dvojna postelja* f dvoy-na pos-tel-ya

double room *dvoposteljna soba* f
 dvo-pos-tel'-na so-ba

drink *pijača* f pee-ya-cha

drive v *voziti* vo-zee-tee

drivers licence *vozniško dovoljenje* m
 voz-neesh-ko do-vol-yen-ye

drug (illicit) *mamilo* m ma-mee-lo

dummy (pacifier) *duda* f doo-da

E

ear *uho* n oo-ho

east *vzhod* m vzhod

eat *jesti* yes-tee

economy class *turistični razred* m
 too-rees-teech-nee raz-red

electricity *elektrika* f e-lek-tree-ka

elevator *dvigalo* n dvee-ga-lo

email *elektronska pošta* f e-lek-tron-ska posh-ta

embassy *ambasada* f am-ba-sa-da

emergency *nujen primer* m noo-yen pree-mer

English (language) *angleščina* f ang-lesh-chee-na

entrance *vhod* m vhod

evening *večer* m ve-cher

exchange rate *menjalni tečaj* m men-yal-nee te-chai

exit *izhod* m eez-hod

expensive *drag* drag

express mail *hitra pošta* f heet-ra posh-ta

eye *oko* n o-ko

F

far *daleč* da-lech

fast *hitro* heet-ro

father *oče* m o-che

film (camera) *film* m feelm

finger *prst* m puhrst

first-aid kit *komplet za prvo pomoč* m
 kom-plet za puhr-vo po-moch

first class *prvi razred* m puhr-vee raz-red

fish *riba* f ree-ba

food *hrana* f hra-na

foot *stopalo* n sto-pa-lo

fork *vilice* f pl vee-lee-tse

free (of charge) *brezplačen* brez-pla-chen

friend *prijatelj/prijateljica* m/f
 pree-ya-tel/pree-ya-tel-yee-tsa

fruit *sadje* n pl sad-ye

full *poln* poln

funny *smešen* sme-shen

G

gift *darilo* n da-ree-lo

girl *dekle* n dek-le

glass (drinking) *kozarec* m ko-za-rets

glasses *očala* n pl o-cha-la

go *iti* ee-tee

good *dober* do-ber

green *zelen* ze-len

guide *vodnik* m vod-neek

H

half *pol* poh

hand *roka* f ro-ka

handbag *ročna torbica* f roch-na tor-bee-tsa

happy *srečen* sre-chen

have *imeti* ee-me-tee

he *on* m on

head *glava* f gla-va

heart *srce* n suhr-tse

heat *vročina* f vro-chee-na

heavy *težek* te-zhek

help v *pomagati* po-*ma*-ga-tee
here *tukaj* too-kai
high *visok* vee-sok
highway *hitra cesta* ① *heet*-ra tses-ta
(go on a) hike v *iti na pohod* ee-tee na po-*hod*
holidays *počitnice* ① pl po-*cheet*-nee-tse
homosexual *homoseksualec* ⓜ ho-mo-sek-soo-*a*-lets
hospital *bolnišnica* ① bol-neesh-nee-tsa
hot *vroč* vroch
hotel *hotel* ⓜ ho-*tel*
hungry *lačen* la-chen
husband *mož* ⓜ mozh

I

I *jaz* yaz
identification (card) *osebna izkaznica* ①
  o-*seb*-na eez-*kaz*-nee-tsa
ill *bolan* bo-*lan*
important *pomemben* po-*mem*-ben
included *vključen* vklyoo-chen
injury *poškodba* ① posh-*kod*-ba
insurance *zavarovanje* ① za-va-ro-*van*-ye
Internet *internet* ⓜ een-ter-net
interpreter *tolmač* ⓜ tol-*mach*

J

jewellery *nakit* ⓜ na-*keet*
job *služba* ① *sloozh*-ba

K

key *ključ* klyooch
kilogram *kilogram* ⓜ kee-lo-*gram*
kitchen *kuhinja* ① koo-heen-ya
knife *nož* ⓜ nozh

L

laundry (place) *pralnica* ① *pral*-nee-tsa
lawyer *odvetnik* ⓜ od-*vet*-neek
left (direction) *levo* *le*-vo
left-luggage office *garderoba* ① gar-de-*ro*-ba
leg *noga* ① *no*-ga
lesbian *lezbijka* ① *lez*-beey-ka
less *manj* man'
letter (mail) *pismo* ⓝ *pees*-mo
lift (elevator) *dvigalo* ① dvee-*ga*-lo
light *svetloba* ① svet-*lo*-ba
like v *všeč biti* vshech bee-tee

lock *ključavnica* ① klyoo-*chav*-nee-tsa
long *dolg* dohg
lost *izgubljen* eez-goob-lyen
lost-property office *urad za izgubljene predmete* ⓜ
  oo-rad za eez-goob-lye-ne pred-*me*-te
love v *ljubiti* lyoo-bee-tee
luggage *prtljaga* ① puhrt-*lya*-ga
lunch *kosilo* ⓝ ko-see-lo

M

mail *pošta* ① posh-ta
man *moški* ⓜ *mosh*-kee
map *zemljevid* ⓜ zem-lye-*veed*
market *tržnica* ① tuhrzh-nee-tsa
matches *vžigalice* ① pl vzhee-*ga*-lee-tse
meat *meso* ⓝ *me*-so
medicine *zdravilo* ⓝ zdra-vee-lo
menu *jedilni list* ⓜ ye-*deel*-nee leest
message *sporočilo* ⓝ spo-ro-chee-lo
milk *mleko* ⓝ *mle*-ko
minute *minuta* ① mee-*noo*-ta
mobile phone *mobilni telefon* ⓜ mo-*beel*-nee te-le-*fon*
money *denar* ⓜ de-nar
month *mesec* ⓜ *me*-sets
morning *dopoldne* ⓝ do-*pol*-dne
mother *mama* ① *ma*-ma
motorcycle *motorno kolo* ⓝ mo-tor-no *ko*-lo
motorway *motorna cesta* ① mo-*tor*-na *tses*-ta
mouth *usta* ⓝ *oos*-ta
music *glasba* ① *glaz*-ba

N

name *ime* ⓝ ee-*me*
napkin *prtiček* ⓜ puhr-*tee*-chek
nappy *plenica* ① *ple*-nee-tsa
near *blizu* blee-zoo
neck *vrat* ⓜ vrat
new *nov* noh
news *novice* ① pl no-*vee*-tse
newspaper *časopis* ⓜ cha-so-*pees*
night *noč* ① noch
no *ne* ne
noisy *hrupen* hroo-pen
nonsmoking *nekadilski* ne-ka-*deel*-skee
north *sever* ⓜ *se*-ver
nose *nos* ⓜ nos
now *zdaj* zdai
number *število* ⓝ shte-vee-lo

O

oil (engine) *olje* ⓝ ol·ye
old *star* star
one-way ticket *enosmerna vozovnica* ⓕ
　e·no·smer·na vo·zov·nee·tsa
open a *odprt* od·puhrt
outside *zunaj* zoo·nai

P

package *paket* ⓜ pa·ket
paper *papir* ⓜ pa·peer
park (car) v *parkirati* par·kee·ra·tee
passport *potni list* ⓜ pot·nee leest
pay *plačati* pla·cha·tee
pen *pisalo* ⓝ pee·sa·lo
petrol *bencin* ⓜ ben·tseen
pharmacy *lekarna* ⓕ le·kar·na
phonecard *telefonska kartica* ⓕ
　te·le·fon·ska kar·tee·tsa
photo *fotografija* ⓕ fo·to·gra·fee·ya
picnic *piknik* ⓜ peek·neek
plate *krožnik* ⓜ krozh·neek
police *policija* ⓕ po·lee·tsee·ya
postcard *razglednica* ⓕ raz·gled·nee·tsa
post office *pošta* ⓕ posh·ta
pregnant *noseča* no·se·cha
price *cena* ⓕ tse·na

Q

quiet *tih* teeh

R

rain *dež* ⓜ dezh
razor *brivnik* ⓜ breev·neek
receipt *račun* ⓜ ra·choon
red *rdeč* rdech
refund *vračilo denarja* ⓝ vra·chee·lo de·nar·ya
registered mail *priporočena pošta* ⓕ
　pree·po·ro·che·na posh·ta
rent v *najeti* na·ye·tee
repair v *popraviti* pop·ra·vee·tee
reservation *rezervacija* ⓕ re·zer·va·tsee·ya
restaurant *restavracija* ⓕ res·tav·ra·tsee·ya
return v *vrniti* vr·nee·tee

return ticket *povratna vozovnica* ⓕ
　pov·rat·na vo·zov·nee·tsa
right (direction) *desno* des·no
road *cesta* ⓕ tses·ta
room *soba* ⓕ so·ba

S

safe a *varen* va·ren
sanitary napkins *damski vložki* ⓜ pl
　dam·skee vlozh·kee
seat *sedež* ⓜ se·dezh
send *poslati* pos·la·tee
service station *servis* ⓜ ser·vees
sex *seks* ⓜ seks
shampoo *šampon* ⓜ sham·pon
share (a dorm) *deliti (sobo)* de·lee·tee (so·bo)
shaving cream *krema za britje* ⓕ kre·ma za breet·ye
she *ona* ⓕ o·na
sheet (bed) *rjuha* ⓕ ryoo·ha
shirt *srajca* ⓕ srai·tsa
shoes *čevlji* ⓜ pl chev·lyee
shop *trgovina* ⓕ tuhr·go·vee·na
short *kratek* kra·tek
shower *prha* ⓕ puhr·ha
single room *enoposteljna soba* ⓕ
　e·no·pos·tel'·na so·ba
skin *koža* ⓕ ko·zha
skirt *krilo* ⓝ kree·lo
sleep v *spati* spa·tee
Slovenia *Slovenija* ⓕ slo·ve·nee·ya
Slovene (language) *slovenščina* ⓕ slo·vensh·chee·na
Slovene a *slovenski* slo·ven·skee
slowly *počasi* po·cha·see
small *majhen* mai·hen
smoke (cigarettes) v *kaditi* ka·dee·tee
soap *milo* ⓝ mee·lo
some *nekaj* ne·kai
soon *kmalu* kma·loo
south *jug* ⓜ yoog
souvenir shop *trgovina s spominki* ⓕ
　tuhr·go·vee·na s spo·meen·kee
speak *govoriti* go·vo·ree·tee
spoon *žlica* ⓕ zhlee·tsa
stamp *znamka* ⓕ znam·ka
stand-by ticket *stand-by vozovnica* ⓕ
　stend·bai vo·zov·nee·tsa
station (train) *postaja* ⓕ pos·ta·ya
stomach *želodec* ⓜ zhe·lo·dets

stop v *ustaviti* oos-*ta*-vee-tee
stop (bus) *postajališče* ① pos-ta-ya-*leesh*-che
street *ulica* ① *oo*-lee-tsa
student *študent/študentka* ⑩/①
shtoo-*dent*/shtoo-*dent*-ka
sun *sonce* ① *son*-tse
sunscreen *krema za sončenje* ① *kre*-ma za *son*-chen-ye
swim v *plavati* *pla*-va-tee

T

tampons *tamponi* ⑩ pl tam-*po*-nee
taxi *taksi* ⑩ *tak*-see
teaspoon *čajna žlička* ① *chai*-na zhleech-ka
teeth *zobje* ⑩ *zob*-ye
telephone *telefon* ⑩ te-le-*fon*
television *televizija* ① te-le-*vee*-zee-ya
temperature (weather) *temperatura* ①
tem-pe-ra-*too*-ra
tent *šotor* ⑩ *sho*-tor
that (one) *tisti* *tees*-tee
they *oni/one* ⑩/① *o*-nee/*o*-ne
thirsty *žejen* *zhe*-yen
this (one) *ta* ta
throat *grlo* ⑩ *guhr*-lo
ticket (entrance) *vstopnica* ① *vstop*-nee-tsa
ticket (travel) *vozovnica* ① vo-*zov*-nee-tsa
time *čas* ⑩ chas
tired *utrujen* oo-*troo*-yen
tissues *robčki* ⑩ pl *rob*-chkee
today *danes* *da*-nes
toilet *stranišče* ⑩ stra-*neesh*-che
tomorrow *jutri* *yoot*-ree
tonight *nocoj* no-*tsoy*
toothbrush *zobna ščetka* ① *zob*-na shchet-ka
toothpaste *zobna pasta* ① *zob*-na *pas*-ta
torch (flashlight) *baterija* ① ba-te-*ree*-ya
tour *izlet* ⑩ *eez*-let
tourist office *turistični urad* ⑩ too-rees-*teech*-nee oo-*rad*
towel *brisača* ① bree-*sa*-cha
train *vlak* ⑩ vlak
translate *prevesti* pre-*ves*-tee
travel agency *potovalna agencija* ①
po-to-*val*-na a-gen-*tsee*-ya
travellers cheque *potovalni ček* ⑩ po-to-*val*-nee chek
trousers *hlače* ① pl *hla*-che
twin beds *ločeni postelji* ① pl *lo*-che-nee *pos*-tel-yee
tyre *guma* ① *goo*-ma

U

underwear *spodnje perilo* ⑩ *spod*-nye pe-*ree*-lo
urgent *nujen* *noo*-yen

V

vacant *prost* prost
vacation *počitnice* ① pl po-*cheet*-nee-tse
vegetable *zelenjava* ① ze-len-*ya*-va
vegetarian a *vegetarijanski* ve-ge-ta-ree-*yan*-skee
visa *viza* ① *vee*-za

W

waiter *natakar* ⑩ na-*ta*-kar
walk v *hoditi* ho-*dee*-tee
wallet *denarnica* ① de-*nar*-nee-tsa
warm a *topel* *to*-pe-oo
wash (something) *prati* *pra*-tee
watch *zapestna ura* ① za-*pest*-na *oo*-ra
water *voda* ① *vo*-da
we *mi* mee
weekend *vikend* ⑩ *vee*-kend
west *zahod* ⑩ za-*hod*
wheelchair *invalidski voziček* ⑩
een-va-*leed*-skee vo-*zee*-chek
when *kdaj* kdai
where *kje* kye
white *bel* be-oo
who *kdo* kdo
why *zakaj* za-kai
wife *žena* ① *zhe*-na
window *okno* ⑩ *ok*-no
wine *vino* ⑩ *vee*-no
with *z/s* z/s
without *brez* brez
woman *ženska* ① *zhen*-ska
write *pisati* pee-*sa*-tee

Y

yellow *rumen* roo-*men*
yes *da* da
yesterday *včeraj* vche-rai
you sg inf/pol *ti/vi* tee/vee
you pl *vi* vee

festivals in central europe

The Berlin Love Parade in June is the largest techno party in the world. Hordes of tourists come to **Germany** for the famous beer festival in Munich, the *Oktoberfest* – one of Europe's biggest and most drunken parties from late September to early October.

The Prague Spring in May, one of Europe's biggest festivals of classical music, kicks off the summer in the **Czech Republic**. The town of Prachatice goes fairly wild during the mid-June Gold Trail Festival with medieval costumes, fencing tournaments and fireworks.

People from all over Europe camp and party at the Sziget Festival in **Hungary**, a week-long world music bash in early August on Budapest's Óbuda Island. The Gyula Theatre Festival has spectacular performances in the castle courtyard during July and August.

The Dominican Fair in Gdańsk is the oldest shopping fair in **Poland**, held in August and accompanied by street theatre, concerts, parades and races. The May Juvenalia in Kraków is a student carnival with fancy dress, masquerades and dancing in the street.

In July, artists from all over Europe come to Kežmarok for the biggest Craft Fair in **Slovakia**, with food, drinks and live music. Rumours that the Bojnice Castle is haunted are kept alive by the International Festival of Spirits and Ghosts, held in early May.

Kurentovanje, a rite of spring celebrated in February, is the most extravagant folklore event in **Slovenia**, held in Ptuj. Maribor hosts both the International Puppet Festival in July and August and a renowned theatre festival in the second half of October.

What kind of traveller are you?

A. You're eating chicken for dinner *again* because it's the only word you know.

B. When no one understands what you say, you step closer and shout louder.

C. When the barman doesn't understand your order, you point frantically at the beer.

D. You're surrounded by locals, swapping jokes, email addresses and experiences
– other travellers want to borrow your phrasebook or audio guide.

If you answered A, B, or C, you NEED Lonely Planet's language products ...

- **Lonely Planet Phrasebooks** – for every phrase you need in every language
  you want

- **Lonely Planet Language & Culture** – get behind the scenes of English as it's
  spoken around the world – learn and laugh

- **Lonely Planet Fast Talk & Fast Talk Audio** – essential phrases for short trips and
  weekends away – read, listen and talk like a local

- **Lonely Planet Small Talk** – 10 essential languages for city breaks

- **Lonely Planet Real Talk** – downloadable language audio guides from
  lonelyplanet.com to your MP3 player

... and this is why

- **Talk to everyone everywhere**
  Over 120 languages, more than any other publisher

- **The right words at the right time**
  Quick-reference colour sections, two-way dictionary, easy pronunciation,
  every possible subject – and audio to support it

Lonely Planet Offices

Australia
90 Maribyrnong St, Footscray,
Victoria 3011
☎ 03 8379 8000
fax 03 8379 8111
✉ talk2us@lonelyplanet.com.au

USA
150 Linden St, Oakland,
CA 94607
☎ 510 893 8555
fax 510 893 8572
✉ info@lonelyplanet.com

UK
72-82 Rosebery Ave,
London EC1R 4RW
☎ 020 7841 9000
fax 020 7841 9001
✉ go@lonelyplanet.co.uk

lonelyplanet.com